Pathways to Empathy

Work and Everyday Life
Ethnographic Studies on Work Cultures

Series of the Commission "Working Cultures" in the Deutsche Gesellschaft für Volkskunde (German Society for European Ethnology and Folklore)

Edited by Irene Götz, Gertraud Koch, Klaus Schönberger and Manfred Seifert

Volume 6

Gertraud Koch is professor and *Stefanie Everke Buchanan* is a research fellow in the Department of Communication and Cultural Management at Zeppelin University.

Gertraud Koch, Stefanie Everke Buchanan (Hg.)

Pathways to Empathy

New Studies on Commodification, Emotional Labor, and Time Binds

Campus Verlag
Frankfurt/New York

Bibliographic Information published by the Deutsche Nationalbibliothek.
The Deutsche Nationalbibliothek lists this publication in the Deutsche Nationalbibliografie;
detailed bibliographic data are available in the Internet at http://dnb.d-nb.de
ISBN 978-3-593-39894-5

Copyright © 2013 Campus Verlag GmbH, Frankfurt-on-Main
Cover design: Campus Verlag, Frankfurt-on-Main
Typeset: Tomislav Helebrant
Printing office and bookbinder: CPI buchbuecher.de, Birkach
Printed on acid free paper.
Printed in Germany

This book is also available as an E-Book.
www.campus.de
www.press.uchicago.edu

This book is dedicated to

Arlie Russell Hochschild

In the 30 years since the publication of her ground-breaking *The Managed Heart*, she has passionately pursued the seismographic detection of subtle shifts and cumulative changes at the interface of our working and private lives, fuelled by the creeping commodification of our everyday relationships. Each of the contributors to this edited collection shares the common experience of being intellectually inspired by her perceptive, articulate commentaries, with their wealth of pioneering and innovative ideas.

Contents

Emotion, Body Work and Autonomy

Taking on an Idea

Introduction:
Getting There: From Impediments to Pathways to Empathy[1]

Gertraud Koch and Stefanie Everke Buchanan

Across Europe and the United States of America, over the last decades, we hear an ever louder call for an expansion of the market, reduced regulation, and shrinking of government services. Indeed, in the eyes of many, the market can do no wrong, and the government—outside of its military function—can do little right. Since the 1970s, we have witnessed the rise of global corporate giants, the reduced power of labor unions and increased co-optation of governments by business. To be sure, market forces have risen alongside other trends—the rise of science, technology and a rationalization of life reflected in all parts of life (Larsen 2011; Löfgren 2006 on meta-narrative). Taken as a whole, the free-market *zeitgeist* has produced a powerful—and as yet under-theorized—impact on our lives. As a *worker*, the pre-Fordist employee is now the post-Fordist "entre-ployee". She assumes risks and lives with insecurity like an entrepreneur. But she works for a boss, like an employee. As a *consumer*, the individual who once turned to family, friends and church to meet personal needs now turns—in the absence of government services—to market services, i. e., to babysitters, eldercare workers, for pay dating services, life coaches. As *private individuals*, we draw from a market-colonized culture, ideas and images of the self. The individual is adviced to develop a "personal brand". The internet dater is advised to count his "R.O.I", i.e., return on investment. All this takes place within a larger culture of "blur" between companies seeking to add emotional appeal to the goods and services they sell, and individuals who seek to draw useful tips for successful living from the market (Illouz 2007). Workers bring to work personal ideas, tastes, habits. And for its part, the workplace exercises great

1 We would like to express our gratitude to a number of individuals for their help in the realization of this volume. Paul Brook was a constant source of advice and inspiration throughout the project. Anja Lesche was indispensable with her formidable organizational skills. Teresa Stumpf and Anne Kruse diligently and carefully checked the bibliographies and analyzed the manuscripts for the index. And Spring Gombe-Götz and Dr. Katrin Götz-Votteler proofread all articles with remarkable professional care and attention to detail.

influence over every aspect of the private individual (Moldaschl and Voss 2002; Hochschild 1983, 2003; Sieben and Wettergren 2010).

Arlie Hochschild has studied the impact of capitalist forces on intimate life in many ways and from many perspectives. Her work carves an important path between those who barely acknowledge capitalism at all, and those who acknowledge it but assume that its influence is always alienating. Especially in *The Outsourced Self* (2012), she describes a large and well-occupied space for resistance. Adapting Freud's notion of "mechanisms of defense" she describes the various semi-conscious means through which individuals work to *keep personal life personal*. A woman pays a love coach to guide her through the many small acts of looking for love on Match.com—picking a photo to post, a subject line, a self-description, for example. But when the coach says, "Shall I scan the replies you get on line" she says, "No, I'll do that, because when I find my true love I want to tell him that that *it was I* who found him." She purchases a whole service, but elevates one act to symbolize her un-outsourced self. Or a middle-aged daughter comes to love the caretaker she hires to care for her elderly, brain-injured father, and so loves the father *through* an empathic reach to a proxy caregiver. In these ways and more, people carve out ways to detach themselves from a culture of detachment so often connected to market life. They protect both their autonomy and sense of relatedness to others.

In line with this new emphasis in Hochschild's perspective, the authors of these essays are interested in the contradictions, counter moves, resistances and the daily practices individuals use to cope with the promise and demands of the market. For indeed, there are limits to market influence, as Collin Williams shows (2005). To what degree does the individual draw a line between self and the myriad everyday manifestations of market culture? By what feeling rules does he or she say, I will be emotionally attached to this, but I will be detached from that? In addition to rules about *what* to feel—happy, anguished, sad—we encounter rules about *how much* to feel— or even whether to feel anything at all. Given these rules of attachment and detachment, what emotion work does an individual perform in an effort to abide by this rule? Sometimes at a certain point in an interaction, an individual will encounter a moment of anxiety—he is too detached, alienated— and he will counter it using various mechanisms of defense (Hochschild 2011, 2012). At other times, in the quest for efficiency, he finds himself too emotionally attached. ("I don't need to be best friends with the babysitter or have drinks with the dog-walker" one respondent told Hochschild.) It is through our various personal rules of engagement, Hochschild argues, that we regulate capitalism from inside.

It is the purpose of this collection to explore the complex forces of commodification and the many ways we embrace it, resist it and "muddle through". We aim to delineate the strategies by which the individual asserts the un-alienated self, and the public discourses available for trying to seem that way. We aim to theorize the collective strategies by which we might achieve a better balance of social spheres—market, governmental, civic, personal, and so articulate an alternate cultural world in which to assert a humane self.

This shift of perspective from impediments to pathways to empathy is the leading paradigm for the contributions in this volume. In their work, many of these authors have developed ideas about ways in which the individual counters commercialization and point to welcome and unexpected spaces of resistance. The contributions—literally in the sense of "paying tribute to"— demonstrate to how many areas the thoughts of Arlie Russell Hochschild have flowed over the past three decades, and show the wide variety of fields her work has influenced.

The Contributions

Leading into the topic, *Arlie Russell Hochschild* sketches *Empathy Maps* and develops a novel way of looking at ways in which we direct our empathy, zoning people in one area of life to receive much empathy, and those in another area of life, to receive little or any. While proposing a metaphor-driven idea we can apply to all spheres of life, it clearly applies to the division between commercial life (for which the cultural rule is emotional detachment) and personal life (for which the rule is attachment—care, empathy). She thus provides a connection with her detailed studies on the commodification of life in contemporary societies, and simultaneously assumes a changed perspective on them. Her mapping out of the borderlands between alienated and fulfilling lives calls forth the "credit" side of our lives—that which makes up for what commodification sometimes subtracts. Hochschild thus introduces us to a central antagonist who, in everyday life, can be against the depersonalizing effects of commodification.

Empathy is part of human nature, and we may feel it even in the heat of conflict. The feeling can be strong or mild, laced with ambivalence or pure. And there is a "sociology" to empathy. Some social categories of people feel it more than others—women more than men, for example. And we differ in aim—some social groups empathize with the poor, others empathize with the rich. Some cultures provide feeling rules that promote wide-spread, race-blind, empathy. Others don't. Hochschild shows that the links to commodification are far more multi-faceted and contradictory than we might first assume. In her paper, she maps out a landscape full of pathways which individuals may take on their way to achieving a wide-zone marked for empathy with many others. Without ignoring or downplaying the constraints placed upon individuals by the rules of the post-Fordist world, she also points to a way forward and to strategies for achieving a more humane world.

The section *"Family and Work"* focuses on fields of tension between competing urgency systems of family and work. Competing demands lead to an almost unmanageable 24-hour day, as well as to an emotionally torn biography. The time in the age span between 30 and 45, which frequently sees the concurrent pursuit of career and family, is therefore often described as the rush hour of life. However, family life and work life are not always experienced as areas of tension. Depending on one's own perspective, they can also be experienced as a mutually facilitating, harmonious unity, as demonstrated by two of the studies. The section thus draws a multifaceted image of time binds at home and at work, as well as of how these demands on our time are felt.

In her study on family and work life in the context of late-forming families in Spain, *Nancy Konvalinka* provides insight into the tight squeeze experienced in a societal setting in which traditional views on when to start a family compete with limits set by human biology and market realities. Using theoretical lenses derived from Bourdieu's concepts such as *habitus* as well as the concept of the *life course*, she traces the interplay between emotion and economy and the strains that traditional expectations and new market realities pose and to which individuals feel they must respond on their own—either by arranging for a stay-at-home parent or hiring a caregiver. Either way, they spare the state the need to help out.

Using a highly unusual research strategy, *Jeremy Schulz* interviewed men who shared much in common—age, profession, marital status and devotion to their jobs. Only one thing differed: national culture. For one group were American and the other Norwegian, and each reflected a different "logic" toward the deployment of time and energy. The Americans favored a logic of "use your time and energy until you get the job done". They took little account of family and community and so used up their time and energy—revealing haunting parallels to the way in which America, as a nation, "uses up" such resources as oil. While equally motivated, the Norwegian men chose a more "sustainable" approach to their time and energy, mindful in the morning of their attachment to home and community in the evening.

In the study by *Caroline Ruiner*, family and work are experienced as positively related rather than contrary spheres of life by one of her survey groups. From their childhood in an entrepreneurial family, they derive the *cultural capital* to become self-employed and to experience the related temporal as well as risky aspects as positive. The other group of entrepreneurs who cannot draw on family experience in running a business, on the other hand, feels insecure about and overburdened with the demands placed upon them. She accounts for the emergence of both the fearless and fearful approaches to economic insecurity.

The contributions of the *"Labor Feelings"* section take their conceptual lead from emotional labor and feeling rules and develop suggestions how these could be expanded and rendered productive for empirical work. *Paul Brook* as a researcher who is particularly attuned to the spaces for independent action and the individual possibilities for resistance in connection with emotional labor presents the emotional capacity for labor as comparable to the capacity for physical and intellectual work. Like other forms of labor, Brook argues, emotional labor is characterized by indeterminacy and incomplete commodification. He develops a suggestion as to how Hochschild's concept of emotional labor can be linked to the tradition of labor process analysis in a way that yields a unified framework for the conceptualization of and further research on the emotional, intellectual and physical capacity for work.

Wolfgang Dunkel and Margit Weihrich critique the idea of emotional labor, preferring to understand it as interactive service work. Here, too, the clients are involved in the work process and also perform emotional labor in the process of interaction. Dunkel and Weihrich thus sketch the emotion management described by Hochschild as progressive commodification in the service sector as a (new) mode of social relations which serves to provide exchange between people and does not exclusively or even primarily constitute burdensome or alienating moments of a work situation.

In her essay, *Gertraud Koch* takes up the concept of feeling rules for cultural anthropological research as it has so far received surprisingly little resonance in work culture research but has rather remained in the shadow of studies on emotional labor which were oriented at individual and socio-structural aspects. The text demonstrates and makes available the potential of the concept as a point of access for the cultural analysis of work contexts and demonstrates at which points it still requires further elaboration and development via empirically based theoretical work.

The section *"Emotion, Body Work and Autonomy"* gathers empirical case studies which open up their respective fields by use of Arlie Hochschild's concepts from a variety of perspectives. *Sarah Braun* studies a hairdressing salon, and demonstrates through this research how the emotional labor includes a bodily dimension. The atmosphere at the salon, which is sketched as a part of the wellness arrangement in this service industry, also originates from the embodied work of the service providers, that is, the staff—for instance via the embodied moods of the service workers.

Emotional labor and body work also play a decisive role in the empirical field in which *Petra Schweiger* conducted her research on elder care work in a nursing home. In her thick description of the dilemma faced by carers as they encounter more demanding and rationalised conditions of work. She offers deep insight into how economization and rationalization undermine the workers ability to relate humanely with clients. It is in light of these conditions, she argues, that workers employ strategies in order to benefit patients.

In her study of freelancers in the media, *Birgit Huber* argues that the media sector is part of the service sector. But as a part of the creativity industry, it also plays by different rules than those that operate in the trade, care or the wellness sectors. Self-employed web designers can delimit work and private life as they chose, Huber finds, enabling them to actively design life according to their own preferences. Here, clients become friends, and friends turn into customers. The dissolution of boundaries in work and life forms in a self-employed, creative occupation is presented as one opportunity to gain autonomy and lead a largely self-determined life.

Finally in the section *"Scientific Reception"*, *Irene Götz* completes the arc from the introductory sketches of Hochschild's empathy maps by sketching the reception of Hochschild's work in work culture research as a fruitful intellectual exchange. With her infallible sense for empirical fields, in which cultural changes can be "captured" empirically, Hochschild has instigated cultural anthropological research over many years. The contribution reads as an homage to Arlie Russell Hochschild, her ingenious, imaginative, holistic perspective on work, her remarkable contentual power for inspiration, as well as to the exemplary methodological approaches, particularly for cultural anthropological work research, which she has found.

Works Cited

Hochschild, Arlie Russell (1983), *The managed heart: Commercialization of human feeling,* London: University of California Press.

— (2003), *The commercialization of intimate life. Notes from home and work,* Berkeley, London: University of California Press.

— (2011), "Emotional life on the market frontier", in: *Annual review of sociology,* 37, 1, 21–33.

— (2012), *The outsourced self: Intimate life in market times,* New York: Metropolitan Books.

Illouz, Eva (2007), *Cold intimacies,* Oxford, Malden: Polity Press.

Larsen, Tord (2011), "Acts of entification. The emergence of thinghood in social life", in: Nigel Rapport (ed.), *Human nature as capacity. Transcending discourse and classification,* New York, Oxford: Berghahn Books.

Löfgren, Orvar (2006), "Cultural alchemy: Translating the experience economy into Scandinavian", in: Barbara Czarniawska and Guje Sevón (eds), *Global Ideas. How Ideas, Objects and Practices Travel in the Global Economy,* Malmö: Liber, 15–29.

Moldaschl, Manfred and G. Günter Voß (eds.) (2002), *Subjektivierung von Arbeit,* München, Mering: Rainer Hampp Verlag.

Sieben, Barbara and Åsa Wettergren (eds.) (2010), *Emotionalizing Organizations and Organizing Emotions,* Basingstoke: Palgrave Macmillan.

Williams, Colin C. (2005), *A commodified world? Mapping the limits of capitalism,* London, New York: Zed Books.

Empathy Maps[1]

Arlie Russell Hochschild

The world is in a race, Jeremy Rifkin argues in his book *The Empathic Civilization*. On the "good" team are all the forces pressing each of us to feel empathy for all other people—and indeed all living creatures—on earth.[2] On the "bad" team are forces which accelerate global warming, destabilize the eco-system on which earthly life depends, causing strife, fear, and a search for enemies. Which team gets to the goal line first, he notes, is up to those alive today.

The market economy is a player in this race—on both teams. On one hand, by setting up networks of cooperating parties, market growth encourages the development of a thin layer of empathy—at least enough to assure peace—in order to conduct business and increase wealth.[3] In this way, the market is on the "good" empathy-enhancing team. On the other hand,

---

1 This essay is happily reprinted with the permission of the author. It was originally published in Arlie Hochschild (2013): *So How's the Family? and Other Essays*. Berkeley: UC Press.

2 In *The Empathic Civilization: the Race to Global Consciousness in a World Crisis*, Jeremy Rifkin (2009) argues that through the broad swath of human history, we have increased—indeed, begun to globalize—our empathy for other people. Some evidence for this comes from the Harvard psychologist, Steven Pinker who argues in his book, *The Better Angels of Our Nature*, that over the centuries, violence has decreased—including tribal warfare, homicide, cruel punishments, child abuse, animal cruelty, domestic violence, lynching, pogroms, and international and civil wars. This Pinker attributes to a growing exercise of self control, reason and empathy. Still, in 2011, we should note no fewer than 37 armed conflicts in the world, in each one of which 25 or more died as a cause of battle during the year. In 2011, thousands died. But eons ago, the proportion of people killed in the armed conflict of tribal societies was ten times greater, Pinker argues. War-related deaths as a proportion of modern populations are about a tenth as high as they once were when the world's people lived in tribes (Uppsala, University Sweden, Department of Peace and Conflict Research, http://www.pcr.uu.se/research/ucdp/definitions; Themner and Wallersteen 2012; Azar 2012).

3 As Adam Smith observed in The Wealth of Nations, "Little else is requisite to carry a state to the highest degree of opulence from the lowest barbarism, but peace, easy taxes, and a tolerable administration of justice." Smith famously argued that self-interest was glue

economic over-development—with its gas-belching industrial smoke stacks, toxic wastes, and accumulation of discarded goods—proceeds headlong and heedless of the welfare of future generations.[4] The market also creates gross inequalities both within nations and between them, causing a sense of injustice, envy and conflict.[5] In these ways, the market is also on the "bad" team.

How could we win this race? By extending lines of empathy between the Midwestern industrialist and the worried resident of a sinking Maldivian island in the rising tide of global warming. By drawing links between the prosperous London businessman and the impoverished Soweto street vendor. By encouraging mothers to stand in the shoes of their children in the upper east side of Manhattan, of course, but also in the shoes of the children left back in Mexico by the Mexican nannies such mothers hire to care for their children. Empathy would have to go global. Harder still, perhaps, it would have to go local—three zip codes down the street, up or down the class ladder. It would have to cross barriers of class, race, and gender.

Hidden Evidence of Empathy

To ground such sweeping talk of empathy, we need to ask what empathy is, to wonder at its complexity, and to explore the hidden patterns it sometimes fits. We need to look at maps. But how can we understand these? Clues can be surprisingly indirect. For decades, researchers had been finding that more women than men said they were depressed, and two researchers, Ronald Kessler and Jane McLeod, wondered why (see Weissman and Klerman 1977; Kessler and McLeod 1984; Nolen-Hoeksema 1987; Piccinelli and Wilkinson 2000). The prevailing theory in the 1980s was that women were more "vulnerable to life-event effects" because of their poor "coping strategies" (Kessler and McLeod 1984: 621). But if this were the case, why would women cope better than men—as they do—with financial bad news, a spouse's death, and

strong enough to bind buyer to seller, but some small measure of trust and empathy is surely also required (Smith 2003: 776).
4 See Chapter 2, "From Consumer Book to Ecological Bust" in Juliet Schor's *Plenitude: the New Economics of True Wealth*, New York: Penguin Press, 2010.
5 In addition, the expansion of the market has greatly widened the gap between rich and poor in the world, creating envy and hardship. As Adam Smith noted, "An industrious and upon that account a wealthy nation, is of all nations the most likely to be attacked" (Smith 2003: 887).

after an initial period, with separation and divorce (see Kessler and McLeod 1984: 620; Gove 1972; Barnett et al. 1987)?[6]

Then the researchers found that when exposed to the same disturbing events in the lives of immediate family and friends—death, accident, illness, divorce or separation, losses in love—women more than men talked about and responded strongly to them. Men knew as much about these events as women did, the researchers surmised, but they didn't discuss them as often or respond as strongly.

Women also participated in wider circles of support. More unhappy, lost, ill people came to them than to men, and the women invited them to do so. When respondents were asked to describe "who helped them during the last period in their life when they needed help with a serious problem [...] women [were] between 30 and 50 percent more likely than men to be mentioned as helpers" (Kessler and McLeod 1984: 628). And more than men, women reached out to others for support—often to other women. So as friends and family sought out women more than men as confidants, especially in times of crisis, women came to hold—to remain mindful of—more stories of distress (see Kessler and McLeod 1984: 629). To some people, it seems to me, holding a story of distress signaled a readiness to help. For others, it was the holding onto painful knowledge alongside another person that *was* the help.

Men were as upset as women by serious life crises that occurred to their *spouses* and *children*. Yet beyond that group, men didn't report getting as distressed as women did (see Kessler and McLeod 1984: 629; Fischer 1982; Gove et al. 1983). So women in this study of Americans of the 1980s were not just feeling down about their *own* bad news, or even their own husband's and children's bad news, but about the bad news of *others* in their larger circle of family and friends. There, they were the designated empathizers—the ones others relied on to stay tuned in.[7] They held in mind the sad news of these others. They charted larger empathy maps.

---

6 Married women also reported higher rates of depression than single or divorced women and the question was, again, why? Did married women cope less well with life than unmarried ones, the researchers wondered? Others speculated that women had been dealt a more depressing role in marriage than men had been, or even that depression-prone women were more drawn to marriage than their counterparts.

7 In her forthcoming book on rich and poor families living in Silicon Valley, Marianne Cooper (2013) compares the way rich and poor define and handle economic insecurities. In the working class, women in poor families become the family's "designated worriers"— the ones who wake up at night with nightmares about paying the bills—while, in the upper-class, it is mainly men who take on this kind of worry.

But why did the news of others depress women? Maybe because people have a greater need to share bad news than good, and bad news is harder to hold, so women get more of it, and feel more blue because of it. Or maybe women's depression had nothing to do with their wider circle of concern but with other matters—like the fact that everyone needs to feel mothered, and that many women feel less mothered by men than men feel by women. Whatever is going on with depression, the key discovery here is something else—the different shapes of men's and women's empathy maps.

A 2002 study of over 1,000 people—part of the General Social Survey, a large, nationally-representative U.S. survey—casts a broader light on such maps. Compared to men, women more often described themselves as "soft-hearted", reported themselves feeling touched by events that they saw happen, and found themselves feeling "tender concerned feelings" for people less fortunate than they.[8] They also held more altruistic values than men, agreeing more strongly, for example, that "people should be willing to help others who are less fortunate". Studies show that in close personal situations, women are much more likely to focus on emotion, to offer and seek emotional support and to use "highly person-centered comforting messages" to help people feel better (Smith, Tom 2003: 647 quoting Burleson and Kunkel 2006). The same was found in studies of young girls and boys (see Smith, Tom 2003: 648). Women make up some three-quarters of caregivers for older relatives and friends, and two-thirds of those caring for grandchildren. Women are somewhat more likely to donate their kidneys (58 percent versus men's 42 percent). And the Yad Vashem archive of data on non-Jews honored for rescuing Jews shows that while men and women helped in equal numbers, among non-married people, more women helped than men (see Smith, Tom 2003: 649; Taylor 2003; Leyens et al. 2007). At work, women predominate in the caring professions—they make up 98 percent of kindergarten teachers, 79 percent of social workers, and 92 percent of registered

---

8 The National Altruism Study, based on data collected from 1,366 people in the 2002 General Social Survey, is one of the few nationally-representative studies we have of empathy (Smith 2003). The report found empathy, altruistic values and helping behaviors all fairly common among Americans. According to the study, three-quarters of Americans said they were "often touched by things that happen," and are "pretty soft-hearted" (p. 3). Forty-three percent "feel selfless caring for others on most days or more often," and 33 percent feel it "once in a while or less often" (p. 3). The study distinguished between altruistic values (agreeing, for example, that it is personally important to assist those in trouble) and altruistic behavior (giving directions, letting someone cut in line, talking to a depressed person, loaning items). Women tended to hold more altruistic values, but they didn't perform more altruistic acts, than men (p. 12). Also see Bernard 1981.

nurses (see Eagley 2009: 649). Maybe because women have babies, evolution gives them an empathy advantage, or maybe it's because the culture encourages empathy more in girls than boys, or maybe both.

But that doesn't mean men don't help other people. In fact, many other studies concluded that, without being asked, men perform more public altruistic *acts* than women (see Eagley 2009: 646–647). They offer directions to the lost. They give up their seats in the bus. They let people cut into line. They gave money to a stranger for the subway. Men received 91 percent of the Carnegie Hero Fund Commission awards given between 1904 and 2008 and 87 percent of the Medal of Bravery awards given out by the Canadian government (see Eagley 2009: 647). So while men aren't the biggest empathizers, they sometimes save the day.

Words, Meanings, Causes of Empathy

We say we "stand in another's shoes." But what exactly are we *doing, feeling* and *thinking* when we stand this way? We see through the other's eyes. We feel as they do. We say to ourselves, "What has happened to you *could* happen to me." And as we imagine this, we are often doing such things as looking a person in the eye, listening closely. We feel curious. Or we come to feel empathy for certain categories of stranger we learn about from others through word of mouth, newspaper, television, a film, a play, or a book.

Empathy differs from feeling—or being held as—responsible for another (see Fischer 1982; 2011; Wellman and Berkowitz 1988; Wellman and Wortley 1990). A nephew might pay a dutiful visit to a grumpy uncle but lack empathy for him. In *All Our Kin*, Carol Stack describes *"kinscription"*, whereby some members of poor black families were delegated to care for others (see Stack 1974). The child of an ill parent is sent to live with a childless aunt. A neighborhood orphan is taken in by his grandmother's friend from church. A family looks after a lonely neighbor. One accepts the possibility of a kin assignment. A responsibility is assigned, and empathy is expected to follow.

But empathy doesn't always lead to caring action. A 27-year-old single photographer I interviewed described his feelings upon learning that his dear friend had been diagnosed with cancer. He was grief-stricken but didn't feel it was his role to help. "I wasn't the first person Steven called", the photographer remembered. "That was his sister, and then a female friend of his and then the two women competed over who could take the best care of him, and called on their families to help. I wasn't part of that." Maybe he would have done something if others hadn't. But, as things stood, he felt empathy but not a sense of responsibility to do something.

So, empathy is *related* to doing things but it isn't the doing of those things. We console a bereaved colleague. We talk over the day with a partner. We pet a dog tied up outside a coffee shop. We leave coins in a homeless man's cup. We pray for others. These are acts of kindness that usually *go with* empathy, but empathy itself is an act of *feeling for* another person.[9] Our hearts can go out to Sudanese war orphans or Congolese rape victims, but we may do nothing to help them. As the philosopher Joan Tronto (1993) points out, caring *about* a person differs from caring *for* a person (for example, arranging for care of an elderly parent), which differs from taking care *of* a person (for example, feeding and dressing him).[10]

How do we distinguish empathy from other things like "understanding", "projection" or "identification"? Empathy is less purely cognitive than "understanding", because it requires imagining what another is feeling. We also sometimes *project* the idea of ourselves onto another person and so replace what we know of the other with what we know of ourselves. A recently-bereaved widow recounted a friend's well-meaning attempt to comfort her, for example:

I knew Adrianne loved me and wanted to comfort me. But I knew my loss reminded her of *her* loss. In the living room that afternoon, I felt the presence of my husband and was trying to absorb all the marvelous recollections friends had shared of him. But Adrianne began rubbing my hand back and forth as if she were sanding it, and told me she knew how upset I must be feeling. But that was her upset, not mine.

The good side of such projection is that we take flight from ourselves; we don't remain detached, aloof, uncaring.[11] The bad side of it, potentially, is

---

9 Do sadists empathize with their victims in the sense of trying to understand what would hurt most so as to better inflict pain? They can exercise something *like* empathy, but I would have to believe such a thought process is more mechanical and somehow bypasses the feeling of standing in a victim's shoes.

10 Tronto (1993: 103) defines care broadly as a "species activity that includes everything that we do to maintain, continue and repair our 'world' so that we can live in it as well as possible".

11 The omnipresence of cell phones has led to a culture of interruption, which may thin and loosen empathic bonds. I interviewed a San Francisco-based psychotherapist whose specialties included helping clients to limit the use of iPhones, Blackberries, and computers during in-person communications with loved ones. As he recounted, "This is a real prob-

that we mistake ourselves for the other person. We see the other as like our generous mother, depressed sister, judgmental colleague, when he or she is not any of these. Projection distorts empathy. Again, we may *identify* with another person; and over a long period of time gradually incorporate him into our personality. (We say, the young boy walks and talks just like his dad.) Empathy doesn't have to stick like that.[12]

That's because empathy is an *art*. It is the art of the surveyor, the draftsman and the reader of the empathy map.[13] A surveyor gauges the height of the mountain, depth of a sea, expanse of the desert. She discovers a reality that exists in places where, generally, she is not. By means of aerial, radar, and sonar testing, the surveyor gathers information about where things are, climates and the possibilities of life. She needs a steady hand to hold her surveying instruments. As a surveyor, the empathizer learns to observe with skill and "steady"—that is, manage—her heart. For example, the plight of another person may evoke anxiety, indignation, or sadness in the empathizer.

A draftsman carefully draws a picture based on the surveyor's report, and the reader reads the draftsman's map. So all told, the empathizer develops the skill of noticing, remembering, and imaginatively reproducing the feelings of another, and accepts in her—or his—own heart the feelings evoked by all that was seen. So empathy maps are not given to us: We develop the art of making them.

Some maps are mere sketches. A recovering alcoholic I talked to explained the simple suggestion of empathy she received from a "buddy" through Alcoholics Anonymous. "They assigned me a buddy who had been through the same struggle as I face. He called me every day and told me a short story. I responded with a story. No questions were asked. I didn't get to know him

---

lem with about 10 percent of my clients but a bit of a problem with nearly all of them." A number of his iPhone-glued clients complained that their own listeners seemed to be tuning an ear for their next call, and so serving a thinner slice of empathy.

12 A big thanks to Neil Smelser in helping me articulate the meaning of empathy. In *The Social Edges of Psychoanalysis,* Neil Smelser (2002) argues that structural forces and social psychological ones are mutually embedded, and that patterns of empathy may be an instance of that.

13 Empathy is also related to, but not the same as, "sympathy". Sympathy is a sentiment of feeling sad on behalf of another person, but without necessarily fully empathizing with all of their experience. If I sympathize, I feel sorry for a person even if I can't imagine being in the same predicament myself. As a term, "compassion" blends empathy with sympathy: "I can imagine myself in those shoes" and "I'm sorry that person is in them". "Altruism" refers to a disposition to act generously, and not to what specifically motivates those acts. "Selflessness", in turn, is altruism extended to the act of casting aside one's own needs.

really well, but he reminded me that I wasn't alone." Other maps can offer rich details of the topography of another person's self.

When we draw a map, we draw boundaries around zones—we empathize with people in the empathy zone, and, but not with those outside it. We imagine certain individuals or types of people as *eligible* for empathy, and others, not. To widen the criteria for entrance into an empathy zone, we try out empathy on a wide variety of people. So we know how it feels to be a helpless, distressed, wailing baby. We know how it feels to learn you got perfect scores in English and Math on the College Board exams. We know how it feels to be a heartless murderer. We know these things because we've cultivated the art of imagining ourselves into other people's minds.

Feeling Rules and Zones of Empathy

In applying this art, we are guided by various tacit moral rules governing our idea of the "right" sort of person to be—the stand-alone individual or helper-cooperator. To some people it's shameful to depend "too much" on others; so at the slightest sign of dependency, one is quickly disparaged as "a clinging vine", "a perpetual child", "a welfare bum". The moral rule carries with it a feeling rule: don't feel sorry. Don't empathize.[14] Others hold different ideas about needs: *i. e.* that it is natural to have them and good to seek help from others. So for them, the feeling rule is: Feel compassion. Empathize. Which rules we hold dear determines who we feel empathy for, and how hard we try to feel it.

Our location in society—and so our experience—also alters our map. We experience different structural pressures. I began to think this over in light of interviews with respondents I interviewed for *The Outsourced Self*.[15] For example, a personal assistant working for an immensely wealthy employer was trying to help her partner work off 50,000 dollars worth of graduate student debt, and to pay for a caregiver for her dying mother who lived 500 miles away.

---

14 Thanks to Gertraud Koch for the connection between moral ideas and feeling rules.

15 In the early 2000s, with the help of Allison Pugh, I conducted a set of exploratory interviews with some 50 individuals on "cultures of care". In these, we asked who a person turned to in their hour of need, and who turned to them. I'm also drawing on various other interviews conducted for *The Outsourced Self* (2012) and *The Time Bind* (1997).

Every time I walked by his million dollar awful art collection, I thought about my partner's school debt. I'd look at the ugliest piece and say to myself, "That piece would buy my mother excellent care, and that piece over there would cancel my partner's debt." I had a hard time empathizing with them over their malfunctioning hot tub, you know?

Paradoxically, some moral rules get in the way of empathy. In the pre-Emancipation South, for example, black slaves were held to be private property and it was deemed wrong to steal—or free—them. To be sure, Quakers, blacks, some indentured servants in similar circumstances, and sympathizers such as those who ran the *Underground Railroad*, proved exceptions. But at the time, the idea that then that Blacks were equal and comparable to Whites in mind, heart and soul was as yet missing, a point central to Mark Twain's classic 1885 novel, *The Adventures of Huckleberry Finn* (Twain 1992).

Twain famously juxtaposes the rule against theft and Huck's great empathy for his beloved friend, Jim, a runaway slave. After a long raft trip down the Mississippi with Jim—"we a-floating along, talking and singing and laughing"—Huck wonders whether to abide by the values he was brought up to believe by the Widow Douglas and his drunken father. Should he return Jim to his owner "like I should", or protect Jim and "go to hell" (Twain 1992: 330)? Huck struggles with himself:

Well, I can tell you it made me all over trembly and feverish, too, to hear him, because I begun to get it through my head that he *was* most free—and who was to blame for it? Why, *me*. I couldn't get that out of my conscience, no how nor no way. It got to troubling me so I couldn't rest; I couldn't stay still in one place. It hadn't ever come home to me before, what this thing was that I was doing. But now it did; and it stayed with me, and scorched me more and more. I tried to make out to myself that *I* warn't to blame, because *I* didn't run Jim off from his rightful owner; but it warn't no use, conscience up and says, every time, "But you knowed he was running for his freedom, and you could a paddled ashore and told somebody." That was so—I couldn't get around that no way ... [I felt] bad and low, because I knowed very well I had done wrong. (Twain 1992: 234, 237)

Holding the deed of ownership of Jim in his hand, Huck said, "I studied a minute, sort of holding my breath, and then says to myself: 'All right, then, I'll *go* to hell'—and tore it up" (Twain 1992: 330). Huck's empathy for Jim grew out of companionship, and it won. He brought himself to tear up his society's empathy map.

In his searing account of his horrific torture at the hand of Japanese POW camp commanders during World War II in Kanburi, Thailand, Eric Lomax faced a more difficult challenge—changing his own map. In his book, *The Railroad Man*, he describes how he came to feel empathy for the Japanese interpreter who helped those who tortured him (Lomax 1995). Captured in Thailand, Lomax, a British Royal Signals officer specializing in railways, was found to have a forbidden map detailing the stations along the Thai-Burma rails. He was severely beaten, had both arms broken, was locked in an oven-like cell, had ants crawling over him, was forbidden to wash or visit a latrine, left thirsty and hungry, and later suffered water forced into his nose and mouth until his belly swelled and he was certain he would die.

Given all this, how could Lomax forgive the Japanese interpreter, a man named Nagase, who witnessed and aided his torturers in a mechanical voice, as Lomax recalled it, "with almost no inflection of interest" (Lomax 1995, 132)? At one point, Lomax recalls:

Then [the non-commissioned officer (NCO)] picked up a big stick, a rough tree branch. Each question from the small man by my side was immediately followed by a terrible blow with the branch from above the height of the NCO's head on to my chest and stomach [...] I used my splinted arms to try to protect my body and the branch smashed onto them again and again [...] The interpreter was at my shoulder, "Lomax, you will tell us. Then it will stop." (Lomax 1995: 143)

Fifty years later, having survived his ordeal and retired from the army, Lomax is overwhelmed by memories of his torturers and fury at them. He has received psychotherapy and married a highly sympathetic woman. He also discovers a book describing himself being tortured, written by Nagase, the Japanese interpreter now a devout Buddhist pacifist and anti-war activist, deeply sorry about the harsh Japanese treatment of Allied prisoners-of-war. Lomax's wife writes to the interpreter, who responds to her, "I will try to find out the way I can meet him if he agrees to see me [...] The dagger of your letter thrusted [*sic*] me into my heart to the bottom" (Lomax 1995: 255). The two men meet in Kanburi, Thailand, the very site of Lomax's torture.

"He was kind enough to say that compared to my suffering his was nothing; and yet it was so obvious that he had suffered too", Lomax reflects. "In all the time I spent in Japan [as a guest of Nagase] I never felt a flash of the anger I had harbored against Nagase all those years [...] As we walked and talked, I felt that my strange companion was a person who I would have been able to get on with long ago had we met under other circumstances. We had a lot in common: books, teaching, an interest in history" (Lomax 1995: 266, 268, 274).

At the end of his visit, Lomax asked to sit alone with Nagase, a plan which frightened Nagase's wife, who feared Lomax might still seek revenge. But that was not to be. Sitting quietly alone with Nagase, Lomax "gave [him] the forgiveness he desired". As Lomax recalled, "I told him that while I could not forget what happened in Kanburi in 1943, I assured him of my total forgiveness. He was overcome with emotion again, and we spent some time in his room talking [...] without haste" (Lomax 1995: 275).

Huck Finn loved Jim. He did what a friend does. He came to *trust* his empathy and screw up his courage to defy an empathy-inhibiting law of his society. Eric Lomax first prepared the way (psychiatry, sympathetic wife, the passage of time) before slowly attuning himself to the much-changed Mr. Nagase. Huck had long felt empathy for Jim; his challenge was to act on it. Lomax's feelings shifted, his zone of empathy slowly widening to include his former foe. Huck Finn was guided by the tacit rules of friendship; he did what a friend does. Eric Lomax was guided by a desire to recover from his rage, and by humanism. On both counts he didn't want to hate anyone.

Getting There

So how do we expand the empathy zones on our maps? One way is via an *unexpected personalizing gesture*. Perhaps the most astonishing example is the famous World War I "Christmas truce" of 1914 on the Western Front. British and German soldiers, sharing little by way of culture and language, and each trained by their respective officers to despise and kill the other, made preliminary gestures of trust in the weeks before Christmas—offers back and forth of cigarettes, for example. On Christmas day, each side raised white flags, climbed out of their trenches, exchanged gifts, played football, sang Christmas songs and even danced with each other. The breakthrough was short-lived. When generals on each side discovered this shocking breach of discipline, the practice was stopped. But such a brave act of trust was based on some sense that "you guys must be feeling like we're feeling". Perhaps it was the daily touch with death; nine million soldiers died in World War I and many must have felt: "What do we have to lose?" What transpired was a surprise attack of empathy.

Many also extend their empathy more gradually through the logic of the *exceptional person*. Some whites have one black friend about whom they say, "he's not like the rest of them". Some Christians have one Muslim friend about whom they also say, "he's an exception". Some straight people have one gay friend, and so on. Such connections cross boundaries, but also re-create them. For each says to himself, in effect, "My friend is wonderful so I can empathize with him, because he's so different from others of his type, with whom I can't empathize". But in other cases, sometimes empathy for one person can be a pathway of empathy with the rest of those within a given category.

We can also expand empathy by establishing common ground through specially designed programs that alter our *exposure* to disdained categories of people. Summertime *Children Create Peace* camps have brought together eight- to twelve-year-old Israeli, Palestinian and Christian children to share an interest in animals (see Thomas 2005).[16] Coming from areas such as Ram-allah, Jenin, Bethlehem, East Jerusalem, and Jericho, areas ever prepared for gun or missile fire, the children learn to share a fascination with giraffes and to extend empathy with each other. Other versions of this experiment exist in different forms in many public schools and colleges. Focusing on children from kindergarten to eighth grade, Mary Gordon established in 1996 the *Roots of Empathy* program, a non-profit organization with 15 centers—twelve in Canada and three in the United States of America. In it, a parent and baby pay a series of visits to a classroom (27 visits in all), and a trained empathy instructor helps the children recognize what the baby is feeling.[17] Even such time-limited exposures can lead to many to begin to redraw their maps.

By whatever means we find to alter them, the maps themselves seem to vary according to our membership in given social categories—gender, race, national origin and also social class. Again the clues can be indirect. A series of studies show that the poor are more generous than the rich. *Independent Sector*, a nonprofit organization that researches charitable giving, reported that households earning less than 25,000 dollars a year gave away an average 4.2 percent of their incomes; those earning more than 75,000 dollars gave away 2.7 percent (Warner 2010). In another study, psychologists Paul K. Piff and Michael W. Kraus found that low-income people were more "gener-ous, charitable, and helpful to others" than were the wealthy. The rich who live in neighborhoods with many other wealthy people give away a smaller share of their income than rich people living in more economically diverse

---

16 The camp was started by the US-based Kabbalah Center and the Palestinian Abu Assukar Center for Peace and Dialogue.

17 Roots of Empathy gave rise in 2000 to another school-based program called Seeds of Em-pathy, focused on 3- to 5-year-olds. See http://www.rootsofempathy.org/en/where-we-are/north-america.html.

communities (Gipple and Gose 2012).[18] The income the rich do give away, another study found, is not directed toward the poor but to cultural institutions—such as the opera, museums, their *alma maters*.[19]

So what's the link between a person's empathy and their generosity? In an experiment, Piff discovered that if higher-income people were shown a sympathy-eliciting video and instructed to imagine themselves as poor, they became more charitable and helpful. And the reverse was also true: when lower-income people were instructed to think of themselves as rich, they became less so (Warner 2010; Piff et al. 2010).

Ideas about our placement in the world alter the maps we draw. And among American college students, ideas conducive to empathy seem to be losing—not gaining—hold. In a study of 13,737 students—some entering college in the late 1970s to early 1980s, some entering in the 1990s, and some in the 2000s, a team of psychologists discovered a decline in what they called "empathic concern"[20], indicated by answers to such questions as "I often have tender, concerned feelings for people less fortunate than me". Maybe today's students are more preoccupied with their own uncertain futures than earlier students were, and so are re-drawing their maps. But if the young express less empathy than the old—as one study suggests—we may be heading for real trouble (Konrath et al. 2011: 183).

In the end, we need to know far more than we do about empathy maps. How can circumstances—like those of the surprising battlefront Christmas dance, the summer camp for children of warring states—enable us to empathize better and more than we do? In empathy, women have taken the lead. But so too have some men—like the fictional Huck Finn and the mercilessly tortured, forgiving, extraordinary Eric Lomax. By itself, more empathy will

---

18 Those who made more than 200,000 dollars a year account for more than 40 percent of taxpayers in a ZIP code.

19 Among those earning less than 14,000 dollars a year, the working poor—families with the same income as welfare recipients but who receive all their money from jobs—also give more than equally poor welfare recipients. Findings from a 2007 report from Indiana University's Center on Philanthropy, as cited in Warner 2010.

20 The study was based on a meta-analysis of 72 studies of American college students (Konrath et al. 2011). In a parallel study, another team of researchers found that 44 percent of students in college between 1966–1978 ("boomers") gave priority to "being very well off financially", while 71 percent of those in college between 1979 to 1999 ("Gen Xers") and 74 percent of those in college between 2000–2009 ("Millenials") (Twenge et al. 2012). This growing preoccupation may reflect a growing fear of economic hardship, a turning inward, and vulnerability to an "empathy squeeze". See Hochschild 2005.

not solve all the world's problems, but having more empathy would make it an entirely different world.

Works Cited

Barnett, Rosalind, Lois Biener, and Grace K. Baruch (eds.) (1987), *Gender and stress*, New York: The Free Press.

Bernard, Jessie (1981), *The female world*, New York: The Free Press.

Brooks, Arthur C. (2008), *The poor give more*, in: American Enterprise Institute, March 3, http://www.aei.org/article/society-and-culture/the-poor-give-more/.

Burleson, Brant R., and Adrianne W. Kunkel (2006), "Revisiting the different cultures thesis: An assessment of sex differences and similarities in supportive communication", in: Kathrin Dindia, and Daniel J. Canary (eds.), *Sex differences and similarities in communication* (2nd ed.), Mahwah, NJ: Erlbaum, 137–159.

Cooper, Marianne (forthcoming Fall of 2013), *Cut adrift: Families in insecure times*, Berkeley, Los Angeles: University of California Press.

Eagley, Alice H. (2009), "The his and hers of prosocial behavior: An examination of the social psychology of gender", in: *American Psychologist*, 64 (8), 644–658.

Fischer, Claude S. (1982), *To dwell among friends: Personal networks in town and city*. Chicago: University of Chicago Press.

Fischer, Claude (2011), *Still connected: Family and friends in America since 1970*, New York: Russell Sage Foundation.

Gat, Azar (2012), "Is war declining—and why?", in: *Journal of Peace Research*, December 21, doi: 10.1177/0022343312461023.

Gipple, Emily, and Ben Gose (2012), "American's generosity divide", in: *The Chronicle of Philanthropy*, August 19, http://philanthropy.com/article/America's-Generosity-Divide/133775/.

Gove, Walter R. (1972), "The relationship between sex roles, marital status, and mental illness", in: *Social Forces*, 51, 1, 34–44.

Gove, Walter R., Michael Hughes, and Omer R. Galle (1983), *Overcrowding in the household: An analysis of determinants and effects*, New York: Academic Press New York.

Hochschild, Arlie Russell (1997), *The time bind. When work becomes home and home becomes work*, New York: Metropolitan Books.

— (2005), "The chauffeur's dilemma", in: *The American prospect*, July, 51–53.

— (2012), *The outsourced self. Intimate life in market times*. New York: Metropolitan Books.

Kessler, Ronald C., and Jane D. McLeod (1984), "Sex differences in vulnerability to undesirable life events", in: *American sociological review*, 49, 620–631.

Konrath, Sara H., Edward H. O'Brien, and Courtney Hsing (2011), "Changes in dispositional empathy in American college students over time: A meta-analysis", in: *Personality and social psychology review*, 15, 2, 180–198.

Leyens, Jacques-Philippe, Stéphanie Demoulin, Jeroen Vaes, Ruth Gaunt, and Maria Paola Paladino (2007), "Infra-humanization: The wall of group differences", in: *Social issues and policy review*, 1, 1, 139–172.

Lomax, Eric (1995), *The railway man*. New York: Norton Books.

Nolen-Hoeksema, Susan (1987), "Sex Differences in Unipolar Depression: Evidence and Theory", in: *Psychological Bulletin*, 101 (2), 259–282.

Piccinelli, Marco, and Greg Wilkinson (2000), "Gender differences in depression. Critical review", in: *British journal of psychiatry: the journal of mental science*, 177, 486–492.

Piff, Paul K., Michael W. Kraus, Stéphane Côté, Bonnie Hayden Cheng, and Dacher Keltner (2010), "Having less, giving more: The influence of social class on prosocial behavior", in: *Journal of personality and social psychology*, 99, 5, 771–784.

Pinker, Steven (2012), *The better angels of our nature: Why violence has declined*. New York: Penguin Books.

Rifkin, Jeremy (2009), *The empathic civilization: the race to global consciousness in a world in crisis*, New York: J. P. Tarcher/Penguin.

Smelser, Neil (2002) [1999], *The social edges of psychoanalysis*, Berkeley: University of California Press.

Smith, Adam (2003), *The wealth of nations*, New York: Bantam Classic.

Smith, Tom W. (2003), *Altruism in contemporary America: A report from the National Altruism Study*, Chicago: National Opinion Research Center.

Stack, Carol (1974), *All our kin: Survival strategies*, New York: Harper Torchback.

Taylor, Shelley E. (2003), *The tending instinct: Women, men and the biology of relationships*, New York: Henry Holt.

Themnér, Lotta, and Peter Wallensteen (2012), "Armed conflicts, 1946–2011", in: *Journal of Peace Research*, 49, 4, 565–575.

Thomas, Amelia (2005), "Israeli and Palestinian children participate in peace camp", in: *Middle East Times*, August 2.

Tronto, Joan (1993), *Moral boundaries: A political argument for an ethic of care*, New York: Routledge.

Twain, Mark (1992) [1885], *The adventures of Tom Sawyer & the adventures of Huckleberry Finn*, Ware: Wordsworth Classics.

Twenge, Jean M., W. Keith Campbell, and Elise C., Freeman (2012), "Generational differences in young adults' life goals, concern for others, and civic orientation, 1966–2009", in: *Journal of personality and social psychology*, 102, 5, 1045–1062.

Warner, Judith (2010), "The charitable-giving divide", in: *The New York Times*, August 22, Sunday magazine, p. MM11, http://www.nytimes.com/2010/08/22/magazine/22FOB-wwln-t.html.

Weissman, Myrna M., and Gerald L. Klerman (1977), "Sex differences and the epidemiology of depression", in: *Journal of health and social behaviour*, 26, 156–182.

Wellman, Barry, and Stephen D. Berkowitz (1988), *Social structures: A network approach. Structural analysis in the social sciences.* Cambridge: Cambridge University Press.

Wellman, Barry, and Scot Wortley (1990), "Different strokes from different folks: Community ties and social support", in: *The American journal of sociology,* 96, 558–588.

Caring for Young and Old: The Care-giving Bind in Late-forming Families

Nancy Konvalinka

This chapter will explore how emotion and economy interact in the fulfillment of intergenerational care-giving in late-forming families in the context of Madrid, Spain, keeping in mind themes such as emotion and commodification, the impact of free-market *zeitgeist* on modern life, and the damage done to people's lives by the cultural dominance of the market.

My discussion will be based mainly on the on-going ethnographic fieldwork that our research group, *Family and Kinship in the 21ˢᵗ Century*, is carrying out on the subject of late-forming families in Madrid and their organization of care-giving for and by members of the different generations.[1] This ethnographic fieldwork includes in-depth interviews with members of late-forming families and with experts in assisted reproduction and adoption, participant observation in families' activities and in events organized by assisted reproduction clinics and other agencies and associations, and the monitoring of statements and perspectives on these issues disseminated by the media.

Theoretical underpinnings

My work draws from three main currents of thought, the current founded by Pierre Bourdieu, the area of life course studies as exemplified in the seminal

---

1 The broader research being carried out by our group is financed by the Spanish Ministry of Science and Innovation (Project title: *Late-forming families: An ethnographic study of family configurations in Madrid and their social implications*. Project reference: FEM2011-30306). My specific research on care-giving in these late forming families is financed by the Wenner-Gren Foundation (Project title: *Late-forming families. The organization of care-giving and the concept of generation*) and by the Universidad Nacional de Educación a Distancia (UNED). I would also like to thank Dr. María Isabel Jociles and Dr. Ana Rivas for including me in their research project (Project title: *Single mothers by choice: Strategies of self-definition, distinction, and legitimization of new family models*. Project reference: FEM2009-07717), material from which I have also used in this paper.

work of Leonard Cain (1964) and developed by many later authors, and Hochschild's work on family, market, and emotional and care-giving work.

Bourdieu's (1977, 1979/1984, 1989) concepts of habitus, difference, preference, and different kinds of capital and the uses people give to them to situate themselves on the social field are especially helpful in understanding people's actions and speech-actions, the decisions people make throughout their lives and the way they speak of these decisions.

The concept of life course, as opposed to the limitations of the concept of life cycle, emphasizes the creation of the life course as a process carried out by specific persons in varying cultural, economic, political, institutional, and increasingly globalized contexts (see Heinz et al. [2009] for a compendium of classic and recent work on the life course concept). Finally, within the work on the life course, Johnson-Hanks (2002) provides the concept of vital conjuncture:

> The analytic concept of vital conjuncture refers to a socially structured zone of possibility that emerges around specific periods of potential transformation in a life or lives. It is a temporary configuration of possible change, a duration of uncertainty and potential. Although most social life may be thought of as conjunctural, in the sense that action is conjoined to a particular, temporary manifestation of social structure, vital conjunctures are particularly critical durations where more than usual is in play, when the futures at stake are significant. (Johnson-Hanks 2002: 871)

This concept of vital conjuncture will help us to understand the construction of life courses and the resulting increase in late-forming families in Spain, as well as the interaction of emotion and economy in the way that these families approach the care-giving that is generally assumed to be the family's responsibility in the Spanish welfare state.

In such works as *The Second Shift* (1989), *The Time Bind* (1997), *The Commercialization of Intimate Life* (2003), and the *Outsourced Self* (2012), Hochschild deals with the pressures people, both people on their own and people wrapped up in family relations, are under to carry out the emotional and care-giving work that they feel is their responsibility. As Hochschild points out, in the US context, there are fewer people at home to do the care-giving and emotional work, job insecurity forces people to devote more and more time to work, leaving less time for care-giving, and, increasingly, people seek to cover these needs by buying services on the market (2003: 1–3). How care-giving is organized in the family has important economic and personal repercussions for an entire series of people: those responsible for the welfare of others, those who need care, those who care for them as family or friends, and those who care for them as hired workers. As we shall see, late-forming families, which concentrate a great deal of care-giving in one or two adults, are a privileged place to study these phenomena.

What is a "late-forming family"?

The concept of *late-forming family* is, in fact, not as easy to define as it would seem. As doctors and other professionals in health and fertility have explained in our interviews with them, the age of 35 is a turning point at which women's fertility decreases, with a drastic drop to near zero after the age of 40. But *early* and *late* are always socially and culturally defined terms (Sampedro et al. 2002; Hernández Corrochano 2012) that depend on a culturally constructed life course model that may or may not define the *right* time for life course transitions. In the case we are dealing with here, the age at first birth is considered late for two reasons: because first births used to occur earlier and because the average age at first birth is now approaching the age at which fertility can become problematic.

Although age at first birth has only been gathered by the *Instituto Nacional de Estadística* (INE) since 1975 in Spain, we can get an idea of the age at which women have begun their families before this date by looking at age at first marriage, particularly because, until quite recently, most births took place within marriage. Following the European pattern determined by Hajnal (1965), the birth rate was, historically, controlled in Spain by late marriage. According to Reher (1997: 154), the age at first marriage for women was 24 in the early twentieth century, and 26 by the middle of the century. These ages at first marriage point to ages at first birth of around 25 and 27, for the early and mid-twentieth century, respectively. In 1975, during a period of relative economic prosperity, age at first birth was 25, dropping slightly through 1979, but later it began to rise, from 25 in 1980 to almost 26 in 1990. In the year 2000, it was slightly over 29, and in in 2011 it was 30.1, although if we consider only the population with Spanish citizenship (that is, if we leave out the immigrant population that brings along different fertility patterns), the age at first birth rises to 30.8 (INE Base). So we are looking at a tendency to delay first births that has lasted for thirty years already. This age at first birth, or at family formation, is *late* with respect to women thirty years ago; it is also *late* with respect to non-Spanish mothers and families (see Konvalinka [2012] for a more detailed analysis).

It should be noted here that, when I refer to family, I am using an inclusive definition that covers heterosexual couples, homosexual couples, and single mothers, including single mothers by choice (see Jociles and Rivas 2009 for the definition and study of single mothers by choice).

As we shall see, while having the first child at age 30 is considered *late* with respect to earlier times, it is not considered *late* at present. For the purposes of our research, we have provisionally defined late-forming families as families that "are made up of parent(s) who are considered biologically and socially older and in which the generational difference between parent(s) and children is higher than the conventionally established difference, that is, around 40 years" (Hernández Corrochano 2012: 92; translated by Konvalinka). Thus, our provisional definition does not disagree with the "medical" definition or with the "demographic" definition, while at the same time we follow the present-day culturally constructed definition of the appropriate age at which to have children, which places "too old" at the limits of fertility.

But this delay, which people in Spain are coming to view as *normal*, can clash with the medical definition, leading to problems of infertility when the decision to have a child is finally made. These problems of infertility can lead the women to resort to assisted reproduction techniques, which may take some time, and to adoption, which can take longer, delaying the arrival of the child even longer. These late-forming families are often *last chance* families; although some have two, many only have one child. (See also Hernández Corrochano [2012] and Konvalinka [2012] on this issue.)

Why is the number of late-forming families increasing?

The economic situation (unemployment, job precariousness [see Götz and Lemberger 2009 on this issue in Germany], and the cost of housing), which is also related to the lengthening of the time many people devote to higher education, is popularly blamed as the main cause for the delay in family formation. For some years now, there has been a heightened awareness in Spain of the difficulty for gaining access to and stabilizing job positions. People—and not only young people—are often given one temporary contract after another, and it is quite common now to reach the age of 30, 35, or even 40 and still have no job security. It is, of course, illegal to fire women for becoming pregnant and giving birth, but with the generalized job insecurity, women are understandably concerned that having a child will affect their chances to remain or become employed. Also, the market requires people who are mobile (Götz et al. 2010) and flexible (Seifert et al. 2007). Job mobility creates many complications for two-earner families and can often lead to temporary geographic separation or to job loss for one of the members. The flexibility required for jobs often means making other obligations, most importantly, family obligations, secondary to work, or at least fulfilling them by hiring labor external to the family from the market.

This difficult employment situation is a factor in the lengthening educational trajectories of young people. On one hand, popular wisdom generally holds that more education increases a person's employability: studying is considered to be the only chance to maximize one's chance to get a job and, if a person has studied hard and long, and still cannot get a job, this at least diminishes the blame that accrues to her or him. On the other hand, given the lack of jobs, continuing to study is a way to fill the time while waiting to enter the work force.

The cost of housing in Spain, whether purchased or rented, is also very high. This is a factor that keeps many young people living with their parents until their thirties, often until they have what they consider to be a stable partner and, usually using the salaries of both partners, they decide to marry or move in together.

However, this relationship between the crisis and late family formation is neither clear nor linear; while there have been and are crisis situations in many contexts in the world, a delay in family formation is not always the automatic result. The *habitus* that was already in place long before the crisis achieved its recent dimensions seems to help to understand why people react to the situation by waiting longer to form their families. Popular discourse in Spain postulates a culturally-determined series of *must-do's*, in a specified order, that must be crossed off the list before one can start a family: education, job stability, purchase of a home, marriage, and, finally, children. Whereas these *must-do's* have been feasible in the past, allowing people to form families in their twenties or early thirties, at present, delays in accomplishing them and reaching the different vital conjunctures of the life course seem to accumulate, delaying family formation for many—sometimes indefinitely. The combination of the crisis situation with a relatively rigid life course *habitus* seems to be the key to this situation. We must also consider the effects of the second contraceptive revolution, in which birth control makes it possible for women to plan their calendar for conceiving and giving birth for when it is most convenient (Segalen 1992: 152). Together with the awareness of the possibilities that the new assisted reproduction technologies offer, women's apparently high level of control over their fertility calendar seems to influence people to put off having children and shouldering the care-giving responsibilities that they involve. Not only do assisted reproduction technologies permit many women who are nearing the end of their reproductive lives, or who are even past the critical time, to have children; the new techniques for vitrifying eggs to be used years later offer the possibility, or at least the illusion, of being able to plan for reproduction at later ages.

I believe that these situational factors and the medical progress in reproductive health, superimposed upon the relatively rigid step-by-step life course model that basically precludes family formation until the previous requirements are fulfilled, are fundamental in understanding the present-day delay in family formation, both for couples, whether married or *de facto*, and for single women.

Why are we interested in studying these families and their intergenerational care-giving practices?

In the social sciences, the most interesting situations to study are often situations that are at the limit, situations in which the more typical tendencies are put under an extra strain or tension, highlighting specific problems. To our knowledge, no other researchers are really focusing on late-forming families and there is, in fact, little awareness that this group exists and may have special needs, particularly in the area of care-giving.

There are many indications that late-forming families face specific challenges that place them under a special care-giving strain. Working Spanish mothers often depend on outside help for caring for their children, either on a daily basis, to take children to and from pre-school and school and to stay with them until the mother returns from work, or at particularly complicated moments, when children are ill and cannot go to pre-school or school, or on school holidays that do not correspond to work holidays. Sometimes this assistance comes from friends, neighbors, or hired babysitters or nannies. If the grandparents live nearby, they are often the main source of childcare.

However, this care-giving is both physical and emotional labor and, as such, requires relatively "young", healthy grandparents. The delay in family formation, in contrast, makes for relatively "old" grandparents: if a woman has a child when she is 40 years old, her parents are likely to be 65 or older at this point and may not be able or willing to care for babies and small children. In fact, they may need care themselves, becoming an additional care-giving responsibility for the newly-formed family.

This situation of older people with very young children and elderly grandparents creates a new version of the "sandwich generation" (Miller 1981; Williams 2004). Originally, the term "sandwich generation" from the 1980s and 1990s, coined in the USA where both healthcare and higher education are a significant economic drain on a family's resources, referred to a concentration of economic responsibilities regarding the generation of a person's parents (specialized elder care) and the generation of a person's post-adolescent/young adult children (college expenses). In the context of late-forming families in Spain, we can recycle this concept to refer to a new kind of sandwich generation in which there is a concentration of care-giving responsibilities regarding a person's parents (the elderly) and a person's children (babies or very young children). In addition, the reduction in birth rates in recent decades has reduced the number of siblings with whom to share the elder-care, a situation pointed out in the US by Hochschild (2003: 1), according to whom there is a "growing care gap" as informal systems of care break down and are not sufficiently replaced either by public or private care-giving.

Having been two-earner families (except, of course, in the case of single mothers by choice), these late-forming families often aspire to maintain their economic position by keeping both jobs. And having worked very hard to achieve job stability, the women are often unwilling to stop working, as it is very difficult in Spain to leave the job market for a few years and then return and find a new job. So, who cares for the child or children? And who cares for the elderly and other family members needing special attention?

Approaches to these care-giving challenges

The possibilities for resolving these difficulties depend to a great extent on the conception of the family as a public issue and therefore the object of public policy or as a private issue and therefore an issue to be dealt with within the family and the nearest kinship group.

In this regard, it is important to understand a bit of the history of family policy in Spain. As Naldini (2003: 75–93) explains, family policy in various forms was very important during the Franco dictatorship. The conservative, right-wing politics supported a male-breadwinner model, encouraging women—after a time of greater freedom and the achievement of many rights during the period immediately previous—to remain at home and devote themselves to the emotional, care-giving labor. Throughout the dictatorship, there were many policies that assisted families, for example, through point systems that adjusted a man's salary according to number of dependants and through bonuses for children born, etc. All of these systems left women in a subordinate, dependent position.

When the dictatorship came to an end and the change was made to a democratic system in 1976, one of the main concerns was equal rights for men and women, particularly in employment. At this point in time, policy gave priority to the consideration of men and women as individuals, as equivalent atoms in the system. Family policy, from this point on, was too reminiscent of the dictatorship and of women's subordination to be popular, and it was gradually phased out and then simply ignored (Naldini 2003: 115–120).

And so, family formation went from being a matter of public interest under the dictatorship to being a matter strictly of private and personal interest to the persons concerned. This, of course, had repercussions particularly for women; although women's position had, formally and constitutionally, become equal to that of men, reality had not yet caught up (and it still hasn't), either in the labor market or in the sharing of housework and care-giving work. So moving the issue to the private sphere has, in effect, meant continuing to discriminate against women.

To exemplify this, there is one conversation of which I have heard innumerable versions. It follows these lines:

Well, when my first child was born, I stopped working. We did the math and, if I earned "100", it would have cost "50" to hire someone to take care of the child at home, plus what my transportation to and from work costs, so in the end I would have been working for less than "50", running around like crazy, with someone else taking care of my child, and it would have been a bad situation for all of us. What's the point of trying to do that? So we decided it was better if I stayed at home. (Amalgam of many women's explanations)

What is actually gender discrimination—starting with the fact that, for a whole series of reasons the husband earns more money than the wife—is masked as a rational decision made in the private sphere by freely acting agents. Individuals are forced to take responsibility for a discriminatory situation that is far beyond their power to resolve and thus, unwittingly, propagate the situation.

But let us return to Naldini's explanation of the issue of Spanish family policy (Naldini 2003: 160–173). With priority given to efforts toward gender equality, family policy of any sort became a taboo subject. The attitude taken was that, after all, no one forces anyone to have a family; if that's what they decide to do, they should figure out how to deal with it, an attitude that disregards children as a public good and the production of children as a public service that allows society to continue to function.

With the decrease in the birth rate, however (18.7 in 1975, dropping to a low of 9.17 in 1996, rising only to 10.75 in 2009 due to immigration), Spain fell far below the replacement rate and there began to be concerns about an aging population and the lack of a younger cohort to support them through the social security pension system. However, family policy still has resonances of right-wing politics and little has actually been done to help people to be able to have the families that they would like to have; any aid that was available is being reduced in the present-day economic crisis.

The families we are studying, even though they are under a greater strain in some senses than families that form earlier, seem not to present many demands to the welfare state, as they seem to work under the assumption that these are private problems that they should resolve on their own. Single mothers by choice, for example, who quite often form their families later, repeatedly state that, when they made the decision to have a child, they first made all the necessary changes in order to be able to take care of the child: job changes to ensure compatible schedules, housing changes in order to be near family members who could help with care-giving, hiring of babysitters and nannies for all contingencies. As one woman, using a colloquial expression, said, "Yo me lo guiso, yo me lo como". This expression (which can be roughly translated as "I cook it, I eat it") is particularly rich in nuances, referring to one's sole, personal responsibility for dealing with the situations in which one places oneself.[2] The situation of single mothers by choice is, of course, an extreme example of personal responsibility; even though these

2 Data from the project Strategies of self-definition, distinction, and legitimization of new family models. Project reference: FEM2009-07717) directed by María Isabel Jociles.

mothers are not actually alone and usually have a carefully crafted web of care-giving aid (see Leyra et al. in press), they seem to feel acutely that the responsibility is theirs alone by their own choice.

The only real demand that the state has attended to is lowering the age for free public pre-school, which begins at age three, and increasing the provision of after-school activities (which must, however, be paid for separately) that keep the children busy and under supervision until a parent can arrive from work to pick them up.

So the solutions to the care-giving and emotional labor dilemmas in all families today, but most especially in late-forming families, in which the care-giving needs can be exacerbated by the lack of assistance from the elderly and the very need for care themselves that these elderly persons may have, must be sought either in the private sphere or in the market when people cannot or will not forgo paid employment to do it themselves.

In the specific cases of single mothers by choice and adoptive families, studies have shown that these groups tend to create social bonds of friendship, often through on-line forums, and, as persons with similar needs and difficulties, help one another, at least with the children and advice about them (Rivas y Jociles 2012). These families, then, are also seeking creative non-market solutions to their care-giving needs.

Another option that families use is to go to the market and hire someone (most often a Spanish-speaking immigrant woman) to provide childcare or elder care. And so part of the emotional work that was once a fundamental aspect of the family is now outsourced to foreign women (see Hochschild 2012). As Hochschild notes, although hiring people for care-giving tasks is not new, there is a certain difference in the nature of home-grown care-giving, which is personal (for better or worse) and market-bought care-giving, which is often less personal but can be more professional (2003: 30–44). This outsourcing, although it is not new, is becoming more and more important as a way for middle and middle-upper class families to enable both members of the couple to remain employed.

The specific characteristics of late-forming families, with the simultaneous care-giving pressures of the elderly and the very young, and with adult members, in either couples or monoparental families, often employed full time, place them in a care-giving bind. The media and comments heard in casual conversation often blame the people involved in the late-forming families for this situation, construing these people as selfish for insisting on achieving too much, on trying to consolidate a certain standard of living before having children, on leaving family formation too late. This view of the issue is often shared by the people who form their families late; they understand their decisions to be personal decisions and take personal responsibility for the difficulties of what is actually a structural situation, a situation in which they are caught between the dynamics of the market and the standard life course model they are expected to follow.

To summarize, I would like to address some of the main issues that guide the discussion in this volume, as they specifically refer to late-forming families in Spain.

What are the effects of the free market *zeitgeist* in the emotion and economy of care-giving in late-forming families in Spain?

In the Spanish context we are studying, the free market *zeitgeist*, which requires unattached individuals—or at least individuals who, willingly or not, put work first, relegating almost everything in their lives to second place—to be mobile and to put up with a high degree of precariousness in employment, diminishes people's capacity to provide personal care-giving. The Spanish welfare state continues to construct most of this work as the family's responsibility, and society continues to construct this work mainly as women's work (López de la Vieja 2012). When there is no stay-at-home adult in a family, the care-giving work must be outsourced, either to other family members and friends or to paid care-givers. With reduced family sizes and late-forming families, there may not be recourse to other relatives such as grandparents who may, in this case, be elderly themselves, unable to take on the responsibility of caring for babies and small children and perhaps in need of care themselves.

How do people, especially the people who form their families late, experience the expanding market?

As has been noted, the market needs "individuals" in order to function. The more disengaged these individuals are—allowing them to work long, flexible hours, to exploit themselves by working evenings, weekends and holidays—the better it is for the market. Of course, the market needs these workers to reproduce themselves, but this is generally not considered to be the problem of the businesses; even though there is more and more legislation regarding the conciliation of work and family life, the current economic crisis inspires people to self-exploit and to avoid anything that can be construed as complaining about their jobs. Phrases such as "You're lucky to have a job" and "There are lots of people who would be glad to have your job" are heard constantly, perhaps less from employers than from peers. In a crisis situation in which people are afraid of losing their jobs and becoming unemployed, they are not very likely to rock the boat and vindicate rights limiting shifts, hours, and workloads. In the case of Spain, the situation of unemployment, descending wages, and job precariousness directly affects people's life courses. Stable jobs are very hard to get and difficult to consolidate and this, in turn, delays people's economic independence, their capacity to purchase or rent a place to live and, as a result, their decisions to form families. People explain that this perception of precariousness makes them feel incapable of planning for the long-term, something that they consider fundamental for family formation. As consumers, these same people must often seek care-giving services for both the young and the elderly in the market, something which is still often difficult to accept. Also, as private individuals, the need to have gainful employment in the market, making one independent economically (eventually), is central to one's self-image.

To what degree does the market envelop the self in present-day Spain?

The workplace can influence ideas, tastes, habits. The effort expended in the workplace, particularly with the self-exploitation resulting from fear of losing one's job, and the resulting exhaustion, highlights the work aspect of care-giving activities. This can be good, in a way, because it makes what was previously invisible work, or what was considered to be non-work, visible. But it can turn all care-giving—visiting the elderly, going to the park with the children—into work, work that must be finished before one can finally sit down at night and have a little time for oneself. This has a particularly strong effect on women whose position is not only more precarious in employment but who are expected, and expect themselves, to carry out a larger part of the family's care-giving work.

What ultimate damage is being done by the cultural dominance of the market?

Once again, I feel it is important to point out that it is not only the market that poses difficulties for family formation, but the way that the new market conditions clash with previously culturally constructed expectations for people's life courses that are proving to be slow to adapt to the new conditions.

The uncertainty and insecurity of the job market today (a trend which was also visible in the late 80s and early 90s), with low salaries (*mil-eurista* is the term used for the working population whose take-home paycheck hovers around one thousand euros a month), act upon a cultural basis that considers that a couple should be able to maintain themselves independently before they marry and have children. People have a hard time finding steady work, they have a hard time saving, a very hard time acquiring housing, and often little confidence that the situation will improve. Together with the second contraceptive revolution, with children being born according to a planned calendar and the number generally limited to one or two, this has contributed to a decrease in the number of children people have and in the postponement of their births. In this situation, the market directly frustrates many people's desire to have children. The lower birth rate, in turn, means that there will be fewer care-givers in families in the future, exacerbating the problem in Spanish society.

Works Cited

Bourdieu, Pierre (1977), *Outline of a theory of practice*, Cambridge: Cambridge University Press.
— (1979/1984), *Distinction. A social critique of the judgement of taste*, Cambridge: Harvard University Press.
— (1989), "Social space and symbolic power", in: *Sociological theory*, 7, 1, 14–25.

Cain, Leonard (1964), "Life course and social structure", in: Robert E. L. Faris (ed.), *Handbook of modern sociology*, Chicago: Rand McNally and Company, 272–309.

Götz, Irene, and Barbara Lemberger (eds.) (2009), *Prekär arbeiten, prekär leben. Kulturwissenschaftliche Perspektiven auf ein gesellschaftliches Phänomen*, Frankfurt: Campus Verlag.

Götz, Irene, Katrin Lehnert, Barbara Lemberger, and Sanna Schondelmayer (eds.) (2010), *Mobilität und Mobilisierung. Arbeit im sozioökonomischen, politischen und kulturellen Wandel*, Frankfurt: Campus Verlag.

Hajnal, John (1965), "European marriage patterns in perspective", in: David Victor Glass, and David E. C. Eversley (eds.), *Population in history: Essays in historical demography*, Chicago: Aldine Publishing Co., 101–143.

Heinz, Walter R., Johannes Huinink, and Ansgar Weymann (eds.) (2009), *The life course reader. Individuals and societies across time*, Frankfurt: Campus Verlag.

Hernández Corrochano, Elena (2012), "Familias tardías: ¿Nuevos retos para la sociedad del bienestar?", in: Nancy Konvalinka (ed.), *Modos y maneras de hacer familia. Las familias tardías, una modalidad emergente*, Madrid: Biblioteca Nueva, 85–95.

Hochschild, Arlie Russell (1989), *The second shift. Working parents and the revolution at home*, London: Piatkus.

— (1997), *The time bind. When work becomes home and home becomes work*, New York: Metropolitan Books.

— (2003), *The commercialization of intimate life. Notes from home and work*, Berkeley: University of California Press.

— (2012), *The outsourced self. Intimate life in market times*, New York: Metropolitan Books.

Instituto Nacional de Estadística, INE Base, Indicadores demográficos básicos. Natalidad y fecundidad. Edad media a la maternidad por orden de nacimiento según nacionalidad (española/extranjera) de la madre, http://www.ine.es/jaxi/tabla.do?per=12&type=db&divi=IDB&idtab=125, 18. 2. 2013.

Jociles, María Isabel, and Ana Rivas (2009), "Entre el empoderamiento y la vulnerabilidad: La monoparentalidad como proyecto familia de las MSPE por reproducción asistida y adopción internacional", in: *Revista de Antropología Social*, 18, 127–170.

Johnson-Hanks, Jennifer (2002), "On the limits of life stages in ethnography: Toward a theory of vital conjunctures", in: *American anthropologist*, 104, 3, 865–880.

Konvalinka, Nancy (2012), "Relaciones de cuidado y redes de parentesco en los nuevos modelos de familias: Las familias tardías", in: Nancy Konvalinka (ed.), *Modos y maneras de hacer familia. Las familias tardías, una modalidad emergente*, Madrid: Biblioteca Nueva, 97–106.

Leyra, Begoña, Laura Alamillos, and Nancy Konvalinka (in press), "Discursos y estrategias de conciliación de la vida laboral, familiar y personal entre las madres solteras por elección", in: María Isabel Jociles Rubio, and Raquel Medina Plana (eds.), *La monoparentalidad por elección: El proceso de construcción de un modelo de familia*, Madrid: Tirant lo Blanc.

López de la Vieja, María Teresa (2012), "El cuidado. Lo público y lo privado", in: Nancy Konvalinka (ed.), *Modos y maneras de hacer familia. Las familias tardías, una modalidad emergente*, Madrid: Biblioteca Nueva, 55–65.

Miller, Dorothy (1981), "The sandwich generation. Adult children of the aging", in: *Social Work*, 26, 5, 419–423.

Naldini, Manuela (2003), *The family in the Mediterranean welfare states*, London: Frank Cass.

Reher, David (1997), *Perspectives on the family in Spain, past and present*, Oxford: Clarendon Press.

Rivas, Ana Mª y Mª Isabel Jociles (2012), "La maternidad tardía: el papel de los foros on-line en el caso de las madres solteras por elección (MSPE)", in: Nancy Konvalinka (ed.), *Modos y maneras de hacer familia. Las familias tardías, una modalidad emergente*, Madrid: Biblioteca Nueva, 119–130.

Sampedro, Rosario, María Victoria Gómez, and Mercedes Montero (2002), "Maternidad tardía. Incidencia, perfiles y discursos", in: *EMPIRIA Revista de metodología de Ciencias Sociales*, 5, 11–36.

Segalen, Martine (1992), *Antropología histórica de la familia*, Madrid: Taurus.

Seifert, Manfred, Irene Götz, and Birgit Huber (eds.) (2007), *Flexible Biografien? Horizonte und Brüche im Arbeitsleben der Gegenwart*. Frankfurt: Campus Verlag.

Williams, Cara (2004), "The sandwich generation", in: *Perspectives on Labour and Income. Statistics Canada Catalogue 75-001-XIE 5 (9)*, 5–12, http://www.statcan. gc.ca/pub/75-001-x/10904/4212007-eng.pdf, 17.11 2010.

Channeling Time and Energy into Work and Home: The Rationales of Americans and Norwegians

Jeremy Schulz

The idea that commodified and economistic "ways of viewing" have reshaped everyday life in recent years has attracted its share of skepticism. It is still unclear, for example, whether and to what extent individuals across Western societies perceive their stocks of financial and social resources as "investments" whose returns are supposed to be maximized (Zelizer 2010; Davis 2009; Williams 2005). After all, as Williams shows in the case of the UK, self-servicing labor and non-monetized exchange still command a large proportion of many individuals' time, attention, and effort. When it comes to everyday practice, it is debatable whether the economic logics of commodity production and monetized commodity exchange have displaced the non-economistic logics such as gift-giving and mutual obligation that operate outside the economic sphere mediated by market relations (Hochschild 2012; 2011; 2004; Williams 2005; Margolis 1998).

But even if we accept the premise that the logics of commodity exchange and economic rationality have actually altered the ways that individuals conceive of their relationships with one another, it is still unclear whether these logics have transformed the ways that individuals perceive, allocate, and handle their inner resources of time, talent, and energy. In addressing this elusive question, this chapter asks how economistic logics enter into individuals' frames of their life realm engagements, the temporal allocations, and their vital energy resources. More specifically, the chapter examines the role of two distinct kinds of economistic logics, the logic of commensuration and the logic of economization, in relation to two different kinds of frames: life realm frames and energy frames. While commensuration has to do with the measurement of qualitatively distinct phenomena according to a common metric, economization has to do with the conservation and replenishment of intrinsically scarce resources. Both the commensurating and economizing logics can be seen as subspecies of the calculative rationality that serves as the hallmark of capitalist practice for Weber (Brubaker 1984; Weber 1946).

The life realm frames appear when individuals characterize their engagements with the two most fundamental "experiential realms" in contemporary commodity-producing society, namely the realm of work and the realm of private life (Nippert-Eng 1995; Hochschild 2003). Such life realm frames can apply both to the day-to-day dispositions of time and energy as well as long-term decisions about careers, jobs, and personal lives which unfold over months, years, and sometimes decades. Energy frames manifest themselves when individuals characterize their strategies for disposing of their vital energies and managing fatigue and tiredness.[1] This chapter asks whether, and to what extent, these frames betray the influence of either the commensurating logic or the economizing logic. To the extent that a *commensurating logic* surfaces in these life realm frames, both realms are represented as reducible to a common underlying denominator rather than as qualitatively distinctive domains (Espeland and Stevens 1998). When housework is commensurated with paid work, for example, cooking, cleaning, and other typically unpaid forms of work are measured according to the same units of marketable output as forms of paid work (Hochschild and Machung 1989). To the extent that energy frames bear the stamp of an economizing logic, they define the conservation of scarce energy—rather than the disposition of surplus energy—as the central challenge in everyday life.

In inquiring into the role of these economistic logics, individuals' frames of life realms and vital energy flows, I delve into the commentaries of successful American and Norwegian business professionals of both sexes and multiple family statuses. I ground the analysis in data drawn from over one hundred professional men and women employed by a variety of corporate private-sector employers located in Oslo and San Francisco.[2] Like San Fran-

---

1 The deeply social character of such energy frames are readily apparent in the existing sociological study of fatigue talk, a Norwegian book entitled *Trøtthetens Tid [The Time of Tiredness]* by Ulla-Britt Lilleas and Karin Widerberg. This study draws on interviews and tiredness diaries to illuminate the "doing" of tiredness and fatigue among adult Norwegians (Widerberg 2006; Lilleas and Widerberg 2001). The study demonstrates that, in order to come to grips with one's own tiredness (or lack thereof), one must by necessity interpret one's own mental and bodily sensations through socially constituted lenses. Even the extent to which we attend to our inner energy flows or tune them out reflects the influence of culturally and socially mediated experiences. As it turns out, age, generation, gender, occupation, and family background all make a large difference to how any given individual experiences tiredness, enacts tiredness, and expresses tiredness to themselves and to others in their social environments.

2 This chapter draws on material collected for my dissertation project. This project examines the impact of the French, Norwegian, and American cultural and social contexts on the

cisco's population, Oslo's population contains a comparatively high proportion of high-earning professionals working in demanding jobs. Each group of respondents in the two sites includes professional men and women spanning multiple occupations. The work hours of the Americans ranged from fifty hours per week on the low end to over sixty-five hours per week on the high end, while the Norwegians logged between forty-five hours per week and slightly over sixty hours per week. As far as their earnings are concerned, the American respondents earned somewhat more than their Norwegian counterparts working in comparable positions in the same occupations.

Drawing on narratives gleaned from these in-depth interviews,[3] I show that the American and Norwegian professionals stand apart where these two economistic logics are concerned. When they talk about their efforts to bring the two life realms into balance, only the Americans articulate narratives that incorporate a commensurating logic; the presence of a non-commensurating logic figures more prominently in the commentaries of the Norwegian respondents. However, the opposite pattern surfaces when these professionals address their strategies for handling their own vital energies. Here the Norwegian respondents adopt an economizing logic whereas the Americans give voice to a non-economizing logic. In the following sections I show how my Norwegian and American respondents articulate these frames in their commentaries about their engagements with work and private life, and their stances towards vital energy and tiredness.

Life Realm Frames: American tradeoffs

In this section, I analyze the ways in which the task of harmonizing the demands of work life and private life is framed in the narratives of the American respondents. It is exclusively in the commentaries of the American professionals that the commensurating framing, a framing signaled by the presence of the term "tradeoffs" appears. Furthermore, over three-quarters of the

---

ways that comparable populations of French, Norwegian, and American managers and professionals constitute their work lives and private lives.

3 This analysis focuses on frames and narratives rather than actual practices. The link between practices and narratives/frames is complex. Moreover, there is usually more intra-group diversity when it comes to practices, since they are more influenced by life circumstances unique to the individual. It is therefore usually easier to discern cross-national divergences where frames and narratives are concerned (see also Schulz 2012; 2011).

American respondents reference such tradeoffs when they touch upon the challenge of harmonizing their commitments to work and private life. The narratives of these men and women thematize tradeoffs between what they gain from boosting their earnings and what they gain from investing more in private life. In doing so, they implicitly commensurate the higher quality of life brought about by increases in purchasing power—typically accompanied by longer work hours and more demanding jobs—with the higher quality of life arising from more personal time. The language of tradeoffs is absent in the narratives of the Norwegians.

In discussing their personal and professional biographies, the Americans recall the numerous "tradeoffs" which have shaped their jobs, career trajectories, and personal lives. At the time of the interview, John was a very successful thirty-five year old American investment banker, with four children and a stay-at-home wife, and logging between 55 and 60 hours at work per week, far fewer hours than he had worked while launching his banking career. John repeatedly cites the long-term and short-term tradeoffs he had to make. On one side of the scale was the option of spending more time at his already-demanding job—and garnering more recognition at work and opportunities for increasing his already considerable earnings. Balanced against this option was the chance to spend more of his scarce free time with his family. Such tradeoffs could be avoided by anyone in his position, claimed John. As he put it:

You have to feel that *the tradeoffs* you are making are worth it … and for me they are worth it … I am always asking myself 'what's the incentive for me to blow it out and have a really great year and work really hard and do these 15 great things at work versus spend time with my four kids? *It's a tradeoff … and I'd assume that anyone would make these tradeoffs …*

Other American professionals cite the "lifestyle tradeoff" involved in demanding, long-hours, business services work. One man who already breached the 65-hour weekly mark on a regular basis balked at the idea of adding another ten hours to his weekly totals. Time scarcity was already a familiar challenge in his life, and he had no wish to "exacerbate" the problem, as he put it. As a new father, he already confronted strains over childcare even though his wife worked significantly fewer hours than he did. However, there was no reason to reject a 75-hour workweek in principle, assuming the longer work hours came with a larger paycheck. This tradeoff could make sense for him and his wife:

If [my wife and I] were in a different place now, where it was more important to make a ton of money or as much money as we could in the next five years, we might be willing to sacrifice the lifestyle entirely, and *then the tradeoff* would be worth it.

His wife contrasted her own very different tradeoff scenario with his work-life tradeoff scenario, associating his tradeoff with his assumption of the provider role:

JS:[4] Would you be inclined to work harder if they added 10 % to your salary?
RES: No, *the tradeoff is not worth it to me* … I think my husband would … he considers himself the primary breadwinner and I do too … and so he fortunately or unfortunately carries the burden of bringing home the bacon, quote-unquote, … although my salary isn't much lower now than his … the long-term trajectory for his salary is higher than mine.

Monica, a forty-five-year-old executive at a large accounting firm, had considered many non-business careers when younger, including medical careers that required much more training. In the end she had opted to launch a career in a very demanding corner of the business world, in large measure because she could not see herself "trading off" more unpaid time spent in education for the possibility of making money as a professional. Indeed, Monica had rejected the idea of becoming a physician primarily because she could not envision investing enormous amounts of time attending medical school when she could be earning money and enhancing her economic security and quality of life. Just as she traded off time against the opportunity to make money when younger, as a busy professional she now trades off longer work hours, as a proxy for her earnings, against more time for the leisure pursuits she enjoys in her private life. She explained this tradeoff scenario in terms of the additional security and standard of living she could obtain by securing a thirty-percent bump in her salary versus a thirty-percent reduction in her work hours:

If I could [get] another thirty percent in pay, I could really improve my financial situation. I could get my own house in a great neighborhood, go on better vacations, save more money for retirement. On the other side, cutting back my hours by thirty percent—with no change in my salary—would certainly improve my personal life. I could spend much more time socializing with my friends and maybe get a serious hobby going.

---

4 In this interview excerpt the initials "JS" stand for the author and interviewer, and the initials "RES" stand for the respondent.

While she was content to continue working the hours she currently worked—around fifty-five hours per week—she could easily envision a different balance between her work hours and her private life. Just as these Americans imagine themselves trading off pay—and thus their standard of living—for a fuller personal life and more private time, they perceive the career choices and decisions of their fellow professionals as driven by similar tradeoffs. One consultant who had worked in both San Francisco and Stockholm took note of the fact that these different groups perceive the same tradeoffs quite differently.

[Professional] people here [in San Francisco] are more willing to make the kind of sacrifices that seem really strange to the Swedes, to work 55 to 70 hours a week is like insanity to the Swedish people ... and I think to the people who work right around here in downtown LA, that's a lot of hours but it's certainly not insanity ... *it's a tradeoff that makes sense to people here* ...

Thus, it is through the framing of tradeoffs that the Americans apply a commensurating rationality to their decisions regarding work hours, routines, and particularly jobs and careers.

Interestingly, these tradeoffs have little to do with ideal allocations of time and energy between work and private life. John, the investment banker we met earlier, had made a major tradeoff when he became an investment banker, a job that made it almost impossible to spend any time with his four children during the early years of their lives. Prior to his promotion to his current position, John routinely worked over eighty hours per week. Yet John explicitly rejects the label of "workaholic" and defines himself as someone who does *not* live for his work. In fact, the long hours he spent at work were at odds with his vision of a more fulfilling life, a life which would be almost entirely devoted to parenting:

Ultimately, I'd love to be at home all the time with my kids ... I'm someone who's happy to come home, I don't need to be in the office ... I love to take vacations, I love to be with my kids ... if I could do my job in four hours a week, I'd do it in four hours a week ... I'd love to do that, but I can't.

As is clear from this commentary, John wishes to be more involved in the upbringing of his children and to spend more time in their company, but realizes that this goal conflicts with his commitment to a greedy job and profession, and a very high salary. His idealized commitment to "active parenting" (Blair-Loy 2003) runs counter to his commitment to supporting the family financially and ensuring an acceptable standard of living for them.

For John, as for many of the parenting Americans of both sexes, family life can serve as life's primary emotional anchorage, even when it is starved of time and energy by work (Orrange 2007; Hochschild 2003: 206–207; Weiss 1990). An acceptable standard of living from John's standpoint includes a multi-million dollar home in a "decent" neighborhood, private school for his four children, and a host of other very expensive goods and services. For John and other hard-driving, high-earning, and ambitious American professionals, one can aspire to be fully invested in one's personal and family life, even as one works long hours and dedicates oneself to a greedy job. But, even as someone who works long hours in a greedy job, out of felt necessity as the family's provider, John still feels that he has some margin for self-directed decision-making relating to his hours. He can adjust his work hours by five to ten hours per week and his income by five to ten percent a year. Within these margins is where he can exercise his autonomy.

Energy Frames: American Expenditurism

When vital energy is conceived as an intrinsically scarce resource, it becomes subject to an economizing logic of budgeting and replenishment, as will be illustrated with the conservationist Norwegians. With the expenditurist Americans, however, the main challenge is not the budgeting and replenishment of this scarce resource, but the lack of suitable opportunities to expend reserves of vital energy that outstrip the demands imposed by life. These American expenditurists not only take evident pride in pushing themselves "to the limit" at work and give little thought to the price they may pay in the future, but seek demanding work precisely so that they can expend energies that would otherwise find no outlet.

Paradoxically, these American expenditurists anticipate the inevitable period of enervation, whether after a week, a month, or a year of leaving nothing behind. Many could recall reaching points of near-total collapse and "heroic exhaustion," in the words of one American engineer. A expenditurist lawyer who aspires to arrive at the end of project cycle with "nothing left in the tank," told me that she does not dwell much on the "hangover" that she admits is the inevitable aftermath of such a heroic expenditure of energy. Many of the expenditurists could envision the day when this hangover would strike. In a reflective moment during our interview, Larry, a management consultant in his forties, speculates in a half-joking tone about the inevitability of his future physical collapse. In the midst of a project that requires him to work over sixty hours per week and commute across the United States on a weekly basis, Larry acknowledges that his body might not cooperate with his punishing work schedule indefinitely:

I might not realize that I'm getting tired because I say 'I'm not tired, I can keep working' ... but one day my body might just say 'no more' ... and give up on me.

The equally expenditurist Sam, an American self-described "hardcore" management consultant not only works double shifts five days a week, but delights in pushing himself to the limit during these grueling marathons; declaring "At midnight when I quit work I don't want to have anything left." This ability to "burn hard" was something he prizes not just in himself, but in others as well. When I asked him who in the business world deserved his admiration, he told me about a CEO who could excel at his job without much sleep. He envies this man for his evident ability to "burn hard, day in and day out":

I read a long, long time ago, I think it was one of the ex-Ford Motors CEOs, the guy from Australia who was kicked out about five or six years ago, I forgot his name. There was a big write-up on him, and they said that one of his secret weapons was that he can get by on very little sleep. He just *burns hard, day in and day out*, and I thought, I hugely admire those types of leaders. That's where I want to end up.

Interestingly, several of the American expenditurists conceive of the workplace both as the primary source of energy and the life realm that warrants the greatest investment of energy. For instance, because Tyler struggles to envision a way of energizing himself mentally outside of work, he remains thankful that his workday lasts long enough to absorb sufficient amounts of energy that would otherwise go to waste. Even though he enjoys an active family life and the company of his wife, he explains that an eight-hour workday would leave him with too much energy to spare. What he craves is the chance to give "150 percent" to his work so that he can say he has "left nothing on the field" when he reaches the end of the workday. Tyler worries that shorter work days, workdays lasting less than ten or eleven hours, would leave him restless and would not provide an outlet for his prodigious energies, energies that should be expended at work and not outside it.

Life Realm Frames: Norwegian Priority-setting

Where roughly three-quarters of the American respondents mention making "tradeoffs" in their commentaries on balancing work and private life, about the same proportion of the Norwegian counterparts speak of "prioritizing" one realm over the other realm. So, for the young and childless engineer Jørgen, private life and free time are more enjoyable than work and therefore merit the designation as a "top priority". Many of the parenting Norwegian professionals of both sexes recall their decisions to give "lower priority to" [nedprioritere] their work lives when they became parents. These men and women also freely criticize the parenting practices of those with the opposite priorities; individuals who "lived for their work" and gave lower priority to their families, in their view, had not simply gone astray but had erred in their prioritization [å ta feil prioritering]. In assessing the priorities of others, these Norwegians make judgments about the fitness of their priorities relative to the priorities of "most people". For instance, in the commentary of a young consultant working out of the Oslo office of a hard-charging global strategy outfit (where 60 to 70-hour workweeks are common) the culture clash between the firm's work expectations and the typical work expectations in the Oslo business world is a matter of discrepant priorities:

I think a lot of people don't understand the priorities of people working here [in this office] and I can understand that ... most people want to find a satisfactory job that can support their lifestyle and enable them to spend time on other stuff but the people here live for their work and most people have never experienced that.

Unlike the vision of tradeoffs upheld by the Americans, the priority framing implicitly claims that work life and private life must be ranked against one another. It denies the possibility of commensurating the two realms, in other words. Indeed, several of the Norwegians assert forcefully that a thriving work life cannot compensate for a deficient private life. As Thorvald explains:

There have been times in my life when my personal relationships were falling apart while my career and work life was going really well. But I figured out that putting more of myself into work, even though I enjoyed my work, could not make up for a terrible personal life. And earning more money could not make me happier either. That's when I realized that there was no amount of work success that could compensate. I had to give more of a priority to my personal life.

Unlike the notion of making tradeoffs, which allows for the commensuration of the two life spheres and renders them subject to commensuration, the concept of setting priorities suggests that the relationship between the two life spheres is something like the "lexicographic" ordering analyzed by philosophers, logicians, and economists (Huemer 1995). In this type of ordering, one cannot trade off increments of improvement in one realm for increments of improvement in the other realm, since the two realms are non-substitutable. To give the sphere of personal life priority over the sphere of work life is, logically speaking, to generate an ordering where no amount of improvement in the second-ranked realm can make up for any decrease in the quality of the first-ranked realm.[5]

Energy Frames: Norwegian Conservationism

When the Norwegian professionals put work life and private life in balance by setting private life as their priority, they implicitly characterize the two life realms as incommensurable, and invoke an anti-economistic understanding of the two realms. However, when they deal with their own vital energies, they adopt an understanding that actually treats these energies in an economistic way, as scarce resources that have to be husbanded and budgeted rationally. With their "conservationist" energy framing, they approach their own vital energies as scarce internal resources calling for good stewardship and careful management. Self-appointed caretakers of their own energy supplies, these men and women made efforts to regulate their energy expenditures at work in order to ensure the availability of an "energy surplus" [overskudd] in the home sphere. Thus, wherever possible, they try to ensure enough private time so that they can recharge their depleted batteries, whether through rest, family time, organized leisure, or purely passive restorative activities such as movie-watching. In this way, they enact what Foucault calls the imperative of "self-care," a directive with a long and distinguished history stretching back to classical times (Foucault 1988: 18–22).

A surprisingly large number of the Norwegian professionals, both women and men, endeavor to preserve their energies at work so that they will not suffer from debilitating energy deficits at home. Anders, a Norwegian management consultant and father to a small boy, made a point of avoiding

---

5 As economists and others have noted, lexicographic rankings can disrupt economic behavior. Such preferences may deny the social actor the capacity to weigh different consumption possibilities against one another by measuring them according to a common metric.

working himself "to the bone" so that he could bring enough energy back to the home environment. By working reasonable *[fornuftig]* hours, he assures himself that he had "enough surplus energy *[overskudd]*" for his other commitments at home, particularly his parenting duties. But a sixty-hour work week, he speculates, would not only make it difficult to participate fully in his home life, but would actually impair his ability to fulfill his duties in the workplace:

If I am to do a good job at work the next day, I can't leave myself completely exhausted today. I don't want tomorrow's workday to pay the price for today's all-nighter. I want to have the mental surplus energy *[overskudd]* to really produce at work the next day—if one consumes so much of one's own energies and motivation [today] that one doesn't want to go to work tomorrow, then that's not good.

The same preoccupation with future shortfalls of energy at home and at work figures in the commentary of another male Norwegian consultant, a younger man without children. In his view, there is little point in over-consuming one's energies during the workday, because this expenditure would inevitably compromise one's capacity to work effectively the following day. Moreover, without adequate private time outside of work, he could not meet the following workday with sufficient reserves of energy. When I asked him whether he could envision working sixty hours a week on a regular basis, he responded:

If I were to go up to sixty hours a week at work … it would interfere with the [non-work] activities I get my energy from. Also, I don't believe that I would get more work done [in this situation]. I wouldn't work that effectively. I think that the hours I get off from work make me ready for the next workday.

Like many of his fellow Norwegian professionals, he worries that an excessive expenditure of effort and energy at work would act counterproductively by reducing his overall efficiency. The same framing and reasoning characterize the remarks of a young Norwegian engineer who had no family whatsoever and therefore few external constraints on his working time. This man rarely worked more than forty-five hours per week. One of his primary criteria for deciding when to call it quits is the relative quality of his work product. When this quality starts to slip, he takes it as a sign that he was wasting his time and his employer's money and that he had reached a point where it was time to quit the office.

Since these Norwegians view the work realm as the primary energy-depleting zone, they take careful note of their energy expenditures while in the workplace. In the words of one Norwegian energy conservationist, it is critical to "listen to one's body" during the periods when work imposes heavy demands on one's time and energy. A number of the Norwegians comment on the way that deadlines and "crunch-times" drain their energies. They lament the rare occasions when this happens, because it makes it difficult for them to work efficiently and also to discharge their parenting duties at home, or engage in the organized leisure pursuits which many of them enjoy in the spare time. When the Norwegians adopt a conservationist approach, they treat energy as an inherently finite resource that has to be replenished on a regular basis and should not be over-consumed during a given time period. In this way, they implicitly budget their accounts of vital energy in ways that mirror the budgeting of money and economic resources. Energy resource is managed as fungible from one time period to the next. Just as one can overdraw one's bank account, one can overdraw one's energy "account". This application of an accounting logic to vital energy, as we will see, is culturally specific. The American expenditurists embrace a decidedly non-economizing alternative to this framing of vital energy resources.

Conclusion: The Two Patterns

The interview evidence presented here suggests that economistic logics do make their presence felt in the commentaries and narratives of successful urban business professionals in the US and in Norway. Both groups adopt a mix of economistic and non-economistic frames in their narratives about allocating time and energy in their everyday lives. Whereas the priority-setting of the Norwegians shields private life from the claims of work life, the expenditurist approach of the Americans actually reinforces the claims of a greedy work life when it comes to vital energy. These four distinctive frames are grouped together in the table below according to their relationship to economistic and non-economistic logics.

First, the American respondents are in a better position to earn comparatively large sums of money in return for large investments of time and energy in work. Thus, it makes more sense to the Americans to trade off additional investments in working life, either measured as increments of work time or more demanding jobs, against private life, and approach their efforts to balance work and private life as a series of tradeoffs. This situation makes the

Advantaged life realm	Form of rationality	
	Economistic	Non-economistic
Work	Trading off private life and time for money and success (commensurating logic)	Expending inexhaustible vital energy (non-economizing logic)
Personal life	Conserving scarce vital energy (economizing logic)	Prioritizing life realms (non-commensurating logic)

Logics and Advantaged Life Realms

logic of commensuration more appealing. It is perhaps more suprising that their energy frames lack any hint of an economizing logic. As we recall from the interviews, these individuals keep their distance from the logic of scarcity when they address their ways of handling vital energy. In their expenditurist narratives, disposing of excess energy is the challenge, not preserving scarce energy. Further research is needed to find out exactly why these Americans adopt such a puzzling perspective on their own resources of vital energy.

The reverse combination appears in the narratives articulated by the Norwegian respondents. These Norwegians resist economistic logics in their conceptions of life realms. But they nevertheless embrace the logic of scarcity where vital energy is concerned. These professionals make their private life a priority *vis-à-vis* their work life, implicitly making a case that the two life realms cannot be translated into a common unit of measurement. Interestingly, none of the Norwegians claim that work ought to take priority over private life. Indeed, the more determined the Norwegians are to limit the amount of time and energy credited to work life, the more they cite their priorities as incompatible with long work days, demanding jobs, and long work weeks. With respect to their vital energies, however, the Norwegians represent their vital energies as scarce, in danger of overuse, and in need of economizing. They therefore speak as if they feel compelled to preserve their energy surplus to avoid overdrawing their energy accounts. And so, the Norwegians are the ones who dispose of their temporal and energy resources in ways that help them to protect private life from the encroachments of greedy work.

So how can we explain these patterns? In accounting for these differences, we must contrast the life circumstances of the two groups, particularly their engagements with work, money, and private life. These differences in frames arise from both the institutional environments in which the two groups work, and the cultural landscapes they inhabit. As the Norwegians exercise more control over their work lives, particularly the proportion of their lives that work consumes, they can more easily adopt the frames favoring the claims of personal life *vis-à-vis* work life. Given their situation, it is easier for them to make private life an inviolate priority rather than represent it as something that can be commensurated with a better standard of living. Living in a more lucrative but more demanding work world, the American professionals conceptualize their work time as an investment that can be adjusted in light of their preferences relating to private life. As the interview evidence shows, it is the American respondents who gravitate towards an economistic logic when they trade off a more fulfilling private life against the better standard of living obtained through a larger paycheck. Whereas the Americans' work environment creates conditions favorable to the adoption of a commensurating logic when it concerns their engagements with work life and private life, it thus facilitates the adoption of an anti-economizing logic when it comes to the management of vital energy. As far as vital energy is concerned, the less predictable work environment of Americans affords them less leeway to budget their energies from day to day and week to week, hindering their attempts to economize their vital energies.

However, the differing work environments of the Norwegians and Americans cannot in themselves account for the divergences in these patterns. In fact, some of the Norwegians who speak of setting priorities and budgeting their vital energies actually work in very demanding and unpredictable jobs and careers. Nevertheless, they embrace the frames that advantage private life versus work life, demonstrating their commitment to the ideal of the multidimensional life. As the interviews suggest, this ideal exerts a stronger grip upon Norwegian professionals than it does among American professionals.

In demonstrating the diversity of frames through which individuals perceive their inner resources, and the uneven penetration of economistic logics, this study suggests that such logics have left some frames untouched even as they have left their imprint on other frames. In Norway, the commensurating framing has gained no real foothold, at least among the professional classes, while the economizing framing holds sway. The reverse situation prevails among the American respondents. It is therefore likely that this commensurating framing surfaces more frequently, at least among the professional classes, in less egalitarian societies with greedier work environments, such as the United States. Conversely, this commensurating framing is less common in Scandinavian societies with an uncommon degree of gender and class egalitarianism, societies where the claims of private life are more strongly sanctioned by the culture.

Works Cited

Brubaker, Rogers (1984), *The limits to rationality*, London: Allen & Unwin.

Blair-Loy, Mary (2003), *Competing devotions*, Cambridge: Harvard University Press.

Davis, Gerald F. (2009), *Managed by the markets: How finance reshaped America*, Oxford: Oxford University Press.

Espeland, Wendy Nelson, and Mitchell Stevens (1998), "Commensuration as a social process", in: *Annual review of sociology*, 24, 313–343.

Foucault, Michel (1988), "Technologies of the self", in: Luther H. Martin, Patrick H. Hutton, and Huck Gutman (eds.), *Technologies of the self: A seminar with Michel Foucault*, Amherst: University of Massachusetts Press, 16–49.

Hochschild, Arlie Russell (2003), *The commercialization of intimate life: Notes from home and work*, Berkeley: University of California Press.

— (2004), "The commodity frontier", in: Jeffrey Alexander, Gary T. Marx, and Christine L. Williams (eds.), *Self, social structure, and beliefs: Explorations in sociology*, Berkeley: University of California Press, 38–56.

— (2011), "Emotional life on the market frontier", in: *Annual review of sociology*, 37, 21–33.

— (2012), *The outsourced self: Intimate life in market times*, New York: Metropolitan Books.

Hochschild, Arlie Russell, and Anne Machung (1989), *The second shift: Working parents and the revolution at home*, New York: Viking.

Huemer, Michael (1995), *Ethical intuitionism*, London: Palgrave McMillan.

Lilleas, Ulla-Britt, and Karin Widerberg (2001), *Trøtthetens tid*, Oslo: Pax Forlag.

Margolis, Diane R. (1998), *The fabric of self: A theory of ethics and emotions*, New Haven: Yale University Press.

Nippert-Eng, Christena E. (1995), *Home and work*, Chicago: University of Chicago Press.

Orrange. Robert M. (2007), *Work, family, and leisure: Uncertainty in a risk society*, Lanham: Rowman & Littlefield.

Schulz, Jeremy (2011), "Framing couple time and togetherness", in: Anita Garey, and Karen Hansen (eds.), *At the heart of work and family*, New Brunswick: Rutgers University Press, 85–99.

— (2012), "Talk of work", in: *Theory and society*, 41, 603–634.

Weber, Max (1946), *From Max Weber: Essays in sociology*. In Hans Gerth and Charles Wright Mills (eds.). New York: Oxford University Press.

Weiss, Robert S. (1990), *Staying the course: The mental and emotional lives of men who do well at work,* New York: The Free Press.

Widerberg, Karin (2006), "Embodying modern times: Investigating tiredness", in: *Time & society,* 15, 105–120.

Williams, Colin C. (2005), *A commodified world: Mapping the limits to capitalism,* London: Zed Books.

Zelizer, Viviana A. (2010), *Economic lives: How culture shapes the economy,* Princeton: Princeton University Press.

Time for Business?! Time Binds of Female Founders and Their Familial Origin

Caroline Ruiner

Introduction

Though a disproportionate rise in self-employment of women can be observed, only 32.1 percent of all self-employed academics were female in Germany in 2011 (Eurostat Labour Force Survey 2012). In search of an explanation for this under-representation, there have been numerous studies on the women's characteristics, their motivation to become self-employed and their economic success (see e. g. Clark and James 1992; Moore and Buttner 1997; Lee and Rogoff 1998; Bruni et al. 2004; Loscocco and Smith-Hunter 2004; Fehrenbach and Lauxen-Ulbrich 2006; Brush et al. 2009). These studies reveal that women establish businesses *differently* to men, i. e. more slowly, more carefully, on a smaller scale, and less oriented to growth and economic profit. Similarly, they more often run single-person enterprises in domestic contexts leading to delimitations and blendings between work-life and life-world.

In this context, entrepreneurial time management is conceived of as being decisive for the success of the self-employed as it depends on their personal strategies and behaviors, how they structure and organize their everyday lives. This requirement has already been taken up by career advice literature with headings such as "Time Management for Entrepreneurs" or "Time Management—Introducing the Entrepreneur's Secret Weapon to Maximizing Productivity". These guidebooks connote that the challenge of entrepreneurial time management can be met and is learnable—it only takes encouragement, a few tips and some information which can be acquired in the appropriate literature, and, where necessary, with the help of coaches. So far, this idea of *making* a successful entrepreneur with the help of training and consulting has been too narrowly discussed, as the questions of how these strategies and behaviors originally emerge, based on the founders' prerequisites, have not yet been asked.

Against this background, the aim of this paper is to focus on the inclination and success of female founders in order to reveal patterns of perceiving, thinking and acting regarding their time and self-management, and to discuss these in the context of the familial culture of origin, as it is assumed that this is where the foundations for the founders' strategies and behaviors are laid.

According to this focus, the title "Time for Business?!" can be understood in two ways: Firstly, it implies the question of whether it is time to start one's own business, that has to be answered by founders regarding their individual life planning and thus addresses their inclination to found a business; secondly, the title contains the question of how time is managed in the everyday life of founders and, regarding their self-management, when it is time to *do* business.

In the next section, the conceptual framework will be presented referring to time and self-management of entrepreneurs in the context of the familial culture of origin. Leading on from this, a research project will be introduced to present qualitative empirical findings on female founders and their familial origin. The inclination to found a business and the daily time management of two women will be exposed exemplarily as their strategies and behaviors can be understood as diametrically opposed. Hereafter, the empirical illustrations will be discussed with reference to the theoretical background.

Conceptual Framework: Time and Self-management of Entrepreneurs and Habitual Dispositions

Time Management and Time Binds

In view of the increasing flexibilization in the modern world of work, Hochschild (1997) presents a revealing view on the time management of contemporary workers. Based on interviews with members of a company, she explored why the organizational arrangement of flexible working hours to support the work-life-balance does not lead to a balance but results in an increase of work. As a reason for the low demand of flexible working hours, Hochschild reveals that the employees' time management follows more or less implicit norms and expectations which lead to *time binds* and contrast the organizational setting of temporal flexibility. Moreover, she emphasizes that the spheres of home and work conflate and are perceived in reverse meanings: The workplace has become a place of recognition and appreciation with a variety of social relationships, friendships and emotional support. In contrast, at home, time is perceived as scarce and stressful and family life is subordinated to efficiency principles, rationalized and partially outsourced (see also Hochschild 2003; 2012) with the result that *home* becomes *work* and *work* becomes *home*.

Hochschild's research focus lies on the development of flexibilization and economization in the modern world (of work) and its effects on the life of individuals and their social relationships. She shows that individuals understand their everyday lives as (more or less) voluntarily self-structured and organized with the result of a self-commodification. However, this development is not to be understood as an individual but as a social phenomenon.

Entrepreneurial Self-management and Subjectivization

The interdependency between the individual and social development is discussed in terms of subjectivization with a focus on the flexibilization of work—especially the flexibilization of working hours—and the resulting dynamics in the relation between work and life. Due to the flexibilization of work, life spheres are less clearly defined and demarcated. Individuals are confronted with scopes of action and the need to arrange work-life and life-world individually and actively, for which they need specific self-management skills.

Bröckling (2007) summarizes the debate on the change of work referring to the *entrepreneurial self*. He points out that the necessity of self-management leads to the necessity of self-optimization, which is not just an individual but a social development in the context of economization. Bröckling argues that the concomitant requirement of *self-control* triggers the constant necessity to change. He states that this change process is oriented to the maxim that individuals are *entrepreneurs of themselves* and should, therefore, utilize their personal resources responsibly and profitably. As a consequence of the desire to self-optimize, this *entrepreneurial self* seeks an ideal which can be characterized by the alignment of one's entire life to the model of entrepreneurship.

In view of the modern scopes of action in the context of employment, Pongratz and Voß (2003) discuss strategies of increased flexibility and self-organization in the workplace which lead to a *subjectivization of work*. This development is identified as twofold: On the one hand, businesses have a growing need for *subjective* inputs and individual performances of their employees, and on the other hand, there is an increase in the individuals' demands for fulfilling and interesting work. Referring to their concept of the *entreployee*, Pongratz and Voß elaborate that individuals in the modern world of work essentially face the following requirements:

- *Self-control* as the intensified ability to plan, control and monitor one's own activities.
- *Self-commercialization* as the intensified active and practical production and commercialization of one's own capacities and potentials on a highly competitive market.
- *Self-rationalization* as the ability to establish a self-determined structuration and organization of one's daily life and long-term plans.

As subjectivization intensifies the interdependencies between individuals and their work (see also Kleemann et al. 2003), the segmentation of work and private life is aggravated, and subsequently, the ability to cope with the requirements mentioned is brought into the arena. Against this background, the concept of subjectivization complements and differentiates Hochschild's perspective on the commodification of the self and commercialization of intimate lives, as specific skills are systematized that are needed to cope with flexibility, and as discussions focus less on the consequences for individuals and their social life, but rather address the social development of individualization in the context of the modern world of work.

Essentially, these discussions on subjectivization refer to employees. However, the effects multiply when the self-employed come into focus. Parasurama and Simmers (2001), for example, emphasize that self-employment is likely to foster subjectivization, as entrepreneurs are responsible for the success of their business, and as self-employment, especially of highly qualified women, is often the result of their desire for personal development and self-realization. Moreover, highly skilled self-employed in particular are confronted with flexibilization and have to deal with scopes of action, as the boundaries between work and life are blurred in space and time. To manage these scopes of action, it is especially the self-employed who require specific self-management skills to handle the interplay between work-life and life-world (see Egbringhoff 2004), and who have to develop a structuration of their everyday (work) lives and to plan, organize and manage time. As the founders' strategies and behaviors are decisive to this process, the question is *how* founders fulfill this requirement and how their strategies emerge.

Entrepreneurial Acting and Habitual Dispositions

The realization and foundation of founders' self-management strategies and behaviors can be analyzed with the theoretical framework of Pierre Bourdieu. His concepts of *habitus* and forms of *capital* are helpful in trying to fathom the *entrepreneurial self*, as they take the founders' resources into account. It is especially the *embodied cultural capital* which helps to focus on the founders' prerequisites. It refers to the "long-lasting dispositions of the mind and body" (Bourdieu 1986, 47) that are preconsciously absorbed in the process of primary socialization within the family. Bourdieu argues that people are exposed to given family-specific cultural practices that are part of the family's day-to-day domestic life leading to routines which provide the basis for the habitus (see also Friedland 2009). Bourdieu (1990) discusses the habitus as becoming operative as a generative principle of perceptions, thoughts and actions. As such, it functions as a "modus operandi" (Bourdieu 1990, 52) and influences essentially what occurs on the horizon of the imaginable, what belongs to unquestioned deep convictions, what is perceived as legitimate, and what behaviors are considered to be appropriate.

De Clercq and Voronov (2009a; 2009b) have already provided valuable insights into the importance of a *practical sense* of entrepreneurs or—as Bourdieu (1990) puts it—a "feel for the game" (ibid., 66) that makes agents understand "what is to be done in a given situation" (ibid., 146). In this sense, the habitus influences *how* people act and organize their everyday lives, when they perceive, for example, that something is *right, on time* or *too early* and, consequently, influences the handling of time. Accordingly, the founders' time and self-management strategies in the founding process will be analyzed in the following, focusing on their patterns of perceiving, thinking and acting, and discussed referring to their familial heritage—the specific endowment with cultural capital—to reveal the influence of the familial culture of origin and to understand the time binds and subjectivizations of new entrepreneurial forms.

Data and Methods

The empirical findings discussed in this article stem from a qualitative study of female founders in Germany[1] exploring the inclination and the success of women founding a business. A total of twenty founders, their families (mother, father and siblings) and their partners were interviewed with the help of guided narrative interviews.

In the interviews, we addressed, among other things, the initiation of founding, current challenges of self-employment and time management, as well as time practice and use of leisure time in the family of origin. Interviews with the founders took approximately two hours; interviews with parents, siblings and partners rarely exceeded 90 minutes. In addition to the interviews, a group discussion with the family members was realized in which key issues of the specific families were addressed.

The sample of participants was sourced through a combination of advertising in the media and snowball sampling. The founders were selected according to four criteria:

1. The female founders should have an academic degree, as it is especially the highly skilled workforce who is confronted with the requirements of the *entreployee*.
2. The women should have founded their business in fields of consulting, education or media, as self-employment in these knowledge-intensive industry sectors demands a highly developed capacity for self-commercialization and self-rationalization.
3. The female founders should have officially been in business for 3–18 months to ensure that the challenges of launching self-employment are present.
4. The self-employment should not have been the takeover of a family business or a franchise company to have similar conditions.

In accordance with the principles of Grounded Theory (Glaser and Strauss 1967), data collection and analysis were intertwined. The process of analysis was realized through individual and team analysis. Once all the interviews of a family case had been conducted, the four members of the research team collectively developed starting points for the case analysis. After listening to

---

1 The project "Entrepreneuresse—On the Scent of Habitus of Founders" was supported by the German Ministry for Education and Research (BMBF) and the European Social Fund (ESF) from 2007 to 2010.

all the interviews of a family case and reading the corresponding transcripts, the team members individually worked out first interpretations regarding the relation of familial habitus and the process of founding. These interpretations were presented in team meetings where divergent interpretations were discussed in terms of communicative validation and subsequently either rejected or modified and developed further. In certain cases, we also analyzed key text passages with the help of a *qualitative sequential method of analysis* (Reichertz 2002) or with the help of the *documentary method* (Bohnsack 2010) to deepen case-specific logics. Based on the interview analysis, we identified family themes as key issues of the specific families on which we focused in the (family) group discussion. The transcripts of the group discussion were analyzed in a similar way to the interview transcripts. Finally, this step further helped to deepen case-specific logics.

After completing the data collection, our analysis focused on a case comparison of all founders, their families and the related specific family themes and we assembled detailed (family) case profiles. The comparison revealed parallels between the cases and showed that the logics partially manifest the same theme with variations.

Though the founders interviewed have, in principal, the same (or similar) structural preconditions, they differ from each other essentially in the way in which they manage (the process of) their self-employment, what is imaginable and conceivable to them, as well as their aims, their problems and their success. The related patterns of perceiving, thinking and acting as expressions of the habitus refer to their individual experiences while growing up in a specific culture of origin. For the purpose of this paper, two founders will be introduced, as their founding strategies and acting are identified as *ideal typically* (Weber 1978) regarding the inclination and process of founding as well as the founding-specific strategies and behaviors in the context of the familial culture of origin and, moreover, show that the logics of founding are closely connected to the specific family logics.

Empirical Illustrations:
Logics of Founding and Familial Values

To discuss the interrelation of founding and family logic, two (family) cases will be presented, firstly, by introducing the founder and the founding process and, secondly, by introducing the family of origin and related familial values.

Mareike Kunze and Her Family of Origin

"I am an entrepreneur"—the Implicitness of Self-employment

Mareike Kunze[2] (born in 1972) can be characterized as being an *entrepreneur to the core*. After completing her studies and obtaining a doctorate degree, she was employed as an executive in a company. She reconstructs this employment as an "intermediate step", a chance to gather the experiences which are necessary for starting her own business, as she always anticipated that she would be self-employed one day.

I was ALWAYS sure about that. I could not imagine having an employer, a boss, orientating myself to organizational structures and being in that forever. Actually, during school and college I was pretty sure that I would be self-employed one day.

The step of starting her own business was a conscious turning away from being permanently employed. Though she perceived her employment as "a kind of a self-employed job", the desire to work autonomously surfaced time and again. When the board of directors changed, it was time for her to say, "Now I go with the flow", and she decided to start her own business. She appointed a date for herself, arranged her withdrawal and, after a year, exited in mutual agreement with her bosses and clients. In 2007, Mareike started her self-employment in the field of human resources development, consulting and coaching services for private enterprises. She hired office space and acquired work orders at the beginning of her self-employment, for example, from the company she was formerly employed by.

By the start of her self-employment, Mareike felt that she had arrived where she belonged. She describes herself as being an "entrepreneur on her own behalf" and regards her self-employment holistically: "It's not just work, but a life concept." The implicitness of being self-employed one day pervades the founder's biography: It seems that her whole life concept was aligned to self-employment, and this, moreover, is her point of reference in each of her explanations.

---

2 The names are pseudonyms that were chosen by the interviewees themselves.

The Practice of Managing Work and Life: the Pursuit of Autonomy

In her everyday life as a founder, Mareike Kunze perceives the possibility of flexible time management that comes along with self-employment as "easing the burden" of having to adapt to predetermined structures and having to squeeze herself into the "corset" of organizational time structures. In her eyes, the flexible organization of her life in a temporal and spatial manner is the "greatest present ever", and she perceives this as "endless luxury, totally luxurious". She pays attention to a strict separation of private and professional life and considers it as *her own* responsibility to deal *well* with *her* time and states: "Good work produces more, but more work does not necessarily produce more."

Mareike has not only organized *her world* according to her ideas since becoming self-employed. Her biography from childhood and studies to professional career has always been self-determined and self-organized and she has always acted independently and self-responsibly. The founder and the family members compare Mareike's lifelong pursuit for autonomy with the figure of *Pippi Longstocking*. The father regards this figure as a role model for his daughter: "*Pippi Longstocking* does everything differently and Mareike liked that a lot." The founder herself talks in the family group discussion about the fictitious figure being the most important person in her life.

If someone asked me today who has been the most important person in my life, I think I would say that this was *Pippi Longstocking*. And I still think she is, the older I get: A girl who goes through life with her own rules, but with common sense and humanity.

The comparison of Mareike Kunze and *Pippi Longstocking* elucidates the pursuit of autonomy and the inward orientation of the founder. Mareike acts independently, proactively and formatively in every life sphere. In doing so, she is unswervingly oriented to her own views throughout her biography; others, even family members, had hardly any input. The predisposition for this attitude can be traced back to her familial culture of origin.

Autonomy as a Familial Value—the Self-employment of Mareike Kunze and the Familial Culture of Origin

The parents' work was very present in family life. They ran a thriving kiosk at a tourist attraction and were self-employed for 30 years. The kiosk was open from 7:00 a.m. to 10:00 p.m. every day of the week during summer, and all the family members helped in the everyday business. The founder underlines: "Gastronomy has no working hours. You begin when it's nice outside and you stop when it's dark." Apart from the common supper, there were no fixed or predetermined duties the daughters had to do. Rather, it was important for the parents to convey that the children should "use the time well, not to fritter it" (mother). Accordingly there were no or hardly any requirements from the parents, but it was up to the daughters to think about how they wanted to fill their daily lives and leisure time and to find a structure by themselves.

All family members were aware of the risks of self-employment and of factors that could have destroyed the parents' source of income from one day to the next. For this reason, the parents pursue the strategy of acting successively and creatively which helps them to handle entrepreneurial risks, i.e. to avoid them in advance. However, witnessing how the parents dealt with uncertainties, as well as seeing that the parents were successful in spite of all the risks did not cause self-employment to lose its attractiveness. It is rather connoted positively in the family members' narrations of both generations. The sister underlines, for example: "Well that [self-employment] means for us a bit of freedom." In particular, the sister states that independence and autonomy are attractive criteria in the context of self-employment: "We try to be in control of our own destiny; to create our lives' journey and be responsible for that."

Accordingly, not only Mareike, but all the members of the Kunze family see the pursuit of autonomy as a key issue, and take the perspective of being self-responsible for how they organize their lives and how they fill scopes (of action). Here, one can speak of an intergenerational transfer (and appropriation) of the interfamilial value of autonomy: All family members talk about being libertarian and decisive, and show a high degree of creative will and proactive behavior. Moreover, they perceive the possibility of realizing (successively) their own ideas (of a good life) in the context of self-employment.

Despite all the similarities between Mareike and her family of origin, there are differences in entrepreneurial acting, particularly regarding the handling of time. The parents' working time was extremely dependent on the kiosk as it was open for about 15 hours a day, eight months a year. The remaining time was more or less devoted to the privacy of the family. Their home was described as a "stronghold" (sister) to which they retreated from work and where they maintained privacy. Though a similar approach can be found in Mareike's acting, as she also pays attention to the demarcation between work and private life, she handles time in a rather *self-governed* way, which is not least the reason why she refused to take over the family business. Thus, in contrast to her parents, who were forced to keep their business running by paying attention to the visiting hours of tourists, she is able to be self-employed and to organize her everyday life in a mostly self-referred fashion.

The familial heritage in the case of Maxie Muster can be discovered in the founding process as well, but in a contradictory manner. Although a continuation of the familial culture of origin can be stated, this proves to be less conducive to self-employment.

Maxie Muster and Her Family of Origin

"I actually cannot state that I am a typical entrepreneur"—
Stopgap Self-employment

Maxie Muster (born in 1978) can, in contrast to Mareike Kunze, be characterized as being a *prototype of an employee*. After completing her studies and obtaining a doctorate degree, she could not find a job, which she ascribes to the bad economic situation. As a result, and though she aspired to be employed in a company, she became self-employed with the help of government grants in 2008 and founded a consulting service to address the online safety awareness of children and teenagers. Consequently, she aims to induce schools, teachers, parents, and pupils to book her consulting services. She works from home and, all-in-all, her self-employment begins poorly: There are only sporadic orders relating to her core business, and she offers computer courses for beginners and works part-time as a waitress to make some money. Maxie is aware of running the risk of failing with her business, and her alternative plan is to work as an employee again.

The step of founding a business can be described as *against her will*. It was a "hard decision" for her to start self-employment because she has a considerable "need for safety" and likes to have a regular income. In this respect, she would have been "happy" to secure a "permanent employment contract" for a "well-paid job" in a "well-known company". Maxie had never perceived self-employment as a possibility, but she completely supports and identifies with the business idea. Thus, as she could not find a job in the area of her choice, and having asked the family members for advice, she *risked* the step and became self-employed.

Maxie Muster describes herself as being "NOT a typical entrepreneur". Rather, she is a "founder" because she perceives herself as still in the initial phase of her self-employment and has to "try and learn" a lot. In particular, that means "breaking away from employee-thinking" and internalizing entrepreneurialism instead.

Because I have always been an employee and that has not been bad at all. One person says now you do this, now you do that. And now I have to do EVERYTHING by myself.

In her explanations, she is oriented to a position of a permanent employee, and she mirrors and compares her situation to this. She continues to think and act like an employee and expects others to tell her what to do next. This outward orientation can be found throughout her biography and seems to be a strategy that she has succeeded with so far. However, this strategy leads to difficulties in the context of her everyday life as an *enforced* founder.

The Practice of Managing Work and Life: Outward Orientation

Maxie Muster deals easily with the contentual work in her daily life, but she has difficulties with the "entrepreneurial trappings around". With regard to time management, she emphasizes that she needs "a lot of discipline to structure the day". She is inclined to be "a bit too sloppy with the timing", especially because she works from home: She sleeps in and drinks coffee with her neighbor during the day, which means that she sometimes has to finish her jobs at night.

Furthermore, she becomes aware of "constantly being an entrepreneur and not only from eight to four", similar to being employed in a company. This also implies for her that she "should not wait for jobs" but be proactive in acquiring orders. Her job acquisition has not been very successful so far, and Maxie asks others, such as her family members, for advice. Having no ideas for self-employed acting, she is oriented to external points of reference, as she perceives this strategy as promising. This outward orientation to others' expectations and guidelines can be found throughout Maxie's biography: She chose main subjects in school which promised the best chances for a well-paid job.

So, I went to school and I chose subjects that could be useful in the future. At no time did I think that's ME, I really want that. It was more that I thought this or that could be useful in a job later on. Then, I even chose my degree based on this principle and I only thought "where can I make a lot of money in the future?".

Her decisions have always been aligned to the thought of which way would foster job-related or economic success, and, especially at the recommendation of her father, she starts a field of study with good prospects.

He [the father] wanted me to do something where I would make good money and where I could have a good job as well.

Maxie reconstructs that her father "gets what he wants", and sums up that the field of study was not her "own decision". After finishing her first degree, Maxie sees herself confronted with expectations which lead her to do something that she "never" wanted to do originally: She did not want to do a doctorate, but when asked by her supervisor *why* she wants to receive a doctor's degree (the question whether she wants to do a doctorate or not had never been asked), she thinks of an appropriate answer. Subsequently, she was hired and, in view of the supervisor's expectations, there was no way back for her. The founder sums up: "Well, that was this thing again: I slid into this, I never wanted to do it. But then I just did it."

Maxie's outward orientation has led her to success so far, but in the context of her self-employment it seems to be inappropriate. Nevertheless, this strategy is rooted in the familial culture of origin.

Safety as a Familial Value—the Self-employment of Maxie Muster and the Familial Culture of Origin

Maxie Muster grew up with a father[3] who says that he is extremely lucky to have been permanently employed. He thought that he had "tremendous luck" when he found life-time employment at a university "without ever being unemployed, even for a day". In daily life, the family members had breakfast and dinner together. The father was working during the day, while the founder and her sister were home alone, and organized their leisure time by themselves. Though the founder perceives that she and her sister could do whatever they wanted, she recalls that meals and appointments, such as for music lessons and other hobbies, structured the day, i. e. worked as an external structure. The daughters learned a "well-ordered day-to-day routine", "to be on time" and the founder states "we pretty much knew what we had to do at any time".

---

3 Maxie's mother died when Maxie was young.

All-in-all, the father was highly involved in the biographical development of his daughters: He told them to learn as much as possible[4], and to get good graduation marks so that they would *succeed* in life and find good (in the sense of safe and well-paid) jobs. He always said: "Someday you have to make good money, and because of that you are doing all this stuff." However, the aspired causality did not eventuate in Maxie's case, and the father states regarding Maxie's self-employment: "Of course it bothers me." He argues that "after such a career" something else could have been expected:

She did everything right that you have to do: being ambitious at school, graduating successfully, studying, PhD, semester abroad.

The father expects *correctly* arranged biographical components to lead *safely* to a permanent, well-paid position. Everything else, such as self-employment, is perceived as a suboptimal alternative. Both daughters state that their father had a "master plan" so that they could get such a job. In this respect, the father had already internalized the external standards and demands of the labor market which influenced biographical decisions, and Maxie's life also seems oriented towards an exemplary CV in which she matches her biography and pragmatically adjusts to (pre)conditions.[5] Her acting is based on the expectations of her father, her supervisor, and subsequently, she tries to find out and to adapt to the expectations of what constitutes a *typical* entrepreneur. In doing so, the orientation to external expectations can still be found in Maxie's self-employment. This outward orientation and pattern of realizing a predetermined biography can be assumed as a distinct form of orientation to safety. As this strategy can be revealed in the narrations of both generations, an intergenerational transmission of the familial value of safety can be identified.[6] In the perspective of the family members, this value can best be pursued by having a permanent employed position. Moreover, even though Maxie is self-employed now, her life as a founder is still oriented to employment, and, in particular, oriented to the temporal and structural conditions of being employed.

---

4 Even during leisure time, the two sisters often played school together, with Maxie in the role of the teacher and her sister as the pupil—and their father tested what the sister had learned.
5 Maxie Muster chose her own pseudonym and it can be translated to *maximum pattern* which could not have been more appropriate for the case and family logic.
6 The founder's focus on safety is even manifested in her business idea (which also constituted the topic of her dissertation).

The Time Binds and Subjectivizations of Female Founders and Their Familial Origin

Time Binds and Subjectivizations of Female Founders

The start of an own business is in particular accompanied with a flexibilization and individualization of working time, as self-employed have to regulate their life spheres and to establish a practical everyday time order. The cases presented support a differentiated analysis of the female founders' time and self-management, since they have similar preconditions but differ essentially in their strategies and behaviors for coping with entrepreneurial scopes of action.

Firstly, regarding the inclination to found a business, the biographical taken-for-grantedness of starting a business can be differentiated: On the one hand, in the case of Mareike Kunze, primary pull factors stimulate the step into self-employment and the founding seems to be a kind of a *biographical implicitness* as it has always been part of her life plan; on the other hand, in the case of Maxie Muster, push-factors *force* the step into self-employment, and the founding is conceived to be *against her will* as it is the only alternative to avoid unemployment, and has been *unimaginable* so far.

Secondly, the analyses of time management and subjectivizations are revealing as they show that the founders' working time arrangements are subject to individual decisions and a matter of self-organization pursuing specific behaviors and strategies. Basically, the daily requirement to manage time can be perceived as *luxury* or, on the contrary, felt or seen as a difficult and challenging *task*. Accordingly, the founders' self-organization of working time (in consideration of market requirements) shows that market values are more or less internalized. Mareike Kunze, with the self-perception of being an *entrepreneur*, acts autonomously, proactively and creatively, oriented to her own ideas and paying attention to a strict separation of private and professional life in order to work efficiently. Maxie Muster, conceived as a *prototype of an employee*, is oriented to employment, external criteria and expectations. She notices and reflects the requirement to regulate and structure herself but, primarily, perceives this as a *burden*. She finds it difficult to uphold boundaries between work-life and life-world and rather acts and structures her day reactively based on the order situation.

The comparison of both cases reveals that Mareike Kunze has internalized entrepreneurial acting, as her whole life concept is aligned to the model of entrepreneurship. She shows the ability to plan and to self-control her activities, to self-rationalize and to establish a self-determined structuration and organization of her daily life and life course. In contrast, Maxie sees it as a task to internalize entrepreneurial acting and to turn away from employee thinking. In the end, *how* founders cope with time and self-management requirements leading to self-commodification depend on their resources and, consequently, especially on their *embodied cultural capital*. Thus, the courses of action perceived and realized, as well as the self-perception of the founder and the (time) management of their everyday lives differ essentially and reveal the naturalness of specific strategies.

The Heterogeneity of the "Habitus" and Familial Heritage

The focus on the "practice of dealing" (Bourdieu 1990) of the two cases shows that heterogenic strategies can arrive at the horizon of the imaginable. A closer look at the patterns of perceiving, thinking and acting—the *embodied cultural capital*—of founders reveals that the underlying principles of structuring turn out to be related to the family of origin. The founders do not reinvent themselves only because they start a business, they rather act in relation to their dispositions and continue to uphold familial values: While Mareike Kunze associates self-employment with autonomy and independency, Maxie Muster perceives self-employment to adversely affect her need for safety and thus pursues other strategies.

Accordingly, the founders consider different behaviors to be appropriate. In doing so, heterogeneity in the process of founding is not chosen randomly and consciously. In accordance to Bourdieu, the underlying patterns of perceiving, thinking and acting can be reconstructed as *strategies of the habitus* which reproduce unconscious practices. Depending on how, i. e. under which conditions, the habitus developed, different practices are experienced as natural, while others are inconceivable (see also Bourdieu 1984). As such, habitual strategies are not adapted consciously to changed contexts by a reflexive process, they will rather be continued as they were developed through the years of habituation—Bourdieu (1990, 54) refers to "the presence of the past".

Therefore, certain values in the everyday life of the family of origin are (not) conveyed, i. e. acquired, and specific presuppositions are created or held back which play a decisive role in later self-employment and coping with flexibility. In this sense, the familial culture of origin can be understood as a heritage which is bequeathed from one generation to another through intergenerational transmission processes (see Bertaux and Bertaux-Wiame 1991). These processes are conceived as relational processes, since familial values, leanings and resources are not simply transferred from one generation to another—the cultural familial heritage rather has to be accepted and adopted by the heirs (see also Büchner and Brake 2006). Thus, from an intergenerational perspective, not only similarities, i. e. equivalent patterns or structures, can be found, but also partial (more or less reflected) rejections and concomitant renewals, albeit with astonishing similarities through generations. Nevertheless, the founders continue to stay related to their family of origin, as strategies and patterns still contain traces of familial leanings (which, at least, serve as a demarcation).

Finally, the familial heritage turns out to be more or less appropriate for the specific field of self-employment. As the basis for the founders' habitus, it lays the groundwork for the entrepreneurial acting and, related to this, the time and self-management of entrepreneurs.

Conclusion

It is especially the highly skilled self-employed who are confronted with flexibilization of work and resulting scopes of action. They have to organize their life spheres individually and actively, and they need specific self-management skills for this. Focusing on time management, and in view of *time binds* in particular, it can be shown that founders cope differently with this requirement.

Though guidebooks stress the learnability of proper strategies to succeed in business, in this paper, time management is not discussed as a result of reflected and learned strategies, but rather regarded as *strategies of the habitus*. The *habitus* as an underlying grammar reproduces practices that determine the organization of the founders' everyday lives and can be studied with regard to their style of *doing business*. Moreover, the family of origin has a formative effect on the founders' acting as it is the fountainhead of specific proclivities.

The empirical illustrations of two female founders' founding processes show that they continue their familial culture of origin and have acquired specific patterns of perceiving, thinking and acting. The habitus substantially determines *how* founders manage their everyday lives and translate self-management requirements. As the two founders' *embodied cultural capital* differs essentially, it was shown that the continuation of the familial culture of origin is more or less *appropriate* for facing the requirements of self-employment, and the familial heritage—according to the specific endowment with cultural capital—can be conceived of either as a resource or as an obstacle for founders.

The familial dispositions transmitted as day-to-day taken-for-grantedness have a stronger effect than has been considered yet. Due to these mostly unconscious and pre-reflexive prerequisites, entrepreneurial time management cannot simply be learned. Even with the help of comprehensive rulebooks, founders with different dispositions will perceive and implement rules in their own specific ways. In this sense, the habitual patterns of perceiving, thinking and acting are the keys to understanding the founding process and to answering the question if it is *time for business*.[7]

Works Cited

Bertaux, Daniel, and Isabelle Bertaux-Wiame (1991), "'Was du ererbt von deinen Vätern …'. Transmissionen und soziale Mobilität über fünf Generationen", in: *BIOS*, 4, 14–40.

Bohnsack, Ralf (2010), "Documentary method and group discussions", in: Ralf Bohnsack, Nicolle Pfaff, and Wivian Weller (eds.), *Qualitative analysis and documentary method in international educational research*, Opladen/Farmington Hills: Verlag Barbra Budrich, 99–124.

Bourdieu, Pierre (1984), *Distinction. A social critique of the judgement of taste*. London: Routledge.

— (1986), "The forms of capital", in: John G. Richardson (ed.), *The handbook of theory and research for the sociology of education*, New York: Greenwood Press, 241–258.

— (1990), *The logic of practice*, Stanford: Stanford University Press.

Bröckling, Ulrich (2007), *Das unternehmerische Selbst. Soziologie einer Subjektivierungsform*, Frankfurt am Main: Suhrkamp.

Bruni, Attila, Silvia Gherardi, and Barbara Poggio (2004), "Going gender, doing entrepreneurship: An ethnographic account of intertwined practices", in: *Gender, Work and Organization*, 11, 406–429.

---

7 I would like to thank Philip Saunders for proofreading this article.

Brush, Candida G., Anne de Bruin, and Friederike Welter (2009), "A gender-aware framework for women's entrepreneurship", in: *International Journal of Gender and Entrepreneurship*, 1, 8–24.

Büchner, Peter, and Anna Brake (2006), *Bildungsort Familie. Transmission von Bildung und Kultur im Alltag von Mehrgenerationenfamilien*, Wiesbaden: VS Verlag.

Clark, Thomas A., and Franklin J. James (1992), "Women-owned businesses: Dimensions and policy issues", in: *Economic Development Quarterly*, 6, 25–40.

De Clercq, Dirk, and Maxim Voronov (2009a), "The role of cultural and symbolic capital in entrepreneurs' ability to meet expectations about conformity and innovation", in: *Journal of Small Business Management*, 47, 398–420.

— (2009b), "Toward a practice perspective of entrepreneurship. Entrepreneurial legitimacy as habitus", in: *International Small Business Journal*, 27, 395–419.

Egbringhoff, Julia (2004), "Welche Lebensführung erfordert der Typus des Arbeitskraftunternehmers? Das Beispiel von Ein-Personen-Selbständigen", in: Hans J. Pongratz, and G. Günter Voß (eds.), *Typisch Arbeitskraftunternehmer? Befunde der empirischen Arbeitsforschung*, Berlin: Edition Sigma, 255–279.

Eurostat Labour Force Survey (2012), http://epp.eurostat.ec.europa.eu/portal/page/portal/employment_unemployment_lfs/data/database (8. 8. 2012).

Fehrenbach, Silke, and Maria Lauxen-Ulbrich (2006), "Gender view on self-employment in Germany", in: *International Journal of Entrepreneurship and Small Business*, 3, 572–593.

Friedland, Roger (2009), "The endless fields of Pierre Bourdieu", in: *Organization*, 16, 887–917.

Glaser, Barney G., and Anselm L. Strauss (1967), *The discovery of grounded theory: Strategies for qualitative research*, Chicago: Aldine Publishing Company.

Hochschild, Arlie R. (1997), *The time bind: When work becomes home and home becomes work*, New York: Metropolitan/Holt.

— (2003), *The commercialization of intimate life. Notes from home and work*, Berkeley: University of California Press.

— (2012), *The outsourced self: Intimate life in market times*, New York: Metropolitan/Holt.

Kleemann, Frank, Ingo Matuschek, and G. Günter Voß (2003), "Subjektivierung von Arbeit. Ein Überblick zum Stand der Diskussion", in: Manfred Moldaschl, and G. Günter Voß (eds.), *Subjektivierung von Arbeit*, München/Mehring: Rainer Hampp, 57–114.

Lee, Myung-Soo, and Edward G. Rogoff (1998), "Do women entrepreneurs require special training? An empirical comparison of men and women entrepreneurs in the United States", in: *Journal of Small Business and Entrepreneurship*, 15, 4–29.

Loscocco, Karyn, and Andrea Smith-Hunter (2004), "Women home-based business owners: Insights from comparative analyses", in: *Women in Management Review*, 19, 164–173.

Moore, Dorothy P., and E. Holly Buttner (1997), *Women entrepreneurs: Moving beyond the glass ceiling*, Thousand Oaks: Sage.

Parasurama, Saroj, and Claire A. Simmers (2001), "Type of employment, work-family conflict and well-being: A comparative study", in: *Journal of Organizational Behavior*, 22, 551–568.

Pongratz, Hans J., and G. Günter Voß (2003), "From employee to 'entreployee'. Towards a 'self-entrepreneurial' work force?", in: *Concepts and Transformation*, 8, 239–254.

Reichertz, Jo (2002), "Objective hermeneutics and hermeneutic sociology of knowledge", in: Uwe Flick, Erich von Kardoff, and Ines Steinke (eds.), *Companion to qualitative research*, London: Sage, 290–296.

Weber, Max [1921] (1978), *Economy and society: An outline of interpretive sociology*, Berkeley: University of California Press.

Selling Feelings for a Wage: A Labor Process Perspective on Emotional Labor Power, Its Indeterminacy and Incomplete Commodification[1]

Paul Brook

Introduction: A meeting of ideas

Arlie Hochschild's (1979; 1983/2003) pioneering contribution to the sociology of work on emotion work has been profound. For over 30 years her innovative *emotional labor* concept has inspired and underpinned an exponential growth in the study of workplace emotion from a range of theoretical perspectives within organization studies (Fineman 1993; Sieben and Wettergren 2010) and many other social science fields (Fineman 2008). Throughout this time her primary definition of emotional labor as "the management of feeling to create a publicly observable facial and bodily display" (1983/2003: 7), as a requirement of paid employment, has been accepted by adherents and critics alike.

For the influential *labor process analysis* tradition (see Thompson and Smith 2009), Hochschild's theorization of emotional labor, as "sold for a wage" (1983/2003: 7) and an additional aspect of labor power, alongside physical and intellectual labor (1979), has ensured its progressive incorporation into the main body of labor process theory (LPT) (Brook 2010). Indeed, the widespread adoption and adaption of Hochschild's emotional labor concept has proved to be a theoretically and empirically enriching experience for labor process analysis (LPA) (Bolton 2005; Warhurst et al. 2009).

While LPA has Marxist origins, principally deriving from Harry Braverman's (1974) seminal *Labor and Monopoly Capital*, it has evolved over the decades into a tradition that encompasses Marxist, post-Marxist, neo-Weberian and other materialist perspectives on the capitalist labor process (Jaros 2010; Thompson and Newsome 2004; Vincent 2011). Nevertheless, common to LPA is the insistence that the labor process is contradictory and structur-

---

1 This chapter is based on arguments drawn from a series of three articles (Brook 2009a; 2009b; 2010).

ally antagonistic owing to the combination of labor power's indeterminacy and the unequal and exploitative nature of the employment relationship. The consequence is that managerial control of the labor process tends to be routinely contested, fragile and partial. Therefore, LPA debates concerning the nature, experience and management of emotional labor have focused on the questions of what is actually sold to an employer by an individual worker and the degree to which it is owned and controlled by the employing organization. These questions also encompass the extent to which emotional labor should be conceptualized as distinctly different from physical and intellectual labor, and whether it is feasible to conceive of a discrete *emotional labor process*.

This chapter critically assesses debates within LPA on Hochschild's concept and subsequent attempts to revise or replace it with a theory of emotion work that is compatible with the principal tenets of LPT. This is followed by a critical defense of Hochschild's concept from a classical Marxist perspective (Callinicos 2007; Rees 1998), which defends and elaborates her central position that emotional labor is an aspect of labor power and therefore common to all forms of jobs, irrespective of whether it is performed as an interactive service encounter with a customer or during a routine meeting between a manager and supervisees in an office, hospital, school or factory. However, Hochschild is also critiqued for inadequately theorizing the contradictory, contested and collective nature of the labor process through her over-individualization of the emotional labor experience and tendency to assume, normatively, near-complete management control. It is then argued that for the emotional labor concept to be compatible with LPT, emotional labor power should be theorized within a unitary concept of labor power, comprising a dynamic, interdependent complex of physical, intellectual and emotional effort. Moreover, such an understanding should be based on the central notion that labor power is inherently indeterminate and therefore a special type of commodity. The chapter concludes by arguing that emotional labor cannot be conceptualized as a distinctly different form of labor power—compared to its physical and intellectual counterparts—on the mistaken basis that it is a deeper, less "detachable" aspect of *the self* and therefore performed within its own discrete emotional labor process.

What is labor process theory?

LPT has retained throughout its waves of development since the 1970s a core set of theoretical propositions (Thompson and Smith 2001; 2009). It commences from the character of labor as a unique commodity due to its indeterminate form after hiring, as yet-to-be-realized labor. Hence, employers have to ensure the conversion of labor power into actual work effort under conditions that permit capital accumulation (Littler 1990; Thompson and Newsome 2004). From this understanding flow a number of sub-propositions:

1. The principal focus should be on the experience of employees during the transformation of their labor power into a productive form, rather than the particular means deployed by the employer (Thompson and Smith 2009).
2. The basis for capitalist employment relations is exploitation and subordination, which produces a "structured antagonism" during the transformation of labor power (Edwards 1990: 128; Thompson and Newsome 2004).
3. The transformation of labor power implies the need for control necessitating managerial institutions applying a variety of strategies and tactics (Thompson and Smith 2001).
4. Labor power's inherent indeterminacy and the employment relation's structured antagonism ensure that management's control is fraught with tensions and contradictions, which manifest as a tendency for workers to resist as well as consent (Edwards 1990; Thompson and Newsome 2004).

Arising from this core theory, LPA is therefore concerned with analyzing capital's expansion of labor power capacities in response to competitive market conditions, in particular (and increasingly), capital's demand for enhanced service via the recruitment and training of specific personality traits (Callaghan and Thompson 2002) and corporeal *display* qualities (Warhurst and Nickson 2009). In keeping with LPT's materialist foundations, interactive service work is understood as not purely an "intangible" experience but as an inherently material process (Pettinger 2006; Warhurst et al. 2009). This is because the means of service production comprise an integration of human and technical aspects of the labor process (Thompson 1983/1989), such as a call center worker using telecommunications technology to interact with a customer. Indeed, all interactive service production tends to rely, in varying degrees, on a mix of fixed capital, technical/logistical support and material retail goods in conjunction with the human element.

For LPT, therefore, the logical consequence of its core principles is that labor's determinate form, such as its use to perform a particular type of customer interaction, is not of primary analytic importance. Instead, the key question is whether labor "has been drawn into the network of capitalist social relations, whether the worker who carries it has been transformed into a wage-worker and whether the labor of the worker has been transformed into productive labor" (Braverman 1974: 362). Thus, because Hochschild's (1983/2003: 7) primary focus is on theorizing emotional labor as a *social form* ("the management of feeling"), as an aspect of wage-labor ("sold for a wage") rather than as an occupationally specific *determinate form* of work (e.g. serving airline customers for profit) there is a conceptual bridge between her theorization of emotional labor and the core tenets of LPT. It is this bridge that has underpinned the progressive incorporation, albeit variously, of her emotional labor concept into LPT (Brook 2010).

Emotional labor (power) in perspective

The incorporation of the emotional labor concept into LPT has been a profoundly critical process (Brook 2010; Warhurst et al. 2009). Writers within the LPA tradition have tended to highlight the inability of Hochschild's concept to capture the complex and contradictory experience of the (emotional) labor process (Bolton 2005; Brook 2009a; Lopez 2010; Taylor 1998; Warhurst et al. 2009). In particular, they highlight a normative tendency in her theorization, which assumes that emotional laborers are passive (Callaghan and Thompson 2002) resulting in management possessing the capacity to exert near complete control over the labor process (Bolton ibid.) through what Hochschild refers to as the *successful transmutation* of their feelings by management, during which "the worker must give up control over *how* the work is to be done" (1983/2003: 119 [Hochschild's emphasis]). This claimed normative passivity stands in stark contrast to LPA's foundational conceptualization of managerial control as structurally contradictory and invariably incomplete (Thompson and Newsome 2004). This is because all labor power is a special type of commodity owing to its inherent indeterminacy.

Even after labor power is purchased by an employer as wage-labor, it is only for a limited period and not in its entirety, as "a lump, once and for all" (Marx 1976/1990: 271), as with buying a photocopier or building. To do so would require the worker to sell their entire physical, intellectual and emotional entity as a slave. Thus, converting their individual self "from the owner of a commodity into a commodity" (Marx ibid.). In addition, and crucially, an employer's purchased labor power is characterized by its perpetual existence as a *yet-to-be realized* value-producing resource that has to be continually trained, directed, controlled, policed and even cajoled into undertaking productive labor in sufficient quantities; of appropriate quality; and in the requisite time and place (Smith 2006). This is because workers retain ultimate ownership of their labor power, even if they relinquish control of its application and management in the labor process for fixed periods (Brook 2009a). It is only the final determinate product (embodying an employee's completed labor) that passes into the employer's *full ownership* (i. e. a standard commodity), as either a tangible good, such as a fast-food meal, or as a completed service interaction. The organization then claims it as its "own" through subsequently taking responsibility for its delivery and consequences, as demonstrated by the provision of service-user and customer complaints procedures, underpinned in large measure by legal liability (Brook 2010).

Labor power, unlike completed labor, therefore, is a living, indeterminate commodity that is inherently unpredictable and intractable. Consequently, an employer is routinely confronted by a structural contradiction at the heart of the capital-labor relation in which both parties are driven to continually contest labor power's price, usage and mode of control. This is because it cannot be physically, intellectually or emotionally detached from the individual self, with the inevitable consequence that the worker "brazenly accompanies [their] labor power right into the workplace and stands protectively by it [arguing] about the terms of its sale" (Rees 1998: 221). In this way, employees remain in ultimate possession of their labor power, whether physical, intellectual or emotional, as a commodity, even if they hire it out for a limited period and in prescribed quantities to an employer (Braverman 1974; Marx ibid.).

Revising Hochschild or moving on?

This foundational understanding of labor power's indeterminacy has pro-found implications for LPA's theoretical engagement with the emotional labor concept. From a LPT perspective, Hochschild's (ibid.) normative as-sumption that management's control is so effective it is able to appropriate workers' feelings via a *transmutation of feelings*[2] appears to be a rare feat, even logically impossible, given the indeterminacy of labor power (Bolton and Boyd 2003; Brook 2010; Callaghan and Thompson 2002; Lopez 2006; Taylor 1998). For this principal reason, theoretical interventions within LPA have sought to revise, even replace, Hochschild's concept. A notable con-tribution is by Taylor (1998: 99), who offers instead a more nuanced inter-pretation of Hochschild's stark distinction between emotional *surface acting* (externalized behavioral compliance) and *deep acting* (akin to Stanislavski's method acting), thereby conceptualizing emotional labor as routinely com-prising an "incomplete transmutation of feelings"; whereas Lopez (2006), in his study of care homes, argues for more flexibility in Hochschild's concept to allow emotional labor to be understood as on a continuum, where there are coercive *feeling rules*[3] at one extreme and authentic emotional care (facili-tated by a loosening of management's codified feeling rules) at the other. For Bolton, however, Hochschild's normative tendencies are so deeply embedded that they generate a "one-dimensional analysis" (ibid.: 2), which effectively disallows the possibility of employees' independent emotional agency, as her analysis of management control is "ultimately absolutist" in its consequences (Bolton and Boyd 2003: 290).

In short, there is a high level of agreement within LPA that Hochschild's theorization is stunted in its ability to capture the contradictory and con-tested nature of workplace relations. However, the degree of critique is varied and the range of proposed remedies is wide. At one end are Taylor (1998) and Lopez (2006), who want to retain Hochschild's core concept, whilst reorienting it to capture the incompleteness of managerial control via revis-ing its conceptual components. At the other end is Bolton's (ibid.; Bolton and Boyd 2003) influential critique, which seeks to move on from what she

---

2 Hochschild claims that she chose the term *transmutation* because it is a "grand word" (ibid., 19) that expresses the grievous nature of the process, rather than adopting it to imply a complete mutation of a worker's feelings.

3 Codified *feeling rules* refer to management's requirements that employees adhere to pre-scribed emotional behavior, even feelings, in defined workplace social contexts/service in-teractions (see Hochschild 1979).

calls the "emotional labour bandwagon" (ibid.: 53) with its accompanying one-sided portrayal of workplaces, populated by passive, even crippled, actors who are wholly subordinated to managerial control. In her accompanying re-theorization (ibid.; Bolton and Boyd 2003), the foundational tenets of Hochschild's concept are marginalized, arguably even rejected (Brook 2009b). Indeed, the very use of the term emotional labor is effectively jettisoned, as tellingly revealed by the title of Bolton's monograph where she fully elaborates her critique and re-theorization, *Emotion Management in the Workplace* (ibid.).

Bolton's (2010) re-theorization, rather than understanding emotional effort as a core aspect of labor power, relegates emotional labor's conceptual applicability to its final determinate form as a commodified, for profit, customer service product, such as hairdressing or restaurant waiting. Emotional labor, therefore, is no longer a generalized *social form* of wage-labor but rather defined by what Bolton refers to as its *pecuniary* function (a "for sale" service commodity), as part of a wider typology of emotion work comprising: *pecuniary, prescriptive, presentational* and *philanthropic*[4] forms of workplace emotion management. Unlike *pecuniary* work, the latter three variants are not understood as commodity forms but instead are principally defined by the degree of emotional autonomy exercised by the employee and/or the level of emotional authenticity invested by the employee. For Bolton (ibid.), employees always retain ownership of the emotional means of production, in contrast to their physical and intellectual labor (Warhurst et al. 2009).

The argument that workers retain ownership of the emotional means of production and therefore most emotion work remains private emotion management rather than commodified, emotional labor, lifts all but pecuniary emotional labor out of the unitary concept of labor power. This is based on a common argument within much of LPA that the emotional dimension of labor power, unlike physical and intellectual labor, uniformly possesses an exacerbated indeterminacy (Bolton 2010; Callaghan and Thompson 2002; Warhurst et al. 2009). Underlying this argument is the assumption that suc-

---

4 *Prescriptive* emotion management is the codified organizational and/or professional norms required during service interactions; *presentational* emotion management has its source in the individual asserting the basic socialized-self through applying their own personal norms of emotional engagement in addition to any prescribed rules; and *philanthropic* is emotion management that is given as a personal 'gift' by the employee, over and above any managerial, professional or socialized emotional norms. For Bolton (2005: 102), the latter two are "moments of truth"; expressive of employees' "authentic selves" that are beyond management's control or ownership (i.e. commodification).

cessful emotional labor comprises sincere feelings and behavior, which cannot be captured and owned by management. In effect Bolton argues that in contrast to physical and intellectual labor, the vast majority of emotion work is autonomous, even independent, of the valorization process (the realization of exchange-value) through which labor power is transformed into a productive commodity by the employer. In other words, her theorization implies that most forms of non-pecuniary emotion work are not fully "drawn into the network of capitalist social relations" and therefore the labor of the worker has not been transformed into productive labor (Braverman 1974: 362) by virtue of its exacerbated indeterminacy. It is on this basis that she maintains that her understanding of the emotional labor concept (i. e. commodified emotion work) is inapplicable to non-commercial forms of interactive frontline service work, such as public healthcare and education. In addition, this understanding means that the concept of emotional labor is also inapplicable to other *non-service* forms of workplace emotional effort, often required to get the job done, such as performing teamwork based tasks.

In response to Bolton's critique and re-theorization, I argue in detail elsewhere (Brook 2009b; Bolton 2009) that she misunderstands the basis of Hochschild's primary theorization of emotional labor as an aspect of labor power, which therefore means it is already transformed into a—yet to be realized—commodity form when sold for a wage to employers, irrespective of whether its final determinate product form is for profit or not. This is consistent with LPT's foundational understanding that labor power is a special type of commodity that is purchased and exploited through the employment relationship, thus implying that all forms of hired labor power effort are drawn into capitalist production relations as wage-labor, whether they are for directly commercial purposes or public services; and irrespective of whether they comprise "authentic" emotional displays or not. Therefore, the extent to which employees' emotional labor is sincere during interactive encounters is irrelevant as to whether their emotional effort is formally owned and controlled by the employer. Whatever an employee feels or does as part of their job has already passed into the employer's possession as completed labor, albeit in the contested context of the labor process.

The degree to which sincere emotional labor is a pre-requisite for organizational success is dependent on management's definition of what is required by the worker, which in turn is contingent upon the nature of the service product and its labor process. Compare, for example, the depth and quality of emotional sincerity required performing a high volume, directly supervised interaction, such as that of a supermarket check-out operator, where emotionally empty but polite performances are adequate, with that of an oncologist informing a patient confidentially, privately and with empathy that they have cancer and a short time to live. For the latter, the labor process has to allow for a much greater degree of employee autonomy compared to the former. While for the former, emotional sincerity is not required but rather behavioral compliance, although even this requires emotional effort. In this way, the level of emotional labor power's indeterminacy is not uniformly exacerbated but conditional upon the degree of labor process autonomy, largely determined by the nature of the service product, in just the same way as for physical and intellectual labor. Indeed, its degree of indeterminacy is no greater than that of physical and intellectual labor power (see Brook 2010).

The notion that workers retain ownership of the so called *emotional means of production* is also based on a misunderstanding of a core LPT concept. This is because the means of production comprise both the *forces of production*, principally labor power, technical capacity (e.g. training and service technologies) and fixed capital (e. g. retail stores and hospitals), and the necessary *social relations of production* (the employment relationship and accompanying managerial control) to ensure the production of a profit/surplus (Marx 1976/1990). In short, the means of production are where indeterminate human capacities and technical/fixed aspects of the labor process interpenetrate (Thompson 1983/1989: 39). Therefore, it is not feasible for an individual employee to retain ownership of the means of production, as the deployment of emotional effort is but one, if central aspect of it. Equally, it is the employing organization that pre-owns the technical/fixed components, not the employee.

My defense of Hochschild's emotional labor concept against Bolton's critique, however, is also critical from a LPT perspective (see Brook 2009a; 2009b; 2010) for two principal reasons. First, Hochschild's theorization over-emphasizes the individual experience at the expense of the collective response to emotional labor. Second, her concept insufficiently captures the contradictory and contested nature of the labor process, as other LPA writers have argued. The remainder of the chapter explores these criticisms in more detail as part of a critical defense of Hochschild's central contribution to contemporary LPT. In other words, what of Hochschild's emotional labor concept should be retained, revised or replaced in developing a robust integration with LPT?

Retaining Hochschild's foundations

Central to Hochschild's concept is her understanding that emotional labor is an integral aspect of labor power capacity. She states that as "deep gestures of exchange enter the market sector and are bought and sold as an *aspect of labor power*, feelings are commoditized" (1979: 659 [Hochschild's emphasis]). The opening lines of *The Managed Heart* (Hochschild ibid.) then provide a concrete example of how she understands emotional labor as an aspect of labor power capacity, along with physical and intellectual labor, when she compares the work of a boy in a 19th century factory and a flight attendant over a century later:

The work done by the boy in the wallpaper factory called for a co-ordination of mind and arm, mind and finger, and mind and shoulder. We refer to it simply as physical labor. The flight attendant does physical labor when she pushes heavy meal carts through the aisles, and she does mental work when she prepares for and actually organizes emergency landings and evacuations. But in the course of doing this physical and mental labor she is doing something more, something I define as *emotional labor*. This labor requires one to induce or suppress feelings in order to sustain the outward countenance that produces the proper state of mind in others [...]. (ibid.: 6–7; Hochschild's emphasis)

Hochschild then joins her foundational theorization of emotional labor, as an aspect of labor power, with her application of Marx's distinction between *exchange-value* and *use-value* (Marx 1976/1990) in her oft-quoted, primary definition of emotional labor:

[T]he management of feeling to create a publicly observable facial and bodily display; emotional labor is sold for a wage and therefore has *exchange value*. I use the synonymous terms *emotion work* or *emotion management* to refer to those same acts done in a private context where they have *use value*. (ibid.: 7; Hochschild's emphases)

By making this distinction between emotional effort that is bought for a wage, possessing exchange value, and private emotion management with use value, Hochschild demonstrates that her primary analytic focus, like LPT, is on the social form of emotional labor power and its transformation into productive labor (Brook 2010). In addition, her understanding of emotional labor as an aspect of labor power is also indicative of an acceptance of Marxism's and LPT's crucial distinction between *labor* and *labor power*, whereby workers sell their labor power to an employer—as the yet-to-be realized capacity to work—rather than their completed labor in the form of a finished product (Marx 1976/1990; Thompson 1983/1989).

Hochschild's (ibid.) original definition suggests that emotional labor is only constituted by the emotional effort used directly for interactive service. However, she went on to accept that the logical implication of theorizing emotional labor as the emotional aspect of labor power is that a degree of emotional effort is inherent to all forms of labor power:

All in all, we can think of emotion as a covert resource, like money, or knowledge, or physical labor, which companies need to get the job done. Real-time emotions are a large part of what managers manage and emotional labor is no small part of what trainers train, and supervisors supervise. It is a big part of white-collar 'work'. This is true for manufacturing firms [...] but it is far more true in the rapidly expanding service sector—in department stores, airports, hotels, leisure worlds, hospitals, welfare offices and schools. (Hochschild 1993: xii)

Therefore, a large element of employees' emotion management in the workplace (even resisting the urge to say what they actually think to a supervisor) is a "normal" condition of the job, just as physical labor entails a "normal" degree of physical management, such as complying with health and safety rules (e. g. walking not running around machinery). As such, emotional labor power can be understood as comprising three dimensions: an *object* of work to influence others, such as serving customers or managers supervising staff; a *means* to get the job done, such as being patient when frustrated with a task; and a *condition* of performing the work appropriately, as per the requirements of management's feeling rules or adhering to professional/contractual standards of behavior (Dunkel 1988, cited in Sieben and Wettergren 2010: 10–11).

It logically follows that irrespective of whether a worker is principally employed for their emotional, physical or intellectual labor, they can and do perform a mix of all three forms on a daily basis, in all types of organizations; service and non-service, commercial and not-for-profit. Indeed, many workers in a range of employment sectors, not just those engaged in front-line service delivery, are increasingly expected by their employers to offer at least a nominal display of organizational commitment and to be *customer-oriented* (Brook and Pioch 2006) in tandem with their physical and intellectual work. Hence, Hochschild's example of a flight attendant simultaneously undertaking a range of physical, intellectual and emotional tasks, as part of her everyday job, is highly salient for contemporary LPT. This is because it suggests the notion of a discrete *emotional labor process* (see Bolton 2010; Vincent 2011) is conceptually inaccurate as it decouples emotional effort from the routine working experience of combining it simultaneously with physical and intellectual labor in a range of related, non-interactive, service tasks (Brook 2010).[5] Therefore, it is reasonable to infer that Hochschild concurs with Marx that labor-power is "the aggregate of those mental and physical capabilities existing in a human being" (Marx 1976/1990: 270), with her explicit addition of emotional capacity. Like Marx and LPT, Hochschild's concept would appear to assume an integrated unity of an individual's labor power faculties.

Confronting normative and atomizing tendencies

A paradox lies at the center of LPA's critique of Hochschild's concept. The core criticism that she fails to capture the contradictory and incomplete nature of the labor process, thereby portraying employees as passive (Callaghan and Thompson 2002) even "crippled actors" (Bolton ibid.: 48), appears bizarre from even a cursory reading of *The Managed Heart* (Hochschild ibid.). This is because it is replete with detailed discussion and evidence of workers' indifference, resentment, resistance and trade unionism. Does this mean that much of LPA has misconstrued her emotional labor concept or is it because while Hochschild offers a graphic portrayal of workplace tensions and contestation her empirical evidence is not wholly consistent with or fully explained by her theorization? To explain this apparent paradox, I will argue that both explanations are partially correct.

In *The Managed Heart*, Hochschild (ibid.) is at pains to demonstrate how the cumulative effects of labor intensification and job degradation in the US airline industry generated individual and collective resistance by flight attendants through which they openly contested the terms of sale of their labor power:

The company exhorts them to smile more, and "more sincerely", at an increasing number of passengers. The workers respond to the speed-up with a slowdown: they smile less broadly, with a quick release and no sparkle in the eyes, thus dimming the company's message to the people. It is a war of smiles. (ibid.: 127)

---

5 Nevertheless, I accept that *emotional labor process* is a useful shorthand phrase for indicating a focus on the emotional aspect of a labor process (see Bolton 2009).

Hochschild, therefore, theorizes the transmutation of feelings as an unstable condition rather than one with absolutist consequences producing passive workers (Brook 2009b; 2010). Nevertheless, the notion of a successful transmutation appears to assume the possibility of complete management control. Thus, Hochschild is vulnerable to the charge from within LPA of theorizing a normative and therefore passive experience, where misbehavior and resistance emerge only in the event of transmutation's failure (Brook 2009a). By contrast, Taylor (1998: 99) argues that an "incomplete transmutation of feelings" is a common experience. This conclusion is supported by Bolton and Boyd's (2003: 321) finding that "empty performances" are routine amongst airline cabin crew. LPA studies of service work therefore reject the possibility of a wholly successful transmutation. Instead, management control of emotional labor is understood by LPA as frequently variable, contested and double-edged (Filby 1992; Taylor 1998; Warhurst et al. 2009). In addition, the *triadic* nature of the service labor process (organization, worker and service-user) (Lopez 2010) results in a "continual negotiation and re-negotiation over the transformation of labor power into a serviceable product" involving all three parties to varying degrees (Callaghan and Thompson 2002: 251).

While Hochschild's portrayal of the workplace is pitted with a mix of consent, indifference and resistance, her theoretical capacity to capture the full depth and range of employees' agency is stunted by her tendency to dichotomize the distinction between a successful and failed transmutation of feelings. This weakness is compounded by her one-sided emphasis on the harm done to the individual when performing emotional labor—principally the employee's alienation from their emotions and their "real self"—at the expense of explicitly acknowledging that workers continually strive to ameliorate their alienation both individually and collectively (see Brook 2009a). This one-sided emphasis occurs because Hochschild's concept and analysis focuses on the internalized responses of workers to management's attempt to *transmute* their individual feelings, which she theorizes as either *surface acting* or *deep acting*. This focus on the internalized individual experience overshadows her rich mapping of service organizations as contested and collective terrains.

The principal consequence of Hochschild's focus on the individual is that she over-emphasizes the human cost of emotional labor and tends to present the worker as atomized. This is because she insufficiently grounds her analysis in wider organizational social relations, principally the ubiquitous presence of informal workplace cultures, which can provide, to varying degrees, ameliorative support from co-workers (Korczynski 2003), space for misbehavior (Filby 1992; Ackroyd and Thompson 1999) and even open, collective resistance (Baines 2011). Indeed, the triadic nature of service work is fertile ground for workers to build informal solidarity relations with customers (Lopez 2010), as in the case of Villarreal's (2010) study of bus drivers and their passengers; or even formal organizational unity through community unionism, as illustrated by Baines' (2011) study of Canadian and Australian social services practitioners and their clients.

Hochschild's (ibid.) analysis, however, is unable to embrace theoretically this routine experience of the *collective worker* and its wider context of workplace social relations (see Hyman 2006; Mulholland 2004). With her analytic lens zoomed in on the individual, she is unable to capture adequately the implications for workplace relations of employers' demand for collective adherence to the same feeling rules from employees, who are frequently working side-by-side, such as in shops, hospitals and call centers. In short, Hochschild's portrayal of the workplace effectively obscures the conceptual significance of the fact that emotional labor is most often experienced as a managerial demand made on the many, rather than on isolated individuals. If she did so, her analysis would give a much stronger sense that individual reactions to management's demands are frequently part of a wider collective response that constitutes a largely shared activity. It is this shared experience that enables workers to create informal, mutually supportive sub-cultures outside of management control. As suggested above, these "communities of coping" (Korczynski 2003: 55) are also, crucially, a potential source for contesting unacceptable management ideas and demands, which in turn can offer embryonic conditions for the emergence of trade unionism (Taylor and Bain 2003) and the open resistance and unionization vividly documented in *The Managed Heart* (Hochschild ibid.).

In summary, Hochschild fails to acknowledge explicitly the existence and significance of organizational space outside of management control, filled by ameliorative, even resistive, informal networks of workplace ideas and behaviors. The understanding that the collective worker is a key workplace actor is a core feature of LPT owing to its theorization of all forms of wage-labor as a social form. Consequently, for LPT, the collective worker is an inseparable dimension of workplace agency (Mulholland 2004) owing to its interrelationship with the individual being constitutive, integral and dynamic (Hyman 2006). Thus, while Hochschild portrays the individual and collective agency of emotional laborers, contesting the *frontier of control* between capital and labor (Thompson 1983/1989), her theorization is stunted in its ability to explain its structural source, dynamics and consequences in terms of the inherent incompleteness of managerial control.

Conclusion: towards addressing the gaps

Hochschild's pioneering emotional labor concept enables LPT to systematically theorize the centrality of emotional effort in the contemporary service-oriented workplace. In addition, it offers a foundational understanding that emotional labor power is exercised in an integral, interdependent relationship with its intellectual and physical counterparts. Indeed, it has opened the door to a wider array of concepts, in particular *aesthetic labor*, which emphasizes the increasing corporate demand for specific corporeal qualities and displays from employees *(lookism)* that is often combined with the requirement for a degree of sexualized alluring display and/or behavior *(sexual labor)* (see Warhurst and Nickson 2009). More recently, another concept, *body labor*, has emerged that is defined by the "manipulation or touch of another [conscious] body when sold for a wage or commodified" (Cohen 2011: 190). Whether it is aesthetic, sexualized or body labor, each concept stresses that these increasingly prevalent forms of work comprise an interdependent complex of physical, intellectual and emotional effort. Within LPA, emotional labor and these newer concepts are now essential tools to explain the nature and effects of new forms of service-oriented, frequently branded work (see Pettinger 2004) and their labor processes.

For LPT, the question of the nature and content of emotional labor power is ever more important if it is to maintain its conceptual and analytic effectiveness in the face of corporate employers increasingly seeking to mobilize the whole person in their ceaseless search for competitive advantage (Warhurst et al. 2009). To date, this has not been addressed explicitly within LPA debates, especially in terms of articulating a theory of emotion that is consistent with LPT's materialist underpinnings (Thompson and Smith 2009). One possibility is to utilize Bakhtin's (1993) materialist conception of emotion, which he argues is the volitional tone of all human activity.[6] In this way, emotional effort is understood as providing the color and tenor to all

---

6 For more detail on Bakhtin's theory of emotion and its potential integration with LPT, see Brook (2013).

labor, such as the examples of *passionately*, *indifferently* or *reluctantly* speaking to customers. Away from service interactions, examples would be discussing a problem at work *sensitively* with a colleague, *nervously* undergoing an annual appraisal review with the line-manager or even sweeping a floor *cheerfully*. Thus, emotions are not theorized as discrete entities or things but rather as the emotional quality of activity. Consequently, emotional effort is conceptualized as the tonal quality of all instances of labor, whatever the mix of physical, intellectual and interactive activity. The quantity and quality of emotional effort, therefore, is largely determined by the nature of the task. Emotional labor in this sense is something that is undertaken by all employees whenever they perform an element or task as part of their paid work, as Hochschild (1993) acknowledges when she refers to it as a covert resource needed to get the job done.

Emotional labor, as an inseparable aspect of labor power, enjoys the same variable level of indeterminacy as physical and intellectual labor. It does not possess an exacerbated indeterminacy by virtue of its existence as a discrete or semi-detached entity that is somehow a more authentic dimension of the self than its physical or intellectual counterparts. Thus, emotional labor is an integral aspect of labor power; a singular, unique and special type of commodity that is forever possessed, if not fully controlled or formally owned, by the individual worker. As such, it is hired out to an employer as yet-to-be realized labor for a contracted period of time, during which the terms of its sale and use are forever subject to contestation and renegotiation by its bearers, the individual and collective worker. Because emotional labor power cannot be physically detached from the worker, the employer can never fully own and control it as a standard commodity until it is spent or dead labor in the form of a completed intangible interaction or a finished tangible product. In short, buying "alive" feelings for a wage is a perpetually partial and contested form of commodity ownership and control.

Works Cited

Ackroyd, Stephen, and Thompson, Paul (1999), *Organizational misbehaviour*, London: Sage.

Baines, Donna (2011), "Resistance as emotional work: the Australian and Canadian non-profit social services", in: *Industrial Relations Journal*, 42, 2, 139–156.

Bakhtin, Mikhail Mikhailovich (1993), *Towards a philosophy of the act*, Austin (Texas): University of Texas Press.

Bolton, Sharon (2005), *Emotion management in the workplace*. Basingstoke: Palgrave.

— (2009), "Getting to the heart of the emotional labour process: A reply to Brook", in: *Work, Employment and Society*, 23, 3, 549–560.

— (2010), "Old ambiguities and new developments: Exploring the emotional labour process", in: Paul Thompson, and Chris Smith (eds.), *Working life: renewing labour process analysis*, Basingstoke: Palgrave, 205–222.

Bolton, Sharon, and Carol Boyd (2003), "Trolley dolly or skilled emotion manager? Moving on from Hochschild's *Managed Heart*", in: *Work, Employment and Society*, 17, 2, 289–308.

Braverman, Harry (1974), *Labor and monopoly capital*, New York: Monthly Review Press.

Brook, Paul (2009a), "The alienated heart: Hochschild's emotional labour thesis and the anti-capitalist politics of alienation", in: *Capital and Class*, 33, 2, 7–31.

— (2009b), "In critical defence of 'emotional labour': Refuting Bolton's critique of Hochschild's concept", in: *Work, Employment and Society*, 23, 3, 531–548.

— (2010), "An Indivisible Union? Assessing the marriage of Hochschild's emotional labour concept and labour process theory", in: *International Journal of Management Concepts and Philosophy*, 4, 3/4, 326–342.

— (2013), "Emotional labouring and the *living personality* at work: Towards a unified theory of labour power capacities, materialist subjectivity and the dialogical-self", in: *Culture and Organization, 19*, 4.

Brook, Paul, and Elke Pioch (2006), "Culture change management", in: Rosemary Lucas, Ben Lupton, and Hamish Mathieson (eds.), *Human resource management in an international context*, London: Chartered Institute of Personnel and Development, 89–116.

Callaghan, George, and Paul Thompson (2002), "'We recruit attitude': The selection and shaping of routine call centre labour", in: *Journal of Management Studies*, 39, 2, 233–253.

Callinicos, Alex (2007), *Social theory: A historical introduction*, Cambridge: Polity.

Cohen, Rachel Lara (2011), "Time, space and touch: Body work and labour process (re)organization", in: *Sociology of Health and Illness*, 33, 2, 189–205.

Dunkel, Wolfgang (1988), "Wenn Gefühle zum Arbeitsgegenstand werden: Gefühlsarbeit im Rahmen personenbezogener Dienstleistungstätigkeiten", in: *Soziale Welt*, 39, 1, 66–85.

Edwards, Paul K. (1990), "Understanding conflict in the labour process: The logic and autonomy of struggle", in: David Knights, and Hugh Willmott (eds.), *Labour Process Theory*, Basingstoke: Macmillan, 125–152.

Filby, Michael P. (1992), "The figures, the personality and the bums: Service work and sexuality", in: *Work, Employment and Society*, 6 (1), 23–42.

Fineman, Stephen (ed.) (1993), *Emotion in Organizations*, London: Sage.

— (ed.) (2008), *The emotional organization: Passions and power*, Oxford: Blackwell.

Hochschild, Arlie Russell (1979), "Emotion work, feeling rules and social structure", in: *American Journal of Sociology*, 85, 3, 1–33.
— (1983/2003), *The managed heart: Commercialization of human feeling*, London: University of California Press.
— (1993), "Preface", in: Stephen Fineman (ed.), *Emotion in organizations*, London: Sage, ix–xiii.
Hyman, Richard (2006), "Marxist thought and analysis of work", in: Marek Korczynski, Randy Hodson, and Paul Edwards (eds.), *Social Theory at Work*, Oxford: Oxford University Press, 26–55.
Jaros, Stephen (2010), "The core theory: Critiques, defences and advances", in: Paul Thompson, and Chris Smith (eds.), *Working life: Renewing labour process analysis*, Basingstoke: Palgrave, 70–90.
Korczynski, Marek (2003), "Communities of coping: Collective emotional labour in service work", in: *Organization*, 10, 1, 55–79.
Littler, Craig (1990), "The labour process debate: A theoretical review", in: David Knights, and Hugh Wilmott (eds.), *Labour Process Theory*, Basingstoke: Macmillan, 46–94.
Lopez, Steven Henry (2006), "Emotional labor and organized emotional care", in: *Work and Occupations*, 33, 2, 133–160.
— (2010), "Workers, managers, and customers: Triangles of power in work communities", in: *Work and Occupations*, 37, 3, 251–271.
Marx, Karl (1976/1990), *Capital: Volume 1*, London: Penguin/New Left Review.
Mulholland, Kate (2004), "Workplace resistance in an Irish call centre: Slammin', scammin', smokin' an' leavin'", in: *Work, Employment and Society*, 8, 4, 709–724.
Pettinger, Lynne (2004), "Brand culture and branded workers: Service work and aesthetic labour in fashion retail", in: *Consumption Markets & Culture*, 7, 2, 165–184.
— (2006), "On the materiality of service work", in: *The Sociological Review*, 54, 1, 48–65.
Rees, John (1998), *The algebra of revolution: The dialectic and the classical Marxist tradition*, London: Routledge.
Sieben, Barbara, and Åsa Wettergren (eds.) (2010), *Emotionalizing organizations and organizing emotions*, Basingstoke: Palgrave.
Smith, Chris (2006), "The double indeterminacy of labour: Labour effort and labour mobility", in: *Work, Employment & Society*, 20, 2, 389–402.
Taylor, Phil, and Peter Bain (2003), "Subterranean worksick blues: Humour as subversion in two call centres", in: *Organization Studies*, 24, 9, 487–509.
Taylor, Steve (1998), "Emotional labour and the new workplace", in: Paul Thompson, and Chris Warhurst (eds.), *Workplaces of the future*, Basingstoke: Palgrave, 84–103.
Thompson, Paul (1983/1989), *The nature of work: An introduction to debates on the labour process*, Basingstoke: Macmillan.

Thompson, Paul, and Kirsty Newsome (2004), "Labor process theory, work, and the employment relation", in: Bruce Kaufman (ed.), *Theoretical perspectives on work and the employment relationship*, Illinois: International Industrial Relations Association, 133–162.

Thompson, Paul, and Chris Smith (2001), "Follow the redbrick road: Reflections on pathways in and out of the labor process debate", in: *International Studies of Management and Organization*, 30, 4, 40–67.

— (2009), "Labour power and labour process: Contesting the marginality of the sociology of work", in: *Sociology*, 43, 5, 913–930.

Villarreal, Ana T. (2010), "The bus owner, the bus driver, and his lover: Gendered class struggle in the service work triangle", in: *Work and Occupations*, 37, 3, 272–294.

Vincent, Steve (2011), "The emotional labour process: an essay on the economy of feelings", in: *Human Relations*, 64, 10, 1369–1392.

Warhurst, Chris, and Dennis Nickson (2009), "'Who's got the look?' Emotional, aesthetic and sexualized labour in interactive services", in: *Gender, Work and Organization*, 16, 3, 385–404.

Warhurst, Chris, Paul Thompson, and Dennis Nickson (2009), "Labour process theory: Putting the materialism back into the meaning of service work", in: Marek Korczynski, and Cameron L. Macdonald (eds.), *Service work: Critical perspective*, London: Routledge 91–112.

From Emotional Labor to Interactive Service Work

Wolfgang Dunkel and Margit Weihrich

Arlie Hochschild gained international prominence with her path-breaking theoretical and empirical investigation of emotional labor, laying the foundations for innovative approaches to the sociological study both of emotions and of service work (Hochschild 1979; 1983). Common to all her analyses, including her most recent book, *The Outsourced Self: Intimate Life in Market Times* (Hochschild 2012), is the story of how the increasing dominance of economic over social life is breaking down boundaries that once separated the realms of work and the market from those of the home and the self. She investigates these processes, which she calls "commercialization" and "commodification", from the different perspectives of the participants involved. She takes up the perspective of service providers in her study of flight attendants in *The Managed Heart* (Hochschild 1983), arguing that airline companies instrumentalize and trim flight attendants' emotions to conform to market imperatives. Her new study (2012) examines individuals who utilize market-based services for an increasingly large portion of those things previously considered off-limits to the market. Common to both studies is not only Hochschild's critique of the increasingly pervasive commodification of personal life, a tendency that now reaches far into what had been considered very intimate aspects of people's lives; her studies also focus on services. Her social critique is thus based on an analysis of which services are performed in society, how they are performed, and how this has changed radically over the course of time.

We share the view that conclusions can be drawn about the constitution of society by looking at how services and service work are changing. This chapter thus centers on "interactive work" in service relationships or, more specifically, on the way in which service providers and service receivers resolve problems that are endemic to service relationships. We also look at emotional labor in interactive work, but in contrast to Hochschild's intriguing thesis of the increasing commodification of social life, we offer our own reading of the relationships uniting services, market processes, and social development.

This chapter reflects our longstanding interest in the rich conceptual work undertaken by Arlie Hochschild since the 1980s. We thus begin in section 1 by briefly summarizing Wolfgang Dunkel's (1988) suggestion for linking several dimensions of emotional labor, including Hochschild's concepts of emotion work and emotional labor.[1] In our subsequent collaborative work, discussed in section 2, we elaborated an approach to social interaction in service relationships. In our approach, we make three arguments beyond Hochschild's concept of emotional labor. We argue that emotional labor in service relationships is only a part of the gamut of interactive work; that service providers and service receivers are of equal importance in service relationships and should be analyzed simultaneously; and that economic and social aspects are inseparable in service relationships. This concept of "interactive work", which has already served to guide rather large-scale empirical studies on service work[2] (Dunkel and Voß 2004; Dunkel and Weihrich 2012), synthesizes, as elaborated in detail in our contribution in Dunkel and Kleemann (2013), two separate research traditions: the model of strategic interaction (section 3) and qualitative social research on service work inspired by interactionism (section 4). In the conclusion found in section 5, we present an approach, based on the concept of interactive work, that is useful for understanding the changing relationship between services and society. It focuses not on how economic exchanges affect social relations but rather on how social relations are daily recreated through exchanges in service relationships, exchanges that by their very nature link economic exchanges to social interaction. In this way, service relationships reveal themselves to be laboratories of social relations. Services are not the sole outputs of these laboratories—they also produce, for better or for worse, society itself.

---

1 The conceptual synthesis has been widely received in German debates on emotional labor but was first introduced to an international audience much later (Sieben and Wettergren 2010).

2 See especially the work conducted in the "Professionalization of Interactive Work" project, funded by the German Federal Ministry of Education and Research *(Bundesministerium für Bildung und Forschung, BMBF)* and the European Social Fund of the European Union from 2008 to 2012 (see Dunkel and Weihrich 2012).

The Three Dimensions of Emotional Labor

In her early work, Arlie Hochschild makes two fundamental distinctions relevant to emotional labor. She distinguishes between "emotion work", which is a private matter, and "emotional labor", which takes place in the context of employment and is subject to an employer's manipulation. She also makes the now quite well-known distinction between work on the outward representation of emotion ("surface acting") and work on the emotions themselves ("deep acting"). With these categories, Hochschild opens up a dimension of paid work that had previously gone unnoticed and shows just how deeply companies reach in order to get at their employees' productive reserves of labor. She also shows, incidentally, that these forms of corporate manipulation draw on, and reinforce gender stereotypes. A basic assumption is that emotional labor is directed toward one's own emotions and is motivated by a desire to correct the discrepancy between one's personal emotions and the range of emotions, called "feeling rules", considered appropriate for social and business life. Emotional labor means making one's personal feelings conform to feeling rules, thus reducing or even eliminating discrepancies. Dunkel (1988) argues, however, that emotional labor is a broader phenomenon that has three separate definitional dimensions (see Brook in this volume).

The first dimension of emotional labor is that it makes emotions into an *object to be worked on*. In their classic hospital studies, Anselm Strauss and colleagues (1985) showed that different forms of emotional labor emerge depending on which emotional state workers want to effect in the person being "handled". For some, anxiety must be reduced, for others, trust must be built, and for others, sorrow must be soothed. The following types of what they call "sentimental work" are differentiated: "interactional work and moral rules, trust work, composure work, biographical work, identity work, awareness context work, and rectification work" (Strauss et al. 1982: 258). From their perspective, emotional labor is not some kind of pleasant extra, performed to augment "real" work, which in their case was medical and nursing care. It is, in fact, a very necessary part of medical and nursing care involving human beings and is oriented by the trajectory of the patient's illness, and successful emotional healing is a precondition of successful somatic care. In short: Emotional labor is instrumental for goal attainment.

Emotions are objects of emotional labor, but they also can be made into the *means of emotional labor*. As workers perceive and manipulate others' feelings, their own emotions can serve a regulative function. Empathy helps us understand the emotional state of our interaction partners. The expression of friendly or aggressive feelings leads us to respond in the way intended by the person acting out those emotions. Working with feeling is thus the second dimension of emotional labor.

Finally, the third dimension of emotional labor refers to work on one's own emotions. As Hochschild argues, emotions must conform to social norms. She advances the thesis that success in influencing the emotions of others depends on how appropriate one's own emotions are to begin with. Thus, the emotional state of the emotional laborer is a *framing condition* of emotional labor. In this argument, her work shows parallels to psychology research that understands emotional labor as a potential psychological stressor. In particular, the research on job burnout described a syndrome characterized by physical exhaustion coupled with a deep emotional apathy toward other people in work-related personal interactions (Maslach 1982). This research showed that emotions are a scarce resource and that our emotions can, indeed, get used up.

In the more differentiated approach described by Dunkel (1988), the rationality and malleability of emotions are even more strongly emphasized than in Hochschild's work, although in Hochschild's original concept, emotional labor was portrayed as more rational and malleable than in popular notions of emotionality. Emotions are rational in the sense that they give us valuable information about the situations we find ourselves in: Hochschild (1983: 85) defines emotion as "a sense that tells about the self-relevance of reality". Emotions are malleable because we do not have to let them pass over us; we can regulate them, control them, and come to terms with them. Thus, Hochschild certainly did not subscribe to the conventional dualism of emotion versus reason. However, in her analysis she concentrated on the personal price paid by those who have to manipulate their own emotions in order to satisfy someone else's expectations. The real possibility that a person can sometimes obtain a personal benefit through emotional labor by using it to influence others' behavior was left unexplored. Not that Hochschild was unaware of this possibility: She described how service companies regulate the emotional work of their employees, and of course, must have assumed that this work would have corresponding, intended effects on customers. Her absolutely correct finding that this can represent a source of stress for employees led her, however, to downplay the potentially positive aspects of emotional labor for employees.

We argue that such potential positive effects lie, above all, in the fact that emotional labor in service relationships helps employees reach goals—and not only corporate goals but also their own, personal ones. In other words, companies are not the only entities with strategies for emotional labor. Employees, too, have strategies, which leads us to the concept of interactive work.

Interactive Work

The concept of interactive work begins with the observation of a characteristic unique to service relationships: service providers and customers must work together in order to attain a desired service output. They must engage in "interactive work", by which we mean the specific form of work that, by its very nature, can only be performed by service providers and customers together, and is inseparable from other aspects of the work process. This is true for service relationships between customers and employees of service companies as well as for service relationships between clients and experts or patients and doctors.

This perspective forces us to treat customers as active partners in the service relationship, because the service does not get provided without their cooperation. The form and intensity of cooperation between service provider and customer has a direct impact on the success and quality of the service. Service providers do not provide services by themselves. The customer, too, must work.

This verity of this principle can be put to the test in any doctor's office, for example. During the initial diagnostic interview, patients must provide information about their ailment. To do this well, they must be able to articulate medically relevant information, and to perform certain tasks, such as undressing or breathing deeply. For their part, physicians need empathy to obtain unspoken information for their diagnosis, and they must formulate the diagnosis in terms the patient understands. Doctors know, also, that many patients interpret their symptoms, and may have diagnosed themselves before the visit, perhaps relying on information from the internet. When a treatment regimen is prescribed, the doctor must motivate the patient to adhere to it. Treatment success, after all, depends in large part on the patient's cooperation in taking medication exactly as prescribed, or in sticking to a long-term physical therapy program. The conditions of treatment regimens must be adjusted to the patient's situation, and sometimes these terms are negotiated. If the doctor advises additional testing which the patient would have to pay for herself, the patient must decide to accept or reject this advice. The performance of all of these tasks is more likely if the patient and the physician trust each other. Under conditions of trust, patients can safely assume that their doctor is motivated by an interest in their good health, not in personal economic advantage.

In *every* service relationship, customers and service providers must resolve the central problem of how to build up a cooperative relationship. As the example shows, this undertaking is anything but easy. Service providers and customers must resolve three very specific problems that typically stand in the way of cooperation: 1) how to find each other, 2) whether to contribute to an outcome that benefits the other party, and 3) what to do if no mutual benefit is possible at all. These problems, elaborated below, sometimes appear as social dilemmas or social traps that, theoretically speaking, are very difficult to escape (Weihrich and Dunkel 2003).

Customers and service providers must address the barriers to service provision if a service is to be provided successfully, and they must address them within the service relationship itself, face-to-face and in real time. Participants are always acting in the here-and-now, never knowing exactly what will happen in the next moment. Companies do try to regulate such service interactions, for example by establishing feeling rules for their front-line workers, as Arlie Hochschild so vividly described. However, given that service work necessitates interaction among participants who have some degree of freedom, however slight, interaction in service work creates contingencies, and these, in turn, set clear limits on the regulatory power of corporate management. In fact, interactive work is necessary exactly because service provision cannot be governed by general rules. Every service situation creates its own contextual conditions, and services can only be produced from within these situational contexts. Nor are customers, whose participation in the service relationship would require company regulation too, subordinate to the commands of the service providing organization. This becomes quite obvious when customers refuse to stick to the scripts companies write in the hope of imposing order on service interactions. At the same time, employees are expected to represent company interests that are often self-contradictory or that contradict customer wishes. Common, for example, is the expectation that employees improve both cost efficiency and customer satisfaction without losing control over the customer and without violating professional standards. This work on the margins of incommensurate interests is a challenge for employees and customers alike. Employees must find a way to fit company goals to customer wishes, and customers must work on their wishes so as to make them compatible with what the company is offering.

For investigating and understanding the unpredictability of interaction sequences, a new combination of concepts and empirical methods is needed. To this end, our theoretical and empirical approach to the study of service interactions draws on two separate research traditions. The first tradition is connected to a model of strategic interaction in the sense of a "distinctly sociological version of game theory" (Swedberg 2001: 301). The second tradition is based on the results and methods of research on service work inspired by interactionism and from which Arlie Hochschild's work on emotional labor emerged. The model of strategic interaction is useful for identifying problems of action that characterize service relationships. Interactionism helps expose and describe the concrete strategies used by customers and service providers jointly to resolve their respective problems of action as the service situation unfolds (for further elaboration, see our contribution in Dunkel and Kleemann 2013).

A Model of Strategic Interaction

Problems of social interdependence are inherent in service relationships, as they are in all social relationships, and are tied to the fact that actors pursue individual interests even in mutual undertakings. Their interests come in varying constellations of compatibility. One constellation emerges when we try to meet each other and look for an appropriate solution. In this situation, we share a common goal and both make a contribution to the attainment of this goal. In a second constellation, we have a common goal whose benefit we share. In this situation, however, there exists an alternative to cooperation: We both prefer to let the cost of the contribution be borne by the other. In the third constellation, if I attain my goal, you are precluded from attaining yours, and vice-versa, a situation that produces a clear winner and a clear loser. These three constellations correspond to three typical interdependence problems, elaborated below.[3]

---

3 This typology (under various names) was first presented by Ullmann-Margalit (1977) and then further discussed and developed for example in Weihrich (2002), Schmid (2004), Weihrich (2007), and Maurer and Schmid (2010).

Coordination problems: Despite trying, we may fail to attain shared or complementary goals if I do not know whether, or how, you are going to contribute. This may prevent us from coordinating our actions. If a coordinated solution is found, however, it is stable. Because it matches both our interests, neither you nor I expect to gain by defecting.

Contribution problems: Contribution problems are rooted in the fact that each of us has an alternative course of action that is individually more attractive than making a contribution. As long as I am sure that you are making a contribution, I have no compelling reason to contribute because a benefit accrues to me whether I contribute or not. Assuming you and I think alike and withhold our contribution, anticipating or assuming that the other will do the same, this, too, is a stable solution, but the outcome is the failure of cooperation. Therefore we fail to attain any benefit that we might have reached through cooperation. We arrive at the less-than-optimal position of no costs but no gains.

Distribution problems: Incompatible goals create a problem of distribution. If the commodity in question cannot be split up, or if the division, once made, appears unjust to either party, instability results, and there is no chance of reaching even a stable suboptimal outcome. Distributive processes of this type are rife with conflict potential, and the prospect of the protagonists fighting for more can never be ruled out. One should bear in mind, too, that when goods can be shared, any of a number of rules of distribution can be set, thus the rule can always be called unfair retrospectively again and again (see Moore 1978).

These three situations are characterized by different degrees of potential conflict. For coordination problems, stable solutions of mutual benefit are possible. For contribution problems, solutions of mutual benefit are possible but are unstable. For distribution problems, no solution of mutual benefit to the participants is possible at all.

One might object that these problems are resolvable or avoidable if we assume that people value solidarity, are inclined to reach agreement, or make cooperation itself a goal. Nonetheless, we find it useful to accept the theoretical assumption of self-interested, goal-oriented actors who find themselves (specifically because of this orientation) in the interdependence problems described above. Under this assumption, successful cooperation is an art, never something to be taken for granted. Without question, solidarity and agreement are vitally important mechanisms for the resolution of interdependence problems, but even these mechanisms must somehow first be created.

All three interdependence problems arise in service relationships, for these are no pure relationships of market exchange. Rather, they are characterized by the essential fact that service providers and customers jointly create a product through the service: the new haircut, the treatment of an illness, et cetera. Nor can service providers and customers escape this fact of their mutual dependence. In order to attain the desired service outputs, they must work together, creating and maintaining for this purpose a service relationship. Such cooperation cannot be reached without encountering problems and is, in the rule, the result of quite treacherous processes of coordination. Even in exchange relationships, where all participants are similarly interested in having the service produced, the realization of this goal is anything but simple. It is a challenge, rife with potential conflict, and the attempt can fail, as most of us have experienced personally. Success requires that the following problems and difficulties be overcome.

The problem of the definition of the objects and processes of service relationships

This first problem results from the necessity of determining the object of the service relationship and agreeing on how work is to proceed. Before the service can be effected, the participants must define and agree upon the problem to be resolved and what procedures are to be used in its resolution. Erving Goffman (1961) speaks in this context of the definition of the "malfunctioning object". That which is to become the object of a personal service, he noted, must be turned into an object and separated from the person of the customer before the service provider and the customer can come to terms about how it is to be handled. Taking up the above example again, doctors and patients have to determine together what is wrong with the patient during the initial examination. A precondition of success in this joint endeavor is, among other things, the ability to make oneself understood and to set a clear goal for action. In terms of the ideal types of interdependence problems, this is a coordination problem at first, although it can evolve into a different kind of problem in subsequent phases of interaction.

The problem of the incomplete contract

Once the exact object is defined, both participants must find a way to co-ordinate their actions such that this defined object of the service relationship can be handled successfully. Cooperation is made more difficult because no contract can comprehensively regulate the outputs of a service relationship. Neither the object of the service relationship, nor the procedure of its handling, nor the result of the interaction can be determined *ex ante*. This applies also to the respective contributions of service provider and service receiver: Neither participant knows whether the other will honor their contractual promise to contribute to the costs of providing the service. The doctor does not know if the patient will really begin to exercise more, nor does the patient really know if the doctor's advice is good. Thus, services can only be offered as the promise of service—with all the uncertainty inherent in promises made by human beings. This contribution problem is the root of the problem of the incomplete contract.

The problem of opposing interests

Finally, service relationships are not just a matter of successful cooperation. They are also characterized by the fact that a task is completed in exchange for money; thus, service relationships harbor by definition potential distribution problems. Goffman (1961: 336) speaks here of a "kind of matrix of anxiety and doubt". Service providers must always reckon with not getting paid, just as service receivers have to reckon with the possibility of having to pay more than the service is worth. And each knows that the other knows that their relationship is constrained by economic exigencies. As shown above, this applies even to very traditional professions like medicine: The "customers" may wonder if the physician prescribed a certain medication for reasons that have nothing to do with their health.

Interactionism and Qualitative Methods

Whereas the model of strategic interaction shows the pitfalls inherent to service relationships, qualitative research on service interactions, with its instruments and rich background of previous findings, aids us in understanding how real cases of interactive service work are resolved in daily practice. Existing studies of service work contain a wealth of information about strategies used to cope with interdependence problems in the context of service relationships, although not all authors presented this information explicitly for this purpose. Examples can be drawn from among the most renown representatives of sociological research on services: Erving Goffman (1959; 1961; 1969), Anselm Strauss (1978), Robin Leidner (1993), Marek Korczynski (2002)—and Arlie Hochschild. They all share an interactionist perspective on service work and are part of the traditions of phenomenology, symbolic interactionism, and the Chicago School. From their perspective, the following characteristics of service relations come to the fore.

- Interactive work is social interaction that can include a large spectrum of communication channels (auditory, visual, sensory).
- It is challenging work directed toward a goal that lies beyond the interaction itself.
- The participants involved are only in exceptional cases emotionally cool and calculating; they are more typically existentially and emotionally involved in the interaction situation.
- Interactive work in service relations is a complex process with several participants, each with their own view of the process.
- Interactive service work is usually embedded in institutional rules, most especially those of the respective service company; these rules limit employees and customers' freedom of action.
- Interactive work is shaped by society; cultural rules and economic imperatives suffuse the interactions and also determine the kind and level of resources brought in by each participating actor.

These authors teach us one additional lesson. They demonstrate that qualitative methods, especially those developed in the discipline of ethnography, are well adapted for uncovering the many different strategies service providers and service receivers use to resolve their problems of interdependence. For resolving the problem of the definition of the objects and processes of service relationships, participants offer mutual accommodation and they accept established routines or dock onto social conventions. For resolving the problem of the incomplete contract, they rely on trust-building or monitoring mechanisms. The fact that the objects and the processes of service relationships must be negotiated actually provides a good opportunity to obtain information about the trustworthiness of a potential contractual partner and to signal one's own trustworthiness, thus defusing the problem of the incomplete contract. As pertains to the problem of opposing interests, participants can seek either to reconcile their interests or, if one participant perceives the possibility of a winner-take-all outcome, to engage in confrontation. Qualitative scientific analyses show that service providers and customers indeed employ a wide variety of strategies to elicit each other's cooperation. They explain, persuade, instruct, give in, use tactics and empathy, work on their own feelings and on those of their interaction partner, and use gestures and words. In short, they throw themselves into the work with body and soul, and learn how to seize the moment in hundreds of different ways.

Within a recent research project, we investigated the interactive work of customers and service providers using qualitative methods (Dunkel and Weihrich 2012). We found that work on one's own emotions plays a major role in the resolution of interdependence problems, just as Hochschild argues. However, this emotional labor extends far beyond merely adapting one's feelings to the "feeling rules" of the situation. Feelings are worked on in a very strategic manner, for example when persons hide their real emotions in order to position themselves to attain their goals in interactive situations. Or when persons consciously act out the role of a trustworthy person in order to downplay the potential conflict inherent in the problem of the incomplete contract. Or when the interaction partner is browbeaten into submission. Many more such examples could be given, but they all point to something similar: Emotional labor need not be something that is forced or that is associated with personal disadvantage. Emotional labor can be used as a strategy for reaching one's own goals in service interactions. Indeed, as soon as the issue of cooperation between service providers and service receivers is put at the center of empirical investigation, it becomes clear that one very important fact has been overlooked in the research on emotional labor: customers, too, engage in emotional labor.

Nurses, for example, are not the only emotional labor experts. The residents of nursing homes for the elderly are proficient at it too. "You have to be happy", one nursing home resident said in an interview, "that there are such nursing homes and nurses who do the work. So you have to be nice to them". What the resident describes here is strategic labor on the nurses' emotions. It serves to overcome a contribution problem.

Another resident told us how she handled a distribution problem by first working on her own emotions, and then on the emotions of her nurse, in order to present a criticism at the right moment.

And then somebody comes over and you say, "yes, I've been sitting quite a long time here". And then she says, "excuse me, but the service company had to talk to me and they are my boss". That makes me boil on the inside because I'm thinking, "I pay to live here, so actually I'm a boss, too" but don't say anything until the fourth or fifth time, after I've gotten her to laugh, then I say it, that actually, I'm the boss.

Laboratories of Social Relations

The concept of interactive work as described here shows that services are not pure market relations, which means for effecting service delivery, any and all forms of non-market coordination mechanisms come into play: accommodation and convention, trust and control, negotiation and conflict, and so on. Service providers and service receivers use our original social media—feelings, speech, body language, gender—for these purposes, meeting or disappointing general expectations about appropriate social behavior. In the use, expansion, alteration, and institutionalization of coordination mechanisms, actors create interactive capital, and this can be spent for the resolution of social interdependence problems.

Generalizing from observations of what happens in service relationships to speculation about how interactive work fits to larger social processes, we proffer the thesis that service relationships are compact laboratories of social relations. Below, we elaborate four arguments for why this is so and what this tells us about the current and future states of society.

First, the interactive capital that is created in the context of interactive work can also be used outside service relationships and thus affects the more general social bonds that hold society together. Society is made in service relationships insofar as the way in which actors treat each other in interactive work influences the way they treat each other in other situations. The quantitative expansion of service work alone lends credence to this argument, because now, most everyone is involved daily in multiple service relationships, if not as employees then as customers. Because we live in a service-based society, the corresponding interactive work in service relationships has become integrated into our daily routines, and everyone in service societies spends quite a lot of time performing this work. It has become a basis for establishing social bonds of no mean importance indeed.

Second, because non-market, social mechanisms of interaction are of such great importance in the regulation of interactive work in service relationships, we may at some point in the future look back and see, to our surprise, that service relationships served to check the commodification of social life. Within sociology, there have been prominent discussions of an encroachment of market forces on social life (*"Landnahme"*, see Dörre 2011). Similarly, the market is seen to be impinging on social interaction because aspects of life that once were considered very private are now managed by professional service organizations (Hochschild 2003, 2012), a process that most certainly affects emotional states. In our way of thinking, however, not only does the market impinge on interactions in service relationships, but interactions also impinge on the market and in so doing create new bases of solidarity. This can be observed in ordinary service interactions in which employees and customers tacitly agree to ignore external rules (often put in place by the service company) in order to attain a service result that better harmonizes with what they want. Solidarity can emerge also at a collective level. Employees and customers may, for example, cooperate in scandalizing employer practices as occurred in Germany when the service sector union *(ver.di)* successfully campaigned against poor job conditions at the supermarket discount chain Lidl. Customers may also unite in protest against an entire service industry as occurred in the Occupy Wall Street movement. Service relationships thus hold out the potential for solidarity and even for resistance. Formulated in general terms, the trust produced in interactive work represents a social resource that spreads out beyond the context of service relationships via a generalized expectation that other people can be trusted. This generalized expectation can increase the absolute level of trust in society (see Coleman 1990). Of course, the opposite case can also hold. If trust cannot be produced, then distrust follows, as when customers are bound up by comprehensive corporate control regimes that clearly signal a complete lack of trust. What happens then can be seen in societies that suffer from a chronic shortage of mutual trust; these are high-risk zones where private security companies flourish (Gambetta 1993; Weihrich 2011).

Third, we note that the close relationship between services and society does not necessarily mean that civilized social relationships are going to be the "great hope" of the 21st century, a conclusion that one might be tempted to draw from Fourastié's (1949) optimism about the service-based society of the 20ᵗʰ century. It remains to be seen which coordination mechanisms will emerge out of interactive work and which kinds of social bonds will be produced. This is what the laboratory metaphor is meant to imply. There is no way to rule out that interactive work in service relationships will become engulfed and transformed by the often-diagnosed processes of market encroachment, boundary dissolution, and subjectification surrounding service relationships. The ability of companies to standardize services may improve to the extent that they can rationalize away not only employees but interactive work, too. Comprehensive control environments may erode trust and foster a culture of mistrust, making the pursuit of personal advantage ("bargain grabbing" versus "price gouging") more important than the pursuit of service outcomes that are good for both parties. In the end, it may well be that only a purely economic logic dominates.

Fourth and last, we had noted above that service relationships are structured by expectations about how people deal with each other in social interactions. Our empirical investigations show that these expectations are expressed in specific ways. In service relationships, they are expressed, among other ways, in the parties granting each other mutual recognition as whole persons with private interests, specific skills, and limitations. Employees do not wish to be perceived merely as representatives of a company, nor do customers wish to be treated merely as "part of a process". Both parties are sensitive about upholding general rules of fairness. If recognition as a person is denied or if the rules of fairness are flaunted, moral indignation and all the emotions it stirs up are sure to ensue. For this reason service relationships are highly emotional affairs. For work on this kind of quality in services, norms of reciprocity play a central role. Everyone expects reciprocity to be honored, and this expectation is strategically instrumentalized. The adage, "what goes around comes around", is commonly cited by customers and service providers whenever they describe the "chemistry" of a service situation. They thus clearly demonstrate their underlying understanding of the significance of cooperation and the importance of signaling one's own willingness to cooperate. They also reveal their expectation that an offer of cooperation will be accepted. If this expectation is disappointed, the show of moral indignation can be quite dramatic. Considering the additional fact that service relationships increasingly take place between individuals who consider themselves equals (when the co-working customer is no longer king and no longer an uneducated layperson, when the service provider ceases to be a servant and is not honored as a high expert) then service relationships may well continue to feed our need for mutual recognition. In this way, it may well be that within this kind of market-based exchange relationship, interactive capital is produced that serves to limit the encroachment of the market into social relations.

Arlie Hochschild (2012) described the phenomenon that an increasing number of tasks once considered private are being performed by market organizations, arguing that this represents increased commodification and commercialization. In light of what we have presented here, however, one could interpret this differently. The act of outsourcing is itself a matter of interactive work. The nanny has to be persuaded to cooperate, the "wantologist" (a consultant who tells people what they really want) has to be trusted, and so on. Therefore, a quantitative increase of market relationships in daily life need not necessarily mean that solidarity will wane. That depends on how the social dimension of these relationships is structured, and we should not neglect the overall significance of service relationships for society. Our families and our jobs, after all, are not the only nuclei of social reproduction. Society is also made in service relationships.

Translation from the German by Scott Stock Gissendanner

Works Cited

Coleman, James S. (1990), *Foundations of social theory,* Cambridge/London: The Belknap Press.

Dörre, Klaus (2011), "Capitalism, *Landnahme* and social time régimes: An outline", in: *Time & society,* 20, 1, 69–93.

Dunkel, Wolfgang (1988), "Wenn Gefühle zum Arbeitsgegenstand werden. Gefühlsarbeit im Rahmen personenbezogener Dienstleistungstätigkeiten", in: *Soziale Welt,* 39, 1, 66–85.

Dunkel, Wolfgang, and Frank Kleemann (eds.) (2013), *Customers at work. New perspectives on interactive service work,* Houndmills: Palgrave Macmillan.

Dunkel, Wolfgang, and G. Günter Voß (eds.) (2004), *Dienstleistung als Interaktion – Beiträge aus einem Forschungsprojekt: Altenpflege – Deutsche Bahn – Call Center,* München/Mering: Hampp Verlag.

Dunkel, Wolfgang, and Margit Weihrich (eds.) (2012), *Interaktive Arbeit. Theorie, Praxis und Gestaltung von Dienstleistungsbeziehungen,* Wiesbaden: Springer VS Verlag.

Fourastié, Jean (1949), *Le grand espoir du XXeme siècle. Progrès technique, progress économique, progrès social,* Paris: Presses Universitaires de France.

Gambetta, Diego (1993), *The Sicilian mafia. The business of private protection,* Cambridge: Harvard University Press.

Goffman, Erving (1959), *The presentation of self in everyday life,* Garden City, N.Y.: Anchor Books.

— (1961), *Asylums. Essays on the social situation of mental patients and other inmates,* Garden City, N.Y.: Anchor Books.

— (1969), *Strategic interaction,* Philadelphia: University of Pennsylvania Press.

Hochschild, Arlie Russell (1979), "Emotion work, feeling rules, and social structure", in: *American Journal of Sociology,* 85, 3, 551–575.

— (1983), *The managed heart. Commercialization of human feeling,* Berkeley: University of California Press.

— (2003), *The commercialization of intimate life: Notes from home and work,* San Francisco, Los Angeles: University of California Press.

— (2012), *The outsourced self: Intimate life in market times,* New York: Metropolitan Books.

Korczynski, Marek (2002), *Human resource management in service work,* Houndmills: Palgrave Macmillan.

Leidner, Robin (1993), *Fast food, fast talk: Service work and the routinization of everyday life,* Berkeley: University of California Press.

Maslach, Christina (1982), *Burnout: The cost of caring,* Englewood Cliffs: Prentice Hall.

Maurer, Andrea, and Michael Schmid (2010), *Erklärende Soziologie. Grundlagen, Vertreter und Anwendungsfelder eines soziologischen Forschungsprogramms,* Wiesbaden: Springer VS Verlag.

Moore, Barrington (1978), *Injustice. The bases of disobedience and revolt,* White Plains: M. E. Sharpe.

Schmid, Michael (2004), *Rationales Handeln und soziale Prozesse. Beiträge zur soziologischen Theoriebildung,* Wiesbaden: Springer VS Verlag.

Sieben, Barbara, and Asa Wettergren (eds.) (2010), *Emotionalizing organizations and organizing emotions,* Houndmills: Palgrave Macmillan.

Strauss, Anselm L. (1978), *Negotiations,* San Francisco: Jossey-Bass.

Strauss, Anselm L., Shizuko Fagerhaugh, Barbara Suczek, and Carolyn Wiener (1982), "Sentimental work in the technologized hospital", in: *Sociology of health and illness,* 4, 3, 254–278.

Strauss, Anselm L., Shizuko Fagerhaugh, and Barbara Suczek (1985), *Social organization of medical work,* Chicago: University of Chicago Press.

Swedberg, Richard (2001), "Sociology and game theory: Contemporary and historical perspectives", in: *Theory and society,* 30, 301–335.

Ullmann-Margalit, Edna (1977), *The emergence of norms,* Oxford: Clarendon Press.

Weihrich, Margit (2002), "Die Rationalität von Gefühlen, Routinen und Moral", in: *Berliner Journal für Soziologie,* 12, 189–209.

— (2007), "Abstimmungsprobleme und Abstimmungsmechanismen im Theorievergleich", in: Norbert Huchler, G. Günter Voß, and Margit Weihrich, *Soziale Mechanismen im Betrieb. Theoretische und empirische Analysen zur Subjektivierung von Arbeit,* München, Mering: Hampp Verlag, 60–80.

— (2011), "Don Corleone in Gomorrha: Entstehung, Stabilität und Veränderung mafioser Unternehmen", in: Priddat, Birger, and Schmid, Michael (eds.), Korruption als Ordnung zweiter Art, Wiesbaden: Springer VS Verlag, 139–161.

Weihrich, Margit, and Wolfgang Dunkel (2003), "Abstimmungsprobleme in Dienstleistungsbeziehungen. Ein handlungstheoretischer Zugang", in: *Kölner Zeitschrift für Soziologie und Sozialpsychologie,* 55, 758–781.

Feeling Rules—Unfound Treasures for the Study of Work Cultures[1]

Gertraud Koch

Hochschild's concepts in the context of work research

As hardly any other researcher has done in this consistency, international cultural analytical research has been influenced over decades by impulses created by US sociologist Arlie Russell Hochschild over the course of her academic career. Time and again, her contributions on emotional labor (*The Managed Heart*; Hochschild 1983; 2003; 2012), on the mutual relationship of work and family life (*The Time Bind;* Hochschild and Machung 1990; Hochschild 2001), on the global gender-segregated sharing of work (*Global Women;* Ehrenreich and Hochschild 2003) and the increasing commercialization of private and intimate life (*The Commercialization of Intimate Life*; Hochschild 2003; *The Outsourced Self;* Hochschild 2012) have managed to set new conceptual impulses. These have not only been taken up in the different specialized areas of sociology (sociology of work, sociology of the family, sociology of emotions), but have also stimulated new research perspectives in different disciplines (social psychology, economy, history, cultural anthropology et cetera). The fact that her work has developed such a far-reaching influence across the disciplines is probably closely linked to the proximity to everyday life and the practical relevance which Arlie Hochschild develops in her research topics and areas. She is able to translate the areas of social theoretical interest to her into vivid and comprehensible analyses, even when the connections and relations to theory are highly complex. This is demonstrated in an exemplary fashion in her research on emotional labor[2], around

---

1 I would like to thank Paul Brook for his insightful suggestions for the further development of the concept put forward here. While not all of them could be included in this contribution, they will certainly be taken up in future publications.

2 As has been done elsewhere in this volume but not in this contribution emotion work in the sense of a management of emotion is an everyday act, which becomes emotional labor when it is commodified, that is, marketed as part of one's labor power, such as is done in service occupations in which is inclusive but must always also be given to the customer.

which a lively and mature research field has developed to investigate topics of practical relevance such as exploitation of labor, burn-out and mental strains. Contributions from social, psychological as well as economic, labor, and organizational research (Grandey and Brotheridge 2002; Lively 2006; Sieben and Wettergren 2010), sociology of work (Brook 2013 in this volume; Dunkel and Weihrich 2013 in this volume) as well as cultural anthropological work culture research (Götz 2013 in this volume) have taken up Hochschild's approaches in manifold ways, and by means of their research, have also further developed the understanding of emotional labor from a theoretical perspective.

Despite the far-reaching reception of her studies in work research, Hochschild's academic opus is far from exhausted. To date, the concept of *feeling rules* has found little reception, which is astounding given that it provides a point of access for the analysis of the culturality of work contexts at the intersection of individual and social life. The aim of this contribution is to demonstrate the conceptual offer Arlie Hochschild makes with her concept of feeling rules, and to sketch points of access for cultural theoretical development. To this end, as a first step, the design of the concept of feeling rules as well as the perspective of her analysis will be presented. In a second step, the uptake in work research of the concept of feeling rules will be explored. Finally and in conclusion, the cultural analytical potential of the concept of feeling rules and the points of access for cultural analytical work research will be formulated against this background.

How is emotion cultural?—Feeling rules as a link between emotional work and cultural context

Feeling rules are a central element in and for "The Managed Heart". It is their existence which necessitates emotion work, that is, the reflection of individual feelings with the aim of changing them, or showing different emotions than those felt, as private and occupational contexts demand. Feeling rules in this sense are to be conceived of as the intersection of the individual with social and cultural contexts. "The interactive account of emotion points to alternate theoretical junctures—between consciousness of feeling and consciousness of feeling rules, between feeling rules and emotion work, between feeling rules and social structure. (…) [I]t is these junctures we shall explore" (Hochschild 1979: 560).

It may be due to the far-reaching reception and the intensive theoretical elaboration of the concept of "emotional work/labor" in sociological and social-psychological work research (Grandey 2000; Bolton and Boyd 2003; Stuart 2008; Brook 2009) that feeling rules as a frame of reference, and thus also the cultural theoretical aspects in Hochschild's considerations, have had to take a back seat. Studies on emotion work take their point of departure mainly from individual and social structural aspects. They ask about the special requirements of emotional work/labor, the moments and the measure of exploitation of emotional work/labor capacity, the possibilities for designing work processes as well as the (new) quality of social relationships between employer, employee and customer/client. A central point of discussion and dissent against Hochschild's perspective in this is the measure and the inevitability of the alienation of the individual when his or her capacity for emotion work in work processes is commercialized. There has been intensive discussion along these lines about how and how far the subject is changed and formed through the commodification of emotional work to emotional labor, particularly in the service sector. However, little attention has been given to the sources from which the requirements for emotion management are drawn and which are crucial for the necessity of emotion work/labor. Ideologies as ways of interpreting the world, with its normative, moral orders, can be seen as the cultural grounds from which the feeling rules emerge. They can become a means of top-down management for imposing normative-behavioral training and control (Hochschild 1983). Hochschild's own work, the critics say, lacks a detailed description on the *meso*-level to mediate between emotional work/labor at the *micro*-level and societal developments of rationalization and commercialization at the *macro*-level (Tonkens 2012: 199 f.). Even if the considerations on feeling and framing rules as normative-moral points of reference of emotion work/labor are indeed not central for Hochschild, a closer inspection of her key work on emotional work/labor (1979; 1983) shows that clear contours of feeling rules as a mediating concept between individual and societal developments are sketched. Weber's postulation that capitalism forms mankind according to its requirements gains new clarity here. It is the deviation from the feeling rules, that is, emotions which are considered appropriate for a situation, which creates the necessity for emotion work.

Whether the convention calls for trying joyfully to possess, or trying casually not to, the individual compares and measures experience against an expectation often idealized. It is left for motivation ('what I want to feel') to mediate between feeling rule ('what I should feel') and emotion work ('what I try to feel'). Some of the time many of us can live with a certain dissonance between 'ought' and 'want,' or between 'want' and 'try to'. But the attempts to reduce emotive dissonance are our periodic clues to rules of feeling (Hochschild 1979: 565).

Surface-acting, the simulation of the emotions prescribed in the feeling rules, can therefore only be sustained for a limited time. Overcoming this discrepancy requires intensive emotion work and has been thematized as one cause of the phenomena of mental exhaustion and burn-out (Zapf 2002). The adjustment of our own feelings according to the feeling rules thus relieves individuals of the draining emotion work/labor. The "transmutation of feeling" is achieved via "deep acting", that is, the conscious manipulation of our own experience, in the sense of changes and adaptations to existing conventions. This internalized appropriation of feeling rules can thus be understood as a mechanism by which individuals and their social environment are coordinated (Hochschild 1979; 1983).

Social expectations and requirements are, we can conclude, brought to the subjects to a substantial degree via feeling rules assembled into emotional regimes; subjects experience these emotional regimes as an ensemble of informal rules, formal instructions and rules, practices as well as institutionalized behavior. This is true for the world of work, but also for other areas of society as a whole. Emotions can thus be seen as a "lens of the world" for research (Hochschild 2009). In this manner, feeling rules constitute baselines for social exchange according to emotional dispositions as well as to class, ethnicity or gender:

A feeling rule is like these other kinds of rules in the following ways: It delineates a zone within which one has permission to be free of worry, guilt, or shame with regard to the situated feeling. […] Some rules may be nearly universal, such as the rule that one should not enjoy killing or witnessing the killing of a human being, including oneself. Other rules are unique to particular social groups and can be used to distinguish among them as alternate governments or colonizers of individual internal event (Hochschild 1979: 565–566).

Which feelings are perceived as normal, points, according to Hochschild, to existing social conventions. Contrary to many other rules, they resist codification and are employed situationally, following an experience-based, praxeological application. In this praxeological understanding, the assessment of whether an expression of feelings is appropriate to a particular situation is itself a social process in the sense of negotiation. "Any gesture—a cool greeting, an appreciative laugh, the apology for an outburst—is measured against a prior sense of what is reasonably owed another, given the sort of bond involved" (Hochschild 1979: 568).

Many factors, and their interrelationships, determine the appropriateness of feelings. Hochschild points out that the ability to follow certain feeling rules reflects social belonging and thus appoints an individual their place in social life. Feeling rules have a socializing effect for the members of a group and can, conversely, also lead to exclusion. "These rights and duties of feeling are a clue to the depth of social convention, to one final reach of social control" (564). In this sense, "rules for managing feeling" are, as Hochschild puts it, "the 'bottom side' of ideology", while she understands ideology, like in symbolic anthropology (Geertz 1964: 49–76), as an interpretive framework:

[T]hat [interpretive framework] can be described in terms of framing rules and feeling rules. By "framing rules" I refer to the rules according to which we ascribe definitions or meanings to situations. For example, an individual can define the situation of getting fired as yet another instance of capitalists' abuse of workers or as yet another result of personal failure. In each case, the frame may reflect a more general rule about assigning blame. By "feeling rules" I refer to guidelines for the assessment of fits and misfits between feeling and situation. For example, according to one feeling rule, one can be legitimately angry at the boss or company; according to another, one cannot. Framing and feeling rules are back to back and mutually imply each other (Hochschild 1979: 566).

The interpretive framework or, in Hochschild's work, "ideological stance", has a central importance, both for everyday practice and for the analysis of feeling rules, because feelings or the sanction of these feelings can be categorized and processed in a new way according to this framework (Hochschild 1979: 567). From the perspective of cultural theory, the different ideological points of reference of feeling rules are of interest because they mark out the ethical and moral frameworks of experience, and thus the approaches to social reality. Hochschild herself has pointed to different sources of ideologies such as occupations (Hochschild 1979: 572) and socio-cultural factors like class, gender, ethnicity and religion. Feeling rules can become a point of departure for manipulation, mostly in the interest of groups in a higher social position than others. Hochschild, referring to Randall Collins, speaks of emotive technologies via which elites search access to the respective groups:

"Developing his view, we can add that elites, and indeed social groups in general, struggle to assert the legitimacy of their framing rules and their feeling rules. Not simply the evocation of emotion but laws governing it can become, in varying degrees, the arena of political struggle" (1979: 568).

Research on feeling rules and the respective ideologies in the sense of Clifford Geertz (Geertz 1964: 49–76) is seen by Hochschild as a fertile ground for highly different areas of society (1979: 572 and 2009). However, empirically, this poses fundamental questions: Are there indeed feeling rules? How do we know about them? And which characteristics of social exchange can be gleaned from them (ibid.: 553)? For social and cultural analysis, feeling rules become accessible and productive particularly in those areas where changes and shifts become apparent, and also where different feeling rules collide. "Specifically, if we are to understand the origin and causes of change in 'feeling rules'—this underside of ideology—we are forced back out of a study of the immediate situations in which they show up, to a study of such things as changing relations between classes or the sexes" (1979: 557). Feeling rules are an indicator of what is perceived as normal in an ideology, and thus permit conclusions about moral and ethical guidelines for our acts as well as their contribution to a social good.

In summary, the following contours for the concept of feeling rules can be found which can be taken up for cultural analytical research on work: Feeling rules constitute the link between individual experience and social context. They play a significant role in the socialization into the social rules and cultural norms of a group, as well as provide an institutional context for action as we found in organizations. Feeling rules are thus an expression of the view of the world of these groups. The feelings we experience can be placed in very different ideological frames, such as gender-specific feeling rules, or the professional feeling rules of organizations, and many more. Depending on which framing is taken up in a situation, different repertoires of feeling rules can be invoked and form interpretational frameworks for our feelings. A reflected change of frames, such as aggressive behavior of a female manager, can be negatively interpreted as an unfeminine emotional act. However, if frames are changed to a managerial ideology, this can be interpreted as part of the normal repertoire. Such possibilities for reference frames, which in everyday situations usually overlap, extend situational possibilities as well as necessities for interpretation. The sources and backgrounds of these ideologies can be manifold and can be based on socio-structural as well as cultural factors such as class, gender or religion. This potential unlimited openness in the application of feeling rules is limited by framing rules, and thus placed in relation to given social ordering frames. Further, feeling and framing rules also partly become the object of social processes of negotiation *in situ*. Due to their situational and interactional character, feeling and framing rules are to be understood as praxeologically determined concepts.

From the point of view of cultural analysis, framings of feelings establish the relationship to the ideologies within which the feeling rules must be located. Framing rules deliver the instructions on which of the ideologies are to be seen as the appropriate and correct frames of reference for the emotional experience of a social situation. To feel which feelings are considered appropriate in which situations, and to feel what is the right thing to do or not to do, can, in this sense, not be treated as discrete from each other. The discrepancy between feeling rules and felt emotions thus points to a potential conflict between the moral orientations behind them, which are applied unconsciously or reflected actively in order to categorize our experiences. Framing rules therefore reveal something about the relations and the social orders of these ideologies. A central aspect in Hochschild's considerations in this regard is that societal exchange processes become apparent in feeling rules, that they are established and reproduced via them. The socialization via feeling rules can thus be employed and understood as an exercise of power. The measure to which they are then internalized and experienced as "authentic" determines their effectiveness. Feeling the "correct" emotion in a situation goes along with the ability to categorize this situation "correctly" within an existing social order, and to adjust one's own experience along the repertoires of appropriate ideologies. Often it is about "serving" different feeling rules simultaneously and balancing them, for instance by bringing feminine and managerial feeling rules in their party exclusive orientations into a relationship which is experienced as authentic. In situations such as these, when experienced feelings and feeling rules diverge, when new adjustments are called for, in situations of conflict and change, cultural analytical approaches make sense. Thinking along the lines of a praxeological orientation, it is less about ideologies in Clifford Geertz' sense, but rather about regimes or assemblages (Collier and Lakoff 2005; Rabinow 2007) which can be used to capture the mediating level of culture between individual and societal development both theoretically as well as empirically.

Emotional capitalism and feeling rules in contemporary work life

The increased importance of emotions in work life goes along with the cultural historical development of the informalization of feelings which the Dutch sociologist Wouters has described as starting at the end of the 19th century as "controlled decontrolling of emotional control" (Wouters 2009: 192). The new opportunities for showing one's emotion almost becomes an obligation to feel in the working world. The capacity for empathy and emotion management have come to be seen as key qualifications in the area of executives. "[P]rofessional knowledge is no longer considered to be sufficient for doing a job properly. Instead, 'emotional competencies' are now seen as the real driving forces of a successful career" (Becker 2009: 196). The "emotive technologies" (Hochschild 1979, referring to Randall) of present forms of capitalism have developed so far that cultural sociologist Eva Illouz has sketched them as the basic features of emotional capitalism. Historically speaking, it is psychologists who "have been extraordinarily successful in claiming the monopoly over the definition and the rules of emotional life and who thus have established to new criteria to capture, manage, and quantify emotional life" (Illouz 2007: 66). Emotional capitalism still becomes apparent in the marketing of romantic feelings in everyday life, such as in online dating.

Emotional capitalism is a culture in which emotional and economic discourses and practices mutually shape each other, thus producing what I view as a broad, sweeping movement in which affect is made an essential aspect of economic behavior and in which emotional life—especially that of the middle classes—follows the logic of economic relations and exchange (Illouz 2007: 5).

The motives of "rationalization" and "commodification" of emotion are thus inevitable topics in researching modern societies. Emotional abilities which are fundamental for social relationships are instrumentalized for economic processes of exploitation. "Empathy—the ability to identify with another's point of view and with his feelings—is at once an emotional and symbolic skill, for the prerequisite of empathy is that one must decipher the complex cues of other behaviors" (Illouz 2007: 19 f.). The deployment of all abilities, of the entire "cultural baggage" of an individual (Gorz [2003] 2010) is thus called for in the work process. Self-management, self-organization and self-help characterize the repertoire of action in the culture of emotional capitalism on the individual side. In consequence, a therapeutic *habitus* is developed which instructs individuals to help themselves, particularly in emotion management (Illouz 2008). The latter facilitates a work culture which no longer banks on orders and hierarchy, but on cooperation and coordination, which, in the course of democratization and equality, has become an ever more important principle of management in organizations (Illouz 2007).

Empirical research on feeling rules in the current working world, on the other hand, draws a much more complex picture of how emotions are dealt with at work than what could be expected based on the theory of emotional capitalism. Beyond this sociological macro-perspective, a bandwidth of ideological sources becomes apparent which influence the subject via feeling rules. These feeling rules are only partly based on the economic logics of exploitation of commodification and rationalization. Instead, they are largely lodged in cultural contexts, which, in the sense of Hochschild's (1983) considerations, usually follow socio-structural, that is, class- and gender-specific or ethnic backgrounds.

Therefore, feeling rules are often dimensions of occupational roles (Rafaeli and Sutton 1987). In order to be able to cope with occupational tasks, the special demands in dealing with other people in certain occupational fields as a part of the professional culture, in the sense of an occupational ethos and a specific morality, are appropriated. This holds true for a large spectrum of occupations in the medical sector and in education, in the legal field for judges, arbitrators, law enforcement, bailiffs etcetera, but also in public functions such as a member of parliament, political functions etcetera. Various studies have demonstrated this close connection of emotion management and occupational role (Pierce 1995; Zembylas 2002; Stuart 2008; Westaby 2010; Vickers 2011; Yin and Lee 2011; Bryan-Jaykov 2012; Williams 2012). Feeling rules in this sense show an enormous variability, which far exceeds what is investigated in service sector research, in a very general sense, as subjectivization and customer orientation (e. g. Dunkel and Weihrich in this volume, but also Moldaschl and Voß 2002). Particularly highly qualified service occupations such as doctors, teachers, politicians, etcetera, must base their service occupation on an ethos grounded in societal morality. This is partly achieved through specific occupational codices such as the Hippocratic Oath and justifies deviations from the usual service provider-client-relationship (e. g. Stuart 2008). Large parts of their work in these occupational fields must not be subjected to the economic rationale of exploitation of a service provider but must follow ethical and moral guidelines, as for example the scandalous character of economic calculus, for instance in the area of organ donation, demonstrates (Sandel 2012). The intensity with which emotion work must be delivered as part of occupational roles and the resulting discord between feeling roles and experienced emotions vary substantially (Rafaeli and Sutton 1987; Stuart 2008; Henry 2012). Often, the socialization into the professional feeling rules is a significant part of the relevant occupations (Smith and Kleinman 1989; Clanton 2004; Williams 2012). Furthermore, feeling rules vary within professional fields and organizations according to occupational groups. For instance, in the legal field, they are different for lawyers, prosecutors and paralegals (Pierce 1995; Bolton and Boyd 2003) regarding the spectrum of professionally functional and socially acceptable emotions; researchers have also focused on adult education with its education managers and administrative staff (Coupland et al. 2008).

Feeling rules, according to Hochschild, feed on different ideologies, particularly gender-specific and ethnic backgrounds, a fact which has been substantiated in a number of studies (e. g. Rani 2004; Ramos-Zayas 2011). At the workplace, these feeling rules have been adopted based on membership in certain groups with professional and organizational feeling rules. This sometimes necessitates additional emotional work in order to fulfill the professional feeling rules of composure, friendliness and politeness in the face of experiences of discrimination and contempt. Ethnic and gender-related stereotypes can also collide with the professional feeling rules, so that in organizations there can be a second, and usually limiting, set of feeling rules tailor-made for these groups. Feeling rules at the work place are therefore characterized as racialized (Harvey Wingfield 2007; Harvey Wingfield 2010) because ethnic framings reshape the professional ones. More generally speaking, this relates to the matching of individuals and feeling rules in the relevant professional and organizational contexts.

Emotional harmony is an indicator of good fit between person and environment. More specifically, according to person-environment fit theory (Caplan, 1983), an employee will be free from occupational stress to the extent there is a congruence among the behavior expected by role senders, the behavior that an employee expects of himself or herself, and the employee's personal characteristics (Rafaeli and Sutton 1987: 32).

Thus, different ideologies which frame emotions are effective in organizational action which are partly outside of organizational action itself but become tangible or are reproduced in it. The consideration of specific framings and framing rules brings ideologies outside of their influence on the feeling rules inside the organization into focus. These external framings are and act as anything but economic and rational on the working cultures. The intersections and the intersectionality (Crenshaw 1991) of these frames in the sense of their relational arrangement to framing rules are relevant for cultural analysis.

The necessity to develop specific feeling rules in many occupational contexts as part of a professional performance and to deliver emotion work and labor in occupational everyday life lends a different hue to the ethical question brought by Arlie Hochschild in *The Managed Heart* into the academic and societal discussion: How far can the strategic employment of emotionality in interaction extend, and which social follow-on costs are acceptable in society? There are hardly any studies which formulate these ethical and moral questions in connection with their research and thus investigate the borderlands in which, in the relevant fields, the targeted manipulation of emotions is accepted in the ways made possible by our knowledge of psychology and its translation into practical application. For professional sport, the strategic employment of emotions as part of professional business is largely accepted (Clanton 2004) and regulated via feeling rules.[3] In other sectors of work life, such informal rules via which the strategic employment of emotions in work contexts is seen as socially acceptable, have received little or no attention. From the point of view of cultural analysis, the exploration of these borderlands would be highly insightful. Here, the limits which people have set to the ideologies of market and power become apparent and can be systematically investigated. A more intensive, systematic observation of these ways of drawing limits in the face of emotional manipulation via feeling rules provides an empirical point of access to the question "What Money Can't Buy" (Sandel 2012) for different work contexts (and beyond) in how these market logics can be taken up and processed in everyday life (Hochschild 2012). Feeling rules can thus constitute a conceptual framework for the systematic exploration of the economic pervasion of social contexts.

Based on existing research on feeling rules we can summarize: Culturally determined feeling rules, such as those related to gender and ethnicity, counter the commodification of emotions in many ways and work against a purposeful employment of existing emotional work capacities. A large variety of framings can counter or modify economic rationality in work con-

---

3 A further study on this issue addresses the nonprofit sector with its work for good causes (McKeon 2004).

texts. Occupational feeling rules and organizational feeling rules point to further ideological sources which are formative for work cultures beyond the commercial economic ideologies of emotional capitalism. The intersection of these framings and the ordering of these intersections in framing rules thus facilitate an empirical investigation of work cultures which inscribe themselves into the subjects via emotional regimes as central mechanisms of socialization—and not only in times of emotional capitalism.[4] In concrete work contexts, manifold discontinuities of apparently dominating economic regimes of production, such as post-Fordism and emotional capitalism, will become apparent (Beynon and Nichols 2006) and in their sum will provide a more differentiated picture—which to a large degree meets the research interest oriented at contextuality and complexity in cultural anthropological research. Also, the drawing of limits in the face of the commercialization of private and intimate life can be determined more systematically if the social/ cultural, occupational/organizational and commercial/economic framings are made available for analysis in their detailed interaction as ideological resources of working cultures.

Approaching work cultures through feeling rules

From the point of view of cultural analytical work research, the following points of access for the investigation of work cultures arise from Hochschild's concept as well as the empirical studies on feeling rules in the working world.

a) Sources from which feeling rules in the working world are drawn

The cultural contexts from which feeling rules are drawn are manifold in modern societies, and empirical research has paid particular attention to so-cial/cultural, organizational/occupational and commercial/economic ideolo-gies in their influence on work contexts. The ideologies set by organizations, or feeling rules which are drawn from other commercial ideologies, are thus the most important but nevertheless only one of many cultural areas—or rather, cultures of knowledge with a spectrum of different regimes—which

---

4 Social psychology addresses the question of how societal scripts and individual feeling worlds occurs in more detail (e. g. Hoekstra and Stoop 1989; Moon 2006; Jakoby 2012).

form the working world. These three cultures of knowledge as sources of feeling rules are already pointed to in Hochschild's work (1979: 572). They are taken up conceptually in the sociological research on emotional work in an extended sense (Bolton and Boyd 2003; Stuart 2008)[5] and in work and organizational psychology with discipline specific terminology. Here, the potential for interdisciplinary compatibility becomes apparent similar to emotional labor, as well as the necessity of a further conceptual development of feeling rules in this regard. This may answer the questions of which repertoires of feeling rules are available to certain persons and groups in their actions, which cultures and regimes of knowledge they refer to and how they regulate the social exchange in work contexts.

b) Practices of applying feeling rules in concrete work contexts and situations

The conceptual richness of feeling rules for the praxeological analysis of contexts in work culture has become apparent above and can be further substantiated with the aid of studies on the sociology of emotions. These investigate the appropriation and application of feeling rules, conflicts of emotions and regulations of emotions, repertoires of feeling rules, the deviation from feeling rules, the changes of feeling rules over time and how framings determine emotions (Holmes 2004; McGann 2008; Hansen 2011; Nelson 2011; Ortiz 2011; Schulz 2011). These studies point out how feeling rules act as a baseline of social exchange and also form it in relation to objects. The application of feeling rules in everyday work life thus provides information on how the actors relate to symbolic orders and cultural regimes in their action. This raises questions about which feeling rules are taken up in concrete situations and according to which criteria frames are chosen in emotion management or which social exchange occurs.

---

5 Stuart reacts to this conceptual discrepancy in emotion work research differently to the approach suggested here regarding different occupational cultures of emotion with a suggestion for the theoretical extension of the concept of emotional labor by the "convocational emotion" which is supposed to depict particularly those dimensions which are due to professions. "The worker that performs emotional convocation understands their workplace experiences through two sets of feeling rules. These two sets of norms are the rules of the organizational or institutional culture and the rules for work that is vocational in character" (Stuart 2008: 182).

c) Social orders which become apparent in framing rules and are (re-)produced via them

Framing rules form the ideological stance for the feeling rules and thus frame them in a specific way. The feeling rule for managers to be empathetic with their staff presents itself differently as part of the framework of emotional capitalism oriented at subjectivization, self management and therapy compared to a Fordist work regime which orients itself at role models of the family in its understanding of work relationships. If empathy is understood as the ability to understand which feeling rules are relevant for the action of the other in contrast to the projection of our own feelings onto the other (compare with Hochschild in this volume), then emotional capitalism is a particularly effective instrument for steering in the sense of emotional intelligence of others. The persuasive variety is faced with a capacity for empathy without manipulative intent which is oriented at support and the wellbeing of the other. Both forms can be simultaneously present—not only in a given situation, but also within one individual. Mediated via framing rules, the moral orders and regimes of work thus come into focus.

Conclusion

The feeling rules have become apparent in the considerations by Hochschild as well as in a series of empirical studies in their potential conceptual richness for cultural analytical research. This potential has only been partially tapped into in empirical work culture research. Similar to emotional work/labor, the intersection of different disciplines such as work psychology, sociological work research, economics and cultural anthropology presents an opportunity for a conceptual further development of feeling rules according to the three cultural analytical points of access sketched above. To date, there has been little or no focus on the fact that different feeling rules meet in work contexts, that they intersect, interfere or conflict. Little is known about framings of emotion and their embeddedness into framing rules. To this end, much more empirical work is warranted as the basis for a fruitful exchange between theory and practice.

Translated from the German by Stefanie Everke Buchanan

Works Cited

Becker, Patrick (2009), "What makes us modern(s)? The place of emotions in con-temporary society", in: Debra Hopkins, Jochen Kleres, Helena Flam, and Hel-mut Kuzmics (eds.), *Theorizing emotions. Sociological explorations and applica-tions*, Frankfurt, New York: Campus, 195–121.

Beynon, Huw, and Theo Nichols (2006), *Patterns of work in the post-Fordist era: Ford-ism and post-Fordism*, Cheltenham: Edgar Elgar.

Bolton, Sharon C., and Carol Boyd (2003), "Trolley dolly or skilled emotion man-ager? Moving on from Hochschild's managed heart", in: *Work, employment & society*, 17, 289–308.

Brook, Paul (2009), "In critical defence of 'emotional labour': Refuting Bolton's cri-tique of Hochschild's concept", in: *Work, employment & society*, 23, 531–548.

Bryan-Jaykov, Christian (2012), *An analysis of schools from the perspective of teachers' affective-emotional zones*, University of Bath, Thesis (Doctor of Education).

Caplan, Robert D. (1983), "Person-environment fit: Past, present and future", in: Cary L. Cooper (ed.), *Stress research: Issues for the eighties,* Ann Arbor, Michigan: Institute for Social Research, 35–77.

Clanton, Gordon (2004), *Emotion management in professional baseball, basketball, and football. Conference papers—American Sociological Association*, American So-ciological Association, 1–9.

Collier, Stephen J., and Andrew Lakoff (2005), "On regimes of living", in: Aihwa Ong, and Stephen J. Collier (eds.), *Global assemblages. Technology, politics, and ethics as anthropological problems*, Malden, Oxford, Victoria: Blackwell Publish-ing, 22–39.

Coupland, Christine, Andrew D. Brown, Kevin Daniels, and Michael Humphreys (2008), "Saying it with feeling: Analysing speakable emotions", in: *Human Rela-tions*, 61, 327–353.

Crenshaw, Kimberlé W. (1991), "Mapping the margins: Intersectionality, identity politics, and violence against women of color", in: *Stanford law review*, 43, 1241–1299.

Ehrenreich, Barbara, and Arlie Russell Hochschild (2003), *Global woman. Nannies, maids and sex workers in the new economy,* London: Granta Books.

Geertz, Clifford (1964), *The interpretation of cultures,* London: Hutchinson.

Gorz, André (2010), *The immaterial: Knowledge, value and capital.* London and New York, Seagull Books. Original Publication: (2003), *L'immatériel. Connaissance, valeur et capital,* Paris: Editions Galilée.

Grandey, Alicia A. (2000), "Emotional regulation in the workplace: A new way to conceptualize emotional labor", in: *Journal of occupational health psychology*, 5, 95–110.

Grandey, Alicia A., and Céleste M. Brotheridge Brotheridge (2002), "Emotional la-bor and burnout: Comparing two perspectives of 'People Work'", in: *Journal of vocational behavior*, 60, 17–39.

Hansen, Karen V. (2011), "The asking rules of reciprocity", in: Anita Ilta Garey, and Karen V. Hansen (eds.), *At the heart of work and family. Engaging the Ideas of Arlie Hochschild*, New Brunswick, New Jersey, London: Rutgers University Press, 112–123.

Harvey Wingfield, Adia (2007), "The modern mammy and the angry black man: African American professionals' experiences with gendered racism in the workplace", in: *Race, gender, and class*, 14, 196–212.

— (2010), "Are some emotions marked Whites Only? Racialized feeling rules in professional workplaces", in: *Social problems*, 57, 251–268.

Henry, Sue Ellen (2012, in press), "Vulnerability and emotional risk in an educational philosophy", in: *Emotion, space and society*, available online at http://dx.doi.org/10.1016/j.emospa.2012.05.003.

Hochschild, Arlie Russell (1979), "Emotion work, feeling rules and social structure", in: *American Journal of Sociology*, 85, 3, 1–33.

— (1983), *The managed heart. Commercialization of human feeling*, Berkeley, University of California Press.

— (2001), *The time bind. When work becomes home and home becomes work*, New York: Owl Books Holt.

— (2003), *The commercialization of intimate life. Notes from home and work*, Berkeley, Los Angeles, London: University of California Press.

— (2009), "Introduction: An emotions lens on the world", in: Debra Hopkins, Jochen Kleres, Helena Flam, and Helmut Kuzmics (eds.), *Theorizing emotions. Sociological explorations and applications*, Frankfurt and New York: Campus Verlag, 29–37.

— (2012), *The outsourced self: Intimate life in market times*, New York: Metropolitan Books.

Hochschild, Arlie Russell, and Anne Machung (1990), *The second shift. Working parents and the revolution at home*, Avon Books.

Hoekstra, Hans A., and Bert A. M. Stoop (1989), "Feeling rules: testing a model of appraisal-affect relations", in: *European journal of personality*, 3, 229–248.

Holmes, Mary (2004), "Feeling beyond rules. Politicizing the sociology of emotion and anger in feminist politics", in: *European journal of social theory*, 7, 209–227.

Illouz, Eva (2007), *Cold intimacies. The making of emotional capitalism*, Cambridge and Malden: Polity Press.

— (2008), *Saving the modern soul: therapy, emotions, and the culture of self-help*, Berkeley: University of California Press.

Jakoby, Nina (2012), "Grief as a social emotion: Theoretical perspectives", in: *Death studies*, 36, 679–711.

Lively, Kathryn J. (2006), "Emotions in the workplace", in: Jan E. Stets, and Jonathan H. Turner (eds.), *Handbook of the sociology of emotions*, Boston, MA: Springer US, 569–590.

McGann, Kimberly J. (2008), How do I love thee? Romantic feeling rules in greeting cards. *Conference paper—American Sociological Association*, http://citation.

allacademic.com/one/www/research/index.php?click_key=1&PHPSESSID=71d b53989311ba40d9332a761a52df3a, 2. 2. 2013.

McKeon, Tiffiny Guidry (2004), Can you feel the love … or not? Nonprofit organizations and the use of emotion. *Conference papers—American Sociological Association,* http://citation.allacademic.com/meta/p_mla_apa_research_citation/1/0/9/5/2/pages109526/p109526-1.php , 2. 2. 2013.

Moldaschl, Manfred, and G. Günter Voß (2002), *Subjektivierung von Arbeit,* München, Mering: Rainer Hampp Verlag.

Moon, Lyndsey (2006), The Heterosexualisation of Emotion: Sexual Scripts and Feeling Frames. *Conference Papers—American Sociological Association,* http://citation.allacademic.com/meta/p_mla_apa_research_citation/1/0/4/0/1/pages104018/p104018-1.php, 2. 2. 2013.

Nelson, Margarete K. (2011), "Love and gratitude: Single mothers talk about men's contribution to the second shift", in: Anita Ilta Garey, and Karen V. Hansen (eds.), *At the heart of work and family. Engaging the ideas of Arlie Hochschild,* New Brunswick, New Jersey, London: Rutgers University Press, 100–111.

Ortiz, Steven M. (2011), "Wives who play by the rules: Working on emotions in the sport marriage", in: Anita Ilta Garey, and Karen V. Hansen (eds.), *At the heart of work and family. Engaging the ideas of Arlie Hochschild,* New Brunswick, New Jersey, London: Rutgers University Press, 124–134.

Pierce, Jennifer (1995), *Gender trials: Emotional lives in contemporary law firms,* Berkeley: University of California Press.

Rabinow, Paul (2007), *Marking time. On the anthropology of the contemporary,* Princeton: Princeton University Press.

Rafaeli, Anat and Robert I. Sutton (1987), "Expression of emotion as part of the work role", in: *The Academy of Management review,* 12, 23–37.

Ramos-Zayas, Ana (2011), "Learning affect, embodying race: Youth, blackness, and neoliberal emotions in Latino Newark NJ, Brazil, and Puerto Rico", in: *Transforming Anthropology,* 19, 86–104.

Rani, Kawale (2004), "Inequalities of the heart: the performance of emotion work by lesbian and bisexual women in London, England", in: *Social & cultural geography,* 5, 565–581.

Sandel, Michael J. (2012), *What money can't buy: The moral limits of markets,* New York: Farrar, Straus and Giroux.

Schulz, Jeremy (2011), "Framing couple time and togetherness among American and Norwegian professional couples", in: Anita Ilta Garey, and Karen V. Hansen (eds.), *At the heart of work and family. Engaging the ideas of Arlie Hochschild,* New Brunswick, New Jersey, London: Rutgers University Press, 85–99.

Sieben, Barbara, and Åsa Wettergren (2010), *Emotionalizing organizations and organizing emotions,* Basingstoke, New York: Palgrave Macmillan.

Smith, Allen C. III, and Sherryl Kleinman (1989), "Managing emotions in medical school: Students' contacts with the living and the dead", in: *Social psychology quarterly,* 52, 56–69.

Stuart, Kathy Louise (2008), *Emotional labour and occupational identity: Passionate rationality in the New Zealand parliamentary workplace*, PhD diss., Massey University, Palmerston North, New Zealand.

Tonkens, Evelien (2012), "Working with Arlie Hochschild: connecting feelings to social change", in: *Social politics: International studies in gender, state & society*, 19, 194–218.

Vickers, Margaret H. (2011), "Bullying targets as social performers in the public administration workplace", in: *Administrative theory & praxis (M. E. Sharpe)*, 33, 213–234.

Westaby, Chalen (2010), "'Feeling like a sponge': the emotional labour produced by solicitors in their interactions with clients seeking asylum", in: *International journal of the legal profession*, 17, 153–174.

Williams, Angela (2012), "A study of emotion work in student paramedic practice", in: *Nurse education today*.

Wouters, Cas (2009), "The civilizing emotions: Formaliziation and informalization", in: Debra Hopkins, Jochen Kleres, Helena Flam, and Helmut Kuzmics (eds.), *Theorizing emotions. Sociological explorations and applications*, Frankfurt, New York: Campus Verlag, 169–193.

Yin, Hong-biao, and John Chin-Kin Lee (2011), "Be passionate, but be rational as well: Emotional rules for Chinese teachers' work", in: *Teaching and teacher education*, 21, 179–197.

Zapf, Dieter (2002), "Emotion work and psychological well-being: A review of the literature and some conceptual considerations", in: *Human resource management review*, 12, 237–268.

Zembylas, Michalinos (2002), "'Structures of feeling' in curriculum and teaching: Theorizing the emotional rule", in: *Educational theory*, 52, 187–208.

Hairdressers as Managers of Well-being: A Multi-dimensional Perspective of Emotional Labor in the Service Industry

Sarah Braun

In post-Fordist times, society is often described as a service society in Germany, and wellness—a term referring to a combination of physical and emotional *well-being*—is an important keyword. In this situation, the public awareness of human intimacy increases. While emotions used to be seen as an irritation within the workflow, they are now considered a valuable resource enriching the work environment. In the context of a service society, management consultants describe people providing services as "managers of well-being" who offer their customers a "warm, emotional experience" (Zanetti 2007, translated). Newspapers call the wellness sector—the jobs of beauticians, masseuses, and hairdressers—a "Berührungsindustrie", literally a "touch industry" (Haberl 2008; 2009). Workers in this sector know how to "catch people, to deal with their stress, their loneliness, with a world of work and everyday life that is disembodied and desensitized yet increasingly visual and virtual" (Haberl 2009: 67–68, translated).

Within these frames of reference, this article takes one branch of this so called "touch industry" as an example. It is based on an ethnographic case study on a hairdressing salon in a small town in Germany[1] and focuses on the question of how workers produce emotional labor[2] in their daily practices and routines, using both a dual type of body work and of emotional management: By transforming the body of the customers according to their expectations, the hairdressers have to work with their own body styling it according to the atmosphere of the shop and displaying positive emotions. Furthermore, it is considered to be the particular task of the emotional ef-

---

1 This study was originally conducted in the context of a research project at LMU Munich in 2009/10 under the supervision of Irene Götz (see Braun 2010) and eventually resulted in my master thesis. I would like to thank Irene Götz for her effort and the content support of this article.

2 Alongside the emotional labor, treated as a form of service, the aim of this fieldwork was to observe how the emotions of the hairdressers became a capital and an individual resource. The concept of emotional labor was coined by Arlie Russell Hochschild in her study *The managed heart: commercialization of human feeling* (1983, reissued in 2012).

forts of hairdressers to match an individualized customer's personality when styling his or her hair. Moreover, the job requirements for hairdressers are not just to create a hairstyle but also to give the customers a positive feeling of well-being within the salon. Thus, the article, furthermore, highlights how the creation of a particular atmosphere is an essential part of this form of emotional labor.[3]

To exemplify this, two aspects of this kind of work are described in the following case study. Firstly, at a more collective level, the subjectively experienced and carefully produced *atmosphere of wellness* in the salon will be investigated. Secondly, at the level of the individual worker, the emotional practices of the hairdressers in concrete interactions with their customers are analyzed as an integral part of this process of creating an atmosphere of well-being. The work of the hairdresser involves personal interactions and is both a craft and a service.[4] It illustrates how social processes of revaluation transform emotions into a resource, a craft into a service, and empathy into human capital.

When hairdressers create an atmosphere of wellness, personalized services and, as a result, positive emotions of their customers, capitalism is "getting under their skins". Consequently, an additional focus of this article is the question of how service workers handle their particular job requirements. I will outline their strategies of resistance and negotiation and describe how capitalism is managed from the inside. Additionally, this article suggests that emotions should be understood in a relational and multi-perspective manner. First of all, the first chapter gives a brief description of the cornerstones of this vocation and reveals the content of everyday work practices. The aim is to make the emotional labor carried out by hairdressers more explicit and comprehensible.

---

3 Atmosphere is a concept that was coined by the German philosopher Gernot Böhme. According to him, atmospheres can be considered as a category of space and are articulated through cognitive subjects such as memory, perception or emotion. Furthermore, they assemble the reality between subjects and objects (Böhme 1998).

4 In hairdressing, the main buzzword is *customer orientation*, which addresses the personal requirements and the *well-being* of the customers and also codes the practice of the service by the employees.

The Vocational Cornerstones of Hairdressing

It becomes possible to map out the most important vocational cornerstones of hairdressing and the job requirements for hairdressers if the categories of time and space and the different dimensions of the social world are considered. Hairdressing salons are semi-public spaces where social and individual imaginations of body images and hair are processed and materialized in an interactive fashion. This is done in a small space and under conditions of bodily proximity, using allocated slots. Hairdos are, on the one hand, surfaces for the inscription of cultural meanings; they point to gender, social role, and *habitus*. On the other hand, the act of sporting a hairstyle that suits one's personality, age, vocation and social role involves subjective negotiations: hair is an object of strategies in everyday life and of vestimentary practices targeting the body. As a result, it is the object of everyday body and identity work. At present, in an individualized society following the paradigm of self-fulfillment, hairstyles become crystallizations of, and an opportunity for, the inscription of people's personality. This act of inscription takes place within the framework of the many options available for the self. Why do we sport the hairstyle we have and not a different one? What makes a hairstyle suit our personality? In the mirrors of the salon and the mirror images of the customers, individual and societal images of the self and the other are reflected. These images are changing nearly every hour. At the micro-level, the hairdressers are holding the mirror of society in their hands and are working on its imaginations. According to the main buzzword of the trade, *customer orientation*, the emphatic gaze of the hairdresser is of key importance: she "should get the best out of me" "by means of having a feeling for me and my personality"—as the customers put it. As a result, the production and consumption of the service provided occur in interactions with the customers based on direct bodily contact—and in the space of the salon. Today, salons are associated with the keyword wellness, which is of significant importance for the trade and "enables the embodied self to experience itself as a source of pleasure" (Greco 2004: 295). Due to the existence of cut-price salons, the trade displays a high degree of heterogeneity; the promise of wellness is an important distinction setting apart certain salons from competitors. The context described suggests that in this type of work, culture is literally getting under people's skin. This happens, on the one hand, through the creation of a hairstyle intended to help the customer achieve self-fulfillment and, on the other hand, through the production and participation in a sensory-emotional atmosphere marked by well-being and wellness. According to Greco's (2004) notion of wellness, it is imperative that positive moods are produced in a salon—but how exactly does this work?

An Embodied Atmosphere of Wellness: An Example

As soon as the door opens and the customers enter the salon, the hairdressers greet them with a friendly smile, which is accompanied by open, caring gestures and welcoming facial expressions. Once seated, a trainee serves a coffee to them, again smiling friendly and providing them with a nice little surprise: a small chocolate bar called *merci*. The entire bodily and emotional demeanor of the workers is honed perfectly to appear calm, welcoming, and approachable. With jokes and pleasantries, they encourage the clients to talk and unburden. If their gazes meet in the mirror, the hairdresser smiles and the customer smiles back. Such rituals of reciprocal appreciation shape the system of symbolic action at work in the salon.

Some customers told me that "you just have to feel good here" and described their experience of the salon as that of a "cozy living room". And so, I started to focus on the interplay between the materiality of the place and immaterial, "sensory-affective" productions and experiences. It is possible to discern in the materiality of the salon some of the social and cultural conventions and processes of socialization characterizing post-Fordist, service-oriented societies. Just like the entire interior of the salon, the chocolate acts as an amplifier of the feeling of wellness. Moreover, the chocolate is supposed to show the appreciation of the business for its customers. Physical objects, as symbols and condensations of associations ascribed to them, structure the conceptions of meaning on offer in present moments—in this case, an atmosphere of *well-being*. At the same time, following Heidrich (2007), such associations only emerge when a *habitus* is shaped through everyday practices involving physical objects. In the context of the production and creation of atmospheres, it is necessary to pay close attention to this interconnectedness of the material and immaterial aspects of this workplace.

In an atmosphere, we experience a kind of a collage of *sensory-atmospheric* elements. Our senses act as an important filter for our subjective experience of space. A room associated with wellness triggers specific, affective attributions. This is achieved through the lighting, colors and decoration as well as through the use of soothing background music and fragrances, which suit the whole interior fitting. The service workers add to this relaxing atmosphere through their embodied moods and their customer-oriented body language: they use the right *body grammar* and *vocabulary* and pitch their voices accordingly.

In this "cozy living room" characterized by "attention to detail" space, time and social patterns collapse, for the customers, into a non-reflective, intuitive understanding of the salon and its social relations (customers—hairdressers; hairdressers—hairdressers), into an experience of space associated with a feeling of well-being. According to the customers, this experience of space turned the salon into a service space where it was possible to take "a (short) vacation from everyday life". Following Jaeggi (2002), everyday processes of appropriation are about our references to the world and our selves: We do not passively accept these references, but actively examine them and process them individually. The instances to be appropriated, that is, the atmosphere of spaces like the salon, do not remain outside the self. Through appropriation, they become part of it. Since it is not possible for humans to be in the world without emotions, it is not just our senses but also our feelings that can be seen as part of the "human mode of appropriating the world" (Rastetter 2008: 63). Accordingly, customers felt "welcome", "accepted", and "at home" in the configuration of time and space created by the hairdressers, which was based on valuing, respecting and focusing on the individual and her needs. Experiences of space associated with well-being, wellness and a short vacation are "waiting to be activated by the perceivers", as Lehnert puts it (2011: 9). Accordingly, the architecture and the interior of a building "are tasked with, by definition, assigning atmospheric potential and even feelings to objects and spaces" (ibid.: 9–10). Correspondingly, the linkages between space and feelings have a considerable influence on life-styles. In the case of the salon, this is revealed by the fact that the customers are expected to experience a feeling of wellness, causing the workers to engage in the according work and body practices. The comforting chill-out music does not just influence, via the sense of hearing, the atmosphere of the salon, but also the hairdressers' styles of work. They adjust their bodily expressions and voice pitches (which always sound friendly) to situations and the contents of conversations and, in so doing, contribute to composing the *sound of the space*. At the same time, the hairdressers do not act hastily, but carefully and in a manner that helps customers to relax. These body practices extend far beyond just being friendly and smiling all the time; they also include caring touching. The skin boundary can be seen as a key element in differentiated negotiations over emotional relationships (Anzieu 1991); similarly, the sense of touch shapes intersubjective recognition via acts of touching. The ways in which hairdressers treat the hair of their customers and touch their bodies (in a pleasant or an unpleasant way) potentially determine whether customers feel well-treated and at home or not.

Like a mosaic, atmospheres are composed of different units of reference—for example existing knowledge about the quality of atmospheres like wellness, the material composition of an interior, sensory perceptions, the perception of one's own body, and emotions. In the case of the salon, these units of reference also extend into the realms of touching, interactions and the emotional "state of the self"' [Sich-Befinden]. This relational configuration between materiality, immateriality, and the interactive negotiation of atmospheres of well-being characterize, in the last instance, the quality of the mood in the salon and transform the salon into a *feeling space*.[5]

Atmospheric spaces are highly dynamic, process-based and, above all, praxeological. Atmospheres emerging in settings characterized by direct contact between customers and employees are dependent on people. This becomes very clear whenever the constellation of people in a team changes. At the salon studied, customers and colleagues called a hairdresser who openly showed that she was in bad mood and allegedly threw the salon "into disarray" a "bad apple" that must be "removed from the bag" because of its "bad temper". This example reveals that, to a large extent, atmospheres are negotiated interactively and produced primarily through the embodied customer-orientation of the hairdressers. In this context, it is helpful to revisit Elias's concept of *figuration*[6] to describe interdependent networks of relationships as emotional figurations. Their atmospheric quality is shaped, according to

---

5 On the grounds of a dynamic understanding of space, Lehnert explains that "space is constituted by human action (which includes sensory perception); conversely, spaces retroact on people's actions and emotions" (ibid.: 11). The linkage between space and emotion refers to the social construction of spaces. This has been revealed, in the context of the spatial turn, by critical theories of space. If we see space as an object of social action and conflict (Lefebvre 1991) and of social construction, we are no longer forced to see atmospheric spaces as pre-existing entities (Böhme 1998: 12). Accordingly, they are appropriated, shaped and used, in an interactive fashion, by all the actors involved.

6 According to Elias, figurations should be seen as dynamic and open networks of interaction between people who produce a specific balance, in the process of creating meaning, between the self and the "we". There is a dominant level of experience, which allows individuals and collectives to feel, interpret and express themselves. It is shaped and (re-)pro-

the situation, by constantly changing constellations of relationships between people—in this case, between the relationships of hairdressers and customers. Depending on how space is appropriated and negotiated inter-subjectively, the feeling actions and reactions of the actors change, and so does the atmosphere of the salon. For example, if the temporal dimension of the configuration of relationships changes—if certain customers leave and others arrive or if new customers or regulars are present –, the atmospheric quality changes, too. The same can be said about the increasing exhaustion of the hairdressers occurring over the course of the working day. Eventually, their exhaustion affects the energy expended on presenting themselves appropriately, conforming to expectations concerning their role, communicating continuously, smiling and keeping eye-contact. Negative moods and figurations of emotion have to be balanced by the service workers through a dual type of emotional labor, which involves surface and deep acting in the sense of Hochschild (1983/2012).

Atmospheres of wellness are discursive *feeling spaces.* Their meanings are loaded with knowledge about a specific atmosphere and its emotional quality; they represent a feeling of individual well-being seen positively in society, which is offered by post-Fordist service workers and bought by service users. If atmospheres of well-being are being shaken up—for example because there are "bad apples"—points of rupture emerge, which offer valuable insights for the research process. On the one hand, these points of rupture reveal the practices of production involved, that is, the dual types of body work and emotional labor described. On the other hand, it becomes possible to dissect the social ascriptions underpinning these activities. These ascriptions concern feelings and concepts such as wellness and customer orientation. Moreover, they relate to the oft-invoked notion of a *culture of service* and the discursive horizons of knowledge and values informing it, whose materializations include small chocolate bars. These patterns of values and norms classify the activities of the service users on the grounds of the distinction between "right" and "wrong" and capitalize on inner resources by promoting the internalization and incorporation of the *habitus of work* required. The thick description and discussion of atmospheres reveals that hairdressers are *managers of well-being* whose job is about far more than just the physical aspects or the material side of a hairstyle or their contribution to arranging the interiors of salons: the issue of *how* to live our everyday lives is embodied in

---

duced by individuals and their figuration in the collective, taking the form of relational dependence (see Elias 1969; 1982).

everyday work practices. It tells us something about contemporary society and its culturally-rooted horizons of values.

Individualized, Empathetic Work Practices

During my fieldwork I asked the customers what they think is important when they choose a hairdresser. They answered that she "has to have a feeling for me!" This requirement is occasionally connected to the assumption that the cultural activity of wearing a hairstyle is understood as a process of generating meaning and a kind of individualized body management and identity work. The educational material (Schmidt et al. 1997) provided to trainee hairdressers at the salon called this "the inner preference of the customer", which was supposed to be identified with the help of an "empathetic, counseling interview". Accordingly, the main attributes of the work required are being customer-oriented, friendly, and empathetic. After all, the "inner wishes of the customers have to be identified and processed creatively in order to create the ideal hairstyle" (Schmidt et al. 1997: 194). According to the author, the hairdresser "has to try, during an empathetic, counseling interview, to reconcile the wishes of the hairdresser, the individual peculiarities of the person and the opportunities for designing something" (Schmidt et al. 1997: 220). In other words, empathy is a character trait of major importance for good hairdressers. Skills like *having a feeling for customers* and being able to identify hairstyles suitable for their personalities are portrayed as the basis of the creativity of hairdressers. Moreover, they are seen as *emotional capital*[7], that is, a competitive advantage. This suggests that the inner sources of being emotional, empathetic and creative are linked to one another, and that they

---

7 See Illouz (2006). She draws upon Goleman's concept of "emotional intelligence" (1996) and defines *emotional capital* as "a sense of the self, the management of emotions, self-motivation, empathy, and the formation of relationships" (ibid.: 100, translated). Following Bourdieu's theory of capital (1984; 1999), Illouz portrays *emotional capital* as being part of embodied cultural capital. *Emotional capital* appears to mobilize the traits of the habitus that are the least reflective; it exists in the permanent dispositions of the organism and thus is the most bodily section of embodied capital (Illouz 2006: 98, translated). It must be possible to convert cultural behavior into economic or social advantages for it to become capital in the sense of Bourdieu. If this happens, the actors can play with this advantage in an existing social field. Their capital either allows them to enter a field—or they are refused entry on the grounds of a lack of qualifications (ibid.: 98).

have an economic value. For the hairdressers, being empathetic does not just mean identifying the customers' conceptions of the self. In a holistic way, they have to follow the customers' perspective and find out about their preferences: do they prefer to talk or to enjoy the treatment of their hair silently? With the help of their facial expressions, the hairdressers transmit certain moods. For example, if the customers are stressed, the hairdressers try to counterbalance this with their own relaxed way of doing their work—or by giving their customers a massage or a space in which they can talk about their problems and unburden. The acts of empathizing with customers and of reading their feelings, moods, and facial expressions are working tools for the hairdressers. They are the *stage directions* for the individual but coordinated service practices used when hairdressers are dealing with customers, that is, when they are doing dual body work, and when they are managing, suppressing or expressing their own intimate feelings and facial expressions on the grounds of certain acting rules.

Feeling rules as cultural codes

A specific embodied knowledge lies behind the embodied atmosphere of wellness and the individual interactions happening on the grounds of specific acting rules. According to Hochschild's studies (1983/2012), these practices of the service sector refer to cultural norms concerning obligatory and openly expressed emotions. These norms categorize patterns of behavior as either correct or incorrect. Feeling rules act as cultural codes inscribing the role of service worker in the faces of the people employed in the sector. This is the result of the active management of emotions, which aims at presenting positive service feelings that can be sold and bought. Hochschild (1983/2012: 7 and 90) points out that processes of alienation take place in the context of this commodification of intimate resources. At this point, it is evident that the practices of the hairdressers and the management of their emotions and labor are consistent with the buzzword *customer orientation*. According to job descriptions in the field, what is required are people working with joy, a good heart and a good head, and a service-oriented personality. In other words, workers are supposed to be *managers of their selves*. Against this backdrop, it seems apt to use concepts referring to Foucauldian techniques of self-management (Foucault 1993). The hairdressers have internalized the social and professional knowledge[8] of their field; they know how to fix the self of the service provider in their demeanor and how to embody it. In some situations, customer-oriented acting and the production of positive feelings are transformed into body routines—one example is the constant smile. In situations of interaction, the hairdressers have to ensure the well-being of their clients through the active management of emotions.

In the context of hairdressing, both the desire of the customers to "be themselves" and the corresponding forms of *empathetic interaction*, which are based on service orientation, result from social processes of individualization, self-optimizing and self-objectification. These processes also influence the work environment at the level of *subjectification* (Moldaschl et al. 2003): They transform the intimacy of the worker into a tool and resource used in the workflow. If representatives of the profession state that trainees have to have a service-oriented personality, they are turning a craft into a service sector job. As a result of this transformation, the self of the worker enters the market.[9] It is a paradox that intimacy is now a resource for capitalism, yet hairdressers are still underpaid and their vocation has a negative reputation in Germany. Another remarkable aspect of self-optimizing and self-objectification is this: not only are the selves of the service workers shaped through professional acting rules and thus become capitalized, but also the supposedly unique, "personalized self". In the case of the customers, it is supposed to travel from the inside to the outside, which is in line with the values of an individualized society. The hairdressers are responsible for producing and selling this "personalized self".

In this context characterized by atmospheric work, our concept of emotional labor should be broadened—not just by taking into account the bodily-sensory and the spatial-material dimension, but the dual type of identity

---

8 On the one hand, this framework of supposedly *correct* work practices is related to the super-ordinate level of society as a whole, which promotes service- and customer-orientation. On the other hand, the correct behavior is learned and internalized during the apprenticeship—both at vocational schools and in the salons, where work is carried out on the grounds of daily, embodied routines, norms and values specific to the business in question.

9 This means that the selves of the workers are bought, and a number of non-manual skills become very important job requirements: the capacity to be emphatic, enter non-verbal and verbal communication, and be able to manage the emotions and the bodily experience of the customers. If hairdressers have to identify the conception of the self and the personality of one customer after the other, they also perform a kind of personality work, making use of their capacity to change perspective time and again.

work[10] carried out here: On the one hand, the hairdressers give the customers advice on how to discover themselves and reach self-fulfillment; in other words, they become assistants in a process of self-idealization. On the other hand, they have to deal with the fact that their self-evaluations are changing constantly due to changing customers, who have different expectations and ascribe different roles to the hairdressers. The identities offered to the hairdressers by the customers include the close confidant, the comforter, the hair expert—and also the *Friseuse*[11] looked down upon, who only cuts hair, which is a job anyone could do. In this case, handling the various offered roles, the identity work of the hairdressers appears to include a (non-capitalized) type of emotional labor, which they appear to apply to themselves and for creating individual spaces of resistance.

How to handle post-Fordist job requirements: Spaces of resistance

The first visible mechanism of resistance is linked to the identity work of the hairdressers. It can be found in the context of the transformation of hairdressing from a craft into a service and of the reinterpretation of feelings triggered by their commodification. Post-Fordist discourses have re-interpreted the immaterial aspects of work practices and the intimacy of workers by portraying them as resources to be mobilized in the workflow; in doing so, they also allow the hairdressers to revalue their emotional side and to defy the traditional disregard for emotions in economy and society. Hairdressers are often confronted with negative images both in work and in society—for example, with the notion that a hairdresser is "only a superficial, touchy-feely actor, who just cuts hair". In situations like this, the hairdressers hold their own by revaluing their emotions and interpreting them differently: They see them as a foundation of their work and creativity, and as a key element in their self-realization. Hairdressers appreciate and "love", as they put it, the daily experience of customers undergoing positive mood changes, especially if the customers arrive in the salon all stressed and leave with the feeling of having been on a "short, relaxing vacation". Through their work, they are

10 On the concept of identity work, see Keupp et al. (2006) and Rastetter (2008).
11 Translator's note: In German, *Friseuse* is a slightly pejorative, disregarding term for a (female) hairdresser.

able to give other people a small emotional boost, helping them in their everyday life. Along these lines, the hairdressers highlight their emotional closeness to their customers and thus reveal that they are entering a reciprocal social exchange of emotional boosts. Moreover, the emotional aspect of the work offers hairdressers the chance to do meaningful identity work and to integrate acts of self-realization in their work. In some situations, they benefit from their relationships with customers, especially if customers have become friends over the years. In such cases, they talk to customers about their own problems. As one of the hairdressers remarked, "Sometimes, I'm not just an emotional trash can for the customers; sometimes, I can give them [an idea about] a certain part of my problems, too—or they give me a good feeling!" In this way, the commodified culture of capitalism provides orientation and guidance in confusing times and in a globalized and pluralized society that is searching for meaning by focusing on personality and the self.

In a profession like hairdressing, which involves caringly touching more or less unfamiliar bodies and souls on a daily basis, it is not always easy to cope with the emotional closeness to customers. In order to avoid becoming too emotionally attached to certain interactions, stories, and emotional demands or role expectations, the hairdressers develop strategies of drawing boundaries and keeping a distance, as one of them put it by remarking that "I decide who gets to see something of my inner self". One mechanism used by the hairdressers to protect themselves is to make decisions of this kind, which are based on knowing about one's feelings, especially feelings of belonging. This suggests that the hairdressers not only have a feeling for, and knowledge of, the needs of the clients, but also their own needs. They have a reflective approach to themselves, that is, the (emotional) person behind the role of the service worker.

Whenever there are ruptures in the atmosphere of wellness—for example, if the hairdressers have to cope with annoying customers (whom they call "a pain in the neck")[12] –, it is possible that the attitude of the customers clashes with the values and feeling rules of the hairdressers. In these situations, the hairdressers deploy their learned professional knowledge about the body language of service and its meanings. They draw a boundary and keep a distance from the clients by reducing customer-orientated body language.

---

12 The customers in question are usually unfriendly and disrespectful. They tend to talk too much about things the hairdressers do not want to hear—either because these things are too intimate, or because they clash with the values of the hairdressers.

In doing so, they undermine the existing acting rules or use them for themselves by reversing them: They do not keep eye contact in the mirror, do not smile back, do not provide communicative stimuli, and cut the hair more quickly than they do when they like a customer. In other words, they no longer embody and perform the role of a service worker and feel what they have to feel. Instead, they interact on the grounds of their subjective feeling rules, and fix their *own self*, feeling what they feel. At these points of rupture, which concern patterns of behavior, the contrast between the projected position of the service workers and their real feelings and actions reveals the values and expectations affecting post-Fordist employees. This contrast does not only show that there is a capitalization of inner resources in the form of embodied, everyday professional knowledge, but also how this knowledge can be re-interpreted and used by the workers for their own purposes and practices of resistance.

When points of rupture emerge, the function of personal feelings is revealed: They help the individual to appropriate the world and orient themselves in it. Moreover, they are the interface between processes of cognition and the individual, bodily existence. As such, they can be the trigger for actively reinterpreting the world and everyday situations for one's own purposes, dealing with them, and changing them through intervention. For example, this occurs when people struggle to cope with a situation. The awareness of, and feeling for, moods, values and boundaries allow people to break with patterns of interaction (and the social frames of values informing them) and to negotiate them individually. This happens through drawing a boundary with the help of individual emotional work, as well as body work aimed at the self. As a result, these types of work become a *capital resource* for the service worker: on the one hand, they help people to cope with post-Fordist, everyday routines at work; and on the other hand, they allow them to modify the market, starting from the inside. In such a scenario, economic capital, which is represented through the customers and their well-being, and which has to be created and managed, no longer forms the frame of action. Instead, the activities of the workers are about an awareness of, and a feeling for, the self and personal well-being.

Contextualization—"Relationalization"—Multi-perspective Analysis

The example of hairdressing as a service demonstrates how the personal feelings of service workers become, through a dual frame of subjectification, an instrument of work which also represents a form of capital with an exchange value. In this article, attention was drawn to hairdressing as a vocation and to the demands placed on the mostly female workers. Hairdressers are usually not being prepared for these demands adequately (apprenticeships are usually taken up by 15-year old females)—and they have to put up with the negative image of the job, its bad reputation, and wages that are often below the level stipulated in collective bargaining agreements. Moreover, this article can be read as a call for analyzing emotional labor from a multiplicity of perspectives.

Processes of appropriating the atmosphere of spaces, for example the atmosphere of wellness discussed, are characterized by an interplay and interaction of different units of reference. Existing spatial representations and "malleable" present moments pervade one another. Consequently, we can only analyze and understand atmospheres if we contextualize them with reference to their meanings, actors, and practices. Once a certain atmosphere has become an object of research, a space opens up for the "relationalization" of the subject, which involves the self, other people, the materialized environment, and immaterial negotiations over it. If we analyze a concrete, emotional atmosphere like wellness—including all the actors involved, the *why* and *how* of their practices, and all the different atmospheric elements –, we will be able to connect different concepts and establish reciprocal relationships between them. As I have discussed, these concepts consist in the various formations of social, professional and personal *knowledge* about wellbeing; conceptions of service in the area of wellness; the *frames* of societal feeling norms and personal feeling rules; emotions as a capital and resource; sensory perceptions; the materiality and immateriality of experiences of space; and a dual body characterized by identity work. With the help of these concepts, we are able to uncover and dissect culturally coded expectations and desires in post-Fordist society: Thick descriptions and analyses of emotional labor enable us to clarify key terms loaded with different meanings such as customer orientation and wellness, do justice to their complexity, and reveal the cultural evaluations underpinning them.

Like atmospheres, we should conceptualize emotions in a relational manner. We should analyze feelings of well-being by looking at the specific contextual references they carry—be they references to capital or the self –, and also by discussing them with reference to a key term, in this case wellness. This can only be done by also relating them to (a) sensory, embodied perceptions and societal, discursive ascriptions of meaning, (b) forms of knowledge, and (c) values and norms. In this context, emotional labor should include, at the conceptual level, a type of body and identity work. If emotions are grasped in this contextualizing and "relationalizing" manner, their multiple layers are revealed—just as is demanded by a multi-perspective analysis. Emotions should not just be viewed in a one-dimensional fashion, focusing on their capitalized consumption. After all, they are also a bridge between the inner and outer self and contribute to people's capacity to act: Feelings provide us with a bodily experience of our discursive knowledge on everyday life and thus are a signal and an "offer" to provide meaning. They enable us to familiarize ourselves with the world and our everyday life and, at the same time, to intervene in it and change it.

This type of multi-dimensional analysis allows to reflect on the social reality of work in post-Fordist service society, taking into account its capitalized consumption. Moreover, it enables to detect practices of negotiation and resistance, as well as spaces of resistance concerning current challenges in everyday life. Finally, it provides us with the opportunity to ask—in analogy to Hochschild' works (1983/2012)—how we live our intimate lives in a market-dominated society and on the grounds of a value grid shaped by emotional economies. Does society in its present state have an interest in strongly centralizing the self, or rather a *potential self?* Does it have an interest in uniting body, mind and soul (in a feeling reflected in a key term like wellness), while sticking to the assumption that there is a separation between the inner self and the outside world—a separation that directly triggers conflicts? And, last but not least, how are these issues constructed discursively, and why?

Translated from the German by Alexander Gallas

Works Cited

Anzieu, Didier (1991), *Das Haut-Ich,* Frankfurt am Main: Suhrkamp.

Böhme, Gernot (1998), *Anmutungen. Über das Atmosphärische,* Ostfildern vor Stuttgart: Ed. Tertium.

Braun, Sarah (2010), "Niemand geht hier mit einem schlechten Gefühl weg! Eine ethnografische Studie zu emotionaler Arbeit als Dienstleistung in einem Friseursalon", in: Irene Götz, Birgit Huber, and Piritta Kleiner (eds.). *Arbeit in "neuen Zeiten". Ethnografien und Reportagen zu Ein- und Aufbrüchen,* München: Herbert Utz Verlag, 125–145 (Münchner ethnographische Schriften, Band 7).

Bourdieu, Pierre (1984), *Distinction: A social critique of the judgement of taste,* London: Routledge and Kegan Paul.

— (1999), *Weight of the world: Social suffering in contemporary society.* Cambridge: Polity.

Elias, Norbert (1969), *The civilizing process,* Vol. I. *The history of manners,* Oxford: Blackwell.

— (1982), *The civilizing process,* Vol. II. *State formation and civilization,* Oxford: Blackwell.

Foucault, Michel (1993), *Technologien des Selbst,* Frankfurt am Main: Fischer.

Goleman, Daniel (1996), *Emotional intelligence: Why it can matter more than IQ,* New York: Bantam Books.

Greco, Monica (2004), "Wellness", in: Ulrich Bröckling, Susanne Krasmann, and Thomas Lemke (eds.), *Glossar der Gegenwart,* Frankfurt am Main: Suhrkamp, 193–199.

Haberl, Tobias (2008), "Das Geschäft mit der Berührung", in: *SZ-Magazin,* 42, 1–4, http://sz-magazin.sueddeutsche.de/texte/anzeigen/26701.

— (2009), "Mein Körper das Stofftier", in: *SPIEGEL WISSEN,* 1, 66–68.

Heidrich, Hermann (2007), "Dinge verstehen. Materielle Kultur aus Sicht der Europäischen Ethnologie", in: *Zeitschrift für Volkskunde,* 103, 223–236.

Hochschild, Arlie Russell (1983/2012), *The managed heart. Commercialization of human feeling,* Berkeley et al.: University of California Press.

Illouz, Eva (2006), *Emotionales Kapital. Gefühle in Zeiten des Kapitalismus,* Frankfurt am Main: Suhrkamp.

Jaeggi, Rahel (2002), "Aneignung braucht Fremdheit", in: *Texte zur Kunst,* 42, http://www.textezurkunst.de/46/aneignung-braucht-fremdheit.

Keupp, Heiner, Thomas Abe, and Wolfgang Gmür (2006), *Identitätskonstruktionen. Das Patchwork der Identitäten in der Spätmoderne,* Reinbek bei Hamburg: Rowohlt.

Lefebvre, Henri (1991), *The production of space,* Oxford/Cambridge: Blackwell.

Lehnert, Gertrud (2011), *Raum und Gefühl. Der Spatial Turn und die neue Emotionsforschung,* Bielefeld: transcript.

Moldaschl, Manfred, and G. Günter Voß (2003), "Subjektivierung von Arbeit. Ein Überblick zum Stand der Forschung", in: Manfred Moldaschl, and G. Günter Voß (eds.), *Subjektivierung von Arbeit*, München/Mering: Hampp, 57–114.

Rastetter, Daniela (2008), *Zum Lächeln verpflichtet. Emotionsarbeit im Dienstleistungsbereich*. Frankfurt am Main: Campus Verlag.

Schmidt, Wolfgang, Jürgen Ackermann, and Jutta Kehm (1997), *Friseurfachkunde. Beraten, Pflegen, Gestalten*, Bad Homburg vor der Höhe: Gehlen.

Zanetti, Daniel (2007), "Gute Verkäufer müssen wie gute Liebhaber sein", in: *SPIEGEL ONLINE*, 28.12.2007, no page, http://www.spiegel.de/wirtschaft/0,1518,5 25623,00.html.

Emotional Labor and Body Work in a Nursing Home for the Elderly

Petra Schweiger

Neoliberal processes of deregulation, rationalization, and subjectification have been taking place in the Western world for thirty-odd years. Elder-care work—just like any other "female", badly-paid job at the margins of the service sector, for example hair-dressing (see Braun in this edition)—is deeply affected by these processes. The resulting pressures of ecomonization and commodification are reflected in this field of work in a specific way: There is a clash between older, function-oriented conceptions of "good" care and newer, service-oriented ones, which are time-consuming and require empathy (see Götz in this edition). At the same time, there is an intensification of internal evaluations and quality management concerning elder-care work and institutions (see Bröckling 2000), which is driven by external factors. Concepts such as "emotional labor" (Hochschild 1983) help us to grasp this process, as do looking at bodies (Gugutzer 2006) and the management of interactions and feelings (see Dunkel and Weihrich in this edition). Moreover, it is elucidating to view care work as a "knowledge landscape" in which "conceptions, insights and body routines" (Götz 2012: 124 f.) are becoming more differentiated.

Against this backdrop, it becomes possible to examine (a) how employees reconcile their conceptions of "good care", that is, their professional ethos, with the pressures of work and time, which have been reinforced through the forces of rationalization unleashed by neoliberal healthcare reforms, and (b) which strategies they develop in order to cope with the tensions caused by the reforms. My field—a Munich nursing home for the elderly—and my fieldwork formed part of an ethnographic research project called *Late Modern Worlds of Labor,* which took place in 2008–9 under the supervision of Irene Götz, and was based at LMU's Department of European Ethnology.[1]

---

1 Utz-Verlag in Munich has published a book (Götz et al. 2010) assembling twelve case studies connected to the project. The title is *"Arbeit in neuen Zeiten": Ethnografien und Reportagen zu Ein- und Aufbrüchen* ("Work in New Times": Ethnographies and Reports on Break-

The nursing home was originally a family-run organization, which, to a degree, left room for empathy for the elderly and individualized styles of care. During my research in 2008, it was taken over by a large, church-sponsored agency managing nursing homes. This was a rupture not just for the staff, but also for the people in care and their relatives. In particular, the nurses had to cope with a number of structural changes to their everyday work patterns. The structural changes consisted in the rationing of staff and material resources, as well as a stronger degree of planning and control. For the nurses, this meant that they had to (a) look after more people per day, (b) follow set standards of care and systems of classification, and (c) deal with new obstacles to working in line with individual ideals of care. These changes are connected to the restructuring of the German welfare state from the 1990s, which is currently being transformed according to neo-liberal principles. The healthcare system is already under the strains of demographic change and the increase in costs caused by the availability of new treatments; the current restructuring entails the privatization of hospitals and nursing homes, the restriction of treatments covered by public health insurance, and the transfer of the financial and moral burden of keeping healthy to the individual.

I will give now a brief account of three critical incidents from my fieldwork. My aim is to provide a thick description of the dilemmas faced by the nurses working under these conditions:

Example 1: A nurse called Martha "fills up" [eingeben], as the professional jargon has it, a resident[2] of the nursing home with porridge. She tells me that she would rather offer the resident a bread roll because she assumes that this is what the woman prefers to eat. But it is quicker to feed her porridge. Moreover, the resident holds a level-of-care insurance coverage that guarantees more time for care and thus provides both sides with a certain degree of flexibility concerning the economized daily routine of the nursing home.[3]

---

downs and Departures). The research project provided the empirical basis of my Master of Arts, which has also been published in the book series of the Department (Schweiger 2011).

2 Just like the caregivers, I use the term "resident" [Bewohner] for the people in care.

3 The care guidelines say that the people in care should be encouraged to preserve and extend their independence. However, if they become more independent eaters again, that is, if they restart chewing food or moving their hands towards their mouths, they will be downgraded to a level-of-care insurance coverage that restricts their time with their caregivers.

Example 2: A nurse called Sebastian is washing a resident confined to bed. He explains that he is supposed to wash her by making slow, rhythmic and circular movements with his hands. He adds that at each stage of the washing procedure, he is supposed to cover body parts not being washed with a towel. The reason is that the person in care is supposed to sense her body and feel good. Sebastian remarks that he rarely has the time and composure to work this way. With rapid movements of his hands (or of one hand), he fulfills the task in a minimum of time.

Example 3: On a particular ward, the residents are lifted out of bed and into wheelchairs or lavatory chairs more often than on other wards. The ward manager explains that it is important to help the people in care to move between different positions and to enable them to pass stool and water sitting up—the "normal" way, as she has it. Not all employees completely agree with this policy. Elsa, for example, usually has to wash ten residents in three hours and subsequently has to place three other residents on their lavatory seats— at least if she follows the guidelines of the ward manager. After relieving themselves, all three are usually lifted back to bed for a rest. Shortly afterwards, they are made to get up again for lunch. After Elsa has washed the last resident, she says tiredly, yet jokingly, "I should wash myself now, I stink". If the manager is not on the ward, Elsa and her colleagues save their energies by following their own patterns of work. They believe that these patterns are more humane. For example, they disregard fixed duty rosters that assign each resident to an individual nurse and all-in-all spend more time with the residents. Moreover, they avoid doing some of the repositioning procedures prescribed by the care guidelines, which tend to turn into acts of strength for themselves and at least some of the elderly.

Against the backdrop of these three examples, I will discuss three aspects of elder-care work. I will address, with reference to my research field, the following question, which was first posed by A. R. Hochschild: "What is the impact of the free-market *zeitgeist* on modern [working—author's note] life in Europe"? (Koch 2011):

1. Processes of economization and rationalization have pervaded care work to such a degree that the labor process is broken down (or has to be broken down) into discrete steps that can be documented. These steps concern nothing but bodies that need to be washed, repositioned and fed. As a result, care work is often reduced to preserving bodily functions. There is no time for conversation or for attending to individual needs.

2. The practice of care work is diametrically opposed to the ideals informing it.
3. The nurses develop practices addressing these tensions. In so doing, they make use of their feelings, their body knowledge and their (informal) experience.

The Economization and Rationalization of Care Work

The example of Sebastian washing a person in care shows that the ideal of individual care and attention becomes intertwined with certain aspects of rationalization. Sebastian would like to carry out each step in the process of washing more slowly, but at the back of his mind, the clock is ticking. He is thinking of the number of residents he still has to wash and get ready for breakfast. The structure of his morning shift is characterized by alternating phases of work marked by their increasing and decreasing intensity, which have to be approached almost like assembly line work. He describes his experience of fixed work units and intensification thus:

Bang on time and just before the start of work, a coffee and a cigarette, and then off you go. Till half eleven, you have to get things done, and you do it. Then everything calms down a little, everyone relaxes a bit. And then lunch is coming up, after that the visits to the bathroom, handover, repositioning.

The caregivers have to get the work done on time as well as attend to human dignity and welfare. Moreover, they have to connect emotionally with the people in care and make their feelings public: It is expected of the caregivers to preoccupy themselves with the residents—by the families of the residents, but also according to their training, the literature on care, and the mission statement of the nursing home. They are not just supposed to look after people in need efficiently, but also to attend to the "entire" human being—a demanding task for the caregivers, which entails the obligation to invest oneself entirely in the work and adopt a holistic approach to care.

    This requirement connected to subjectification [Subjektivierungsimperativ] has existed ever since "care" emerged as a profession, and it is gaining importance in the course of the internal differentiation taking place in this occupational field. This is suggested by the emergence of professional specializations, for example geronto-psychiatric or palliative care nurse. In light of this, it is possible to speak of a tendency towards "subjectivized Taylorization". This concept—coined by Matuschek, Kleemann und Voß (Matuschek et al. 2008)—refers to a fundamental shift in post-Fordist work organization, including its values and practices: Taylorist forms of heteronomy are combined with forms of work that use the subjectivity of workers, i. e., their so-called soft skills. In this context, we need to mention self-management and the investment of one's personality, feelings and social skills. These aspects of subjectification are introduced into, and valorized by the market. Moreover, they are subject to a Fordist regime of control, which is evidenced by the obligation to document all individual steps in care.

Nevertheless, many caregivers working in the home still aspire to invoke feelings of security and pleasure on the side of the residents. After all, the caregivers' confidence about their ways of life is boosted by personal conversations with the residents about their biographies. Since the introduction of public care insurance in Germany in 1995–6, care work is being allocated through a "care ratio": The number of staff in a nursing home is calculated, among other things, on the grounds of the levels of insurance coverage of its residents. This creates a contradictory situation for the staff: The calculation of the working time and the number of staff needed is based purely on body care, but not on emotional labor in the form of attention and communication (Hochschild 1983), which are also required. The individualized care required is not paid for. As a result, the caregivers are torn between being efficient and committing to their professional ethos. In this respect, care for the elderly resembles quasi-domestic work and other professions traditionally held by women: It is taken for granted that immaterial labor and, above everything, emotional labor are *freebies*, i. e., types of work that cannot be measured and remunerated. The more rationalized work organization becomes, the more this immaterial aspect of (care) work is devalued and restricted in terms of time and importance. This quasi-Taylorization of care work, that is, its transformation into assembly line-type work, just focuses on the concrete, material, physical aspects of work involving bodies.

The conflict between the practice of care work and its general principles

Some of the tensions in the nurses' daily routine also result from the aims and objectives of care work set by vocational schools and textbooks, which tend to be general and demanding yet not free of contradictions. In any case, the conceptions of "good care" held by the employees diverge from them.[4] Let me elucidate with an example: A student nurse has learned, on the one hand, to cater for individual needs, and, on the other hand, to facilitate the preservation or even the improvement of bodily functions and activities. But what is she supposed to do if a resident prefers being transported to the dining room in a wheelchair to straining to get there with a walking frame? In this situation, she may be reminded of her parents, of her experiences in the war zone where she is from, or of her personal professional ethos. She might want nothing but relieve the pain of her counterpart and enable him to lead a pleasant life in accordance with his wishes. One could ask, taking up the initial example of the adequate choice of food (porridge or a bread roll): Should the nurses encourage independence and preserve the chewing function, or should they stick with the time assigned to the task? And which kind of care attends to the dignity of the residents, who often can no longer speak for themselves? Many movements between the bed and the wheelchair in order to use the lavatory sitting up? Or lying in bed with an incontinence pad, which might be less strenuous?

Ideals of care tend to be less than clear. They depend on the general, ethical principles of society, which in turn are reflected in historical and cultural, but also personal and biographical processes. In this context, one should mention the Christian virtue of charity; care and labor of love as practices associated with femininity; and also the (medical) attention to bodily functions, which emerged in the 19th century and boomed in the 1950s and 60s—a time in which the humanities and the social sciences drew on bodily functions in order to explain social relations. Today, the paradigm of holism and the general principles of self-realization and autonomy, freedom and pleasure appear to have marginalized medical conceptions concerning

---

4 Renate Stemmer (2006), a care studies scholar, maps out the dilemma faced by nursing staff when they apply the system of classifications of care. If they adopt an analytical perspective, it enables them carry out targeted and efficient care work with a view to results; yet it prevents them from viewing the person in care, on the grounds of the paradigm of holism, in a comprehensive fashion—as an entity.

the preservation of bodily functions. However, these principles cannot be discussed separately from increasing individualization. They are both a reaction to economization in the areas of care and healthcare emerging in the 1980s and a reflection of neoliberal strategies of subjectification in the health sector (note catchphrases like 'successful' or 'productive aging', and how they invoke an energetic, almost youthful body). All these traditions are reflected in the care guidelines and conceptions of care adopted by the caregivers. In the context of strictly structured routines and a general lack of time, they create a considerable potential for tensions, which include feelings of guilt on the side of the nurses.

Emotional work and body work as strategies of coping with care work

The caregivers, whom I accompanied in their daily routines, tend to adopt strategies that address such tensions. They use their knowledge from experience, in the form of emotional labor and body-work, in order to (a) work efficiently; (b) attend to the needs of colleagues, people in care and their families; and (c) address their own needs, for example the need for regeneration. I will describe all this in due course, and will use, as my conceptual "framework", Gugutzer's systematic sociology of the body (2006).[5]

The strategies of the caregivers are revealed in their *body routines*. With the help of these routines, they actively shape their everyday interactions with the people in care and produce and reproduce (or subvert) their own life-world and their work environment. All caregivers whom I accompanied at work used quick, standardized and routinized handling procedures when they washed and dressed residents. They handled the personal hygiene of residents this way and paid attention to their gestures and reactions in the process. I had the impression that in this situation, the caregivers were comfortable. Ideals of care endorsed in principle receded into the background, for example, instructing residents in combing their hair without help, while

---

5 The body and, in my view, the body practices are both producers and products of society. By observing body practices, that is *body routines* and a suspected *bodily self-will*, Gugutzer shows how sociality is created. With concepts such as *body formation*, *body discourse*, *body experience* and *body representation*, he highlights the making of the body through society.

pragmatic goals moved to the fore, for example, getting all residents to sit at the breakfast table in a clean and orderly state.

One example of such routines and resistant practices is, for example, that the nurses have collective, but also unplanned and individual breaks, which are often used for smoking. In official team meetings or handovers, they exchange ideas and give one another feedback on the practices and handling procedures that make care easier and help save time. In this context, the focus is on the physical aspect of care, while the immaterial aspects are talked about less often. The third example shows how Elsa and her colleagues break away from prescribed routines of work by organizing their practices in an alternative, self-willed way as soon as the ward manager is not present: They do their care work differently, "freely", without allocating the people in care to individual caregivers.

Allowing for an outward retreat, the collective breaks also enable the caregivers to gain to an inner distance from the residents. This happens within the team, too: Team members swap individual residents if they cannot handle them. Distance is also created by reducing communication. A nurse called Hatice says that she has learned to dissociate herself from the residents and to stay "cool" if they ring or want something while she is dealing with other issues. An inner distance to the work is also created with the help of irony, humor and the circumvention of rules and professional norms, that is, textbook techniques of care or the perception of people in care as customers.

The production of closeness is another important technique of coping with the work. It mattered a lot to the nurses with whom they had to work a shift. For a young student nurse, the colleagues represented her substitute family. ("When I get to work, I always tend to say, 'I'm back with my mummies'"). In contrast, she is operating at a distance to the residents: She sees them as customers or clients and perceives her work as the provision of a service. Other caregivers, however, perceive intimate communications with the residents about their biographies as a resource for coping with the work. The residents are often treated like sorely missed grandparents or family members, and are addressed with the German informal *"Du"* and their first name. A nurse called Katica, for example, recognizes herself in both the conversations with the residents about their biographies and her reactions to the emotions expressed by the residents. In so doing, she learns about her own abilities and personal traits. For Katica, this process of self-reflection contributes to the development of her personality and the creation of meaning in her life. These examples reveal that care work involves complex processes of work on the self and the latter's active *management*, as well as a spectrum of personal *rules of engagement*—to use one of Arlie Hochschild's concepts (Hochschild 2011).

In a thoroughly rationalized work environment, the *context-sensitive investment of emotions and the body* is just as important as the *rationing* of this investment. Elsa, for example, places a resident in front of the sink, smiles at her and convinces her to wash herself around "the top". She then races to the next resident in order to get her out of bed and place her on the toilet seat. The first resident is not only turned into a cooperating customer (Voß and Rieder 2005)—the caregiver displays a high degree of flexible self-organization. This enables the nurses to work dynamically and efficiently, and this does not just apply to teams: Individual caregivers also use this strategy and actively set priorities—for example, by choosing to focus on medical care or on conversations with residents, or by ignoring either aspect of the work. When they make decisions, the caregivers are able to rely on their experience—they know with whom to restrict conversation and set other priorities. A statement by a nurse called Adile shows that the separation of emotional labor and efficient work, which is unavoidable due to time constraints, is often difficult. She talks about how she races from one resident to the next—despite the fact that the she does not want to break off conversations.

I always tend to think, it's just a few minutes. You should have stayed and done this or that. Then you leave. But it's a fact that there are only two of us on the late shift—what more can you do?

The caregivers also have heated debates on "good care", for example about the adequate number of phases of activity and rest, or about the question whether the residents should be lifted out of bed by using a patient lift or mere physical strength. These debates show that the caregivers, who work in a badly paid profession mainly taken up by women, need to mediate between conflicting demands and needs—including their own.

The decision of the ward manager that the residents need to be lifted out of bed seven times a day in order to allow for "normal" movements also gives rise to conflicts over power. Moreover, there is an imbalance of power between caregivers and people in care: It is in the discretion of the caregiver to decide whether a resident needs porridge or a bread roll, and the caregiver, at this point, is torn between wanting to provide adequate care and giving in to time constraints. This reveals the power of the general system of care. However, it is worth noting that the people in care can actually resist, for example by refusing to eat or by spitting out tablets.

Bodies and Emotion in the Cultural Studies of Work

Finally, I would like to focus on the impulses for our conceptual and empirical work that are created if we pay more attention to bodies and emotion—both in relation to the embodied knowledge of the people researched as well as in relation to the researcher and the research process. For those professions that are mostly feminized and are located in quasi-domestic sections of the service sector, the body and, closely linked to it, emotions do not just represent instruments of labor; moreover, they serve as a memory for knowledge. At the company level, the body is taken advantage of and utilized at the same time as being subjectified and "taylorized". However, the workers also use it to engage in strategic and antagonistic practices. On the one hand, the bodies and body practices of the caregivers contribute to producing social reality and the reality of work. They do so by involving body routines of care that mediate between the systemic compulsions of work and the independent production of knowledge and reality in the life-world. In this context, it is worth noting that cultural studies of work have not paid enough attention to working bodies and emotions. On the other hand, bodies and body practices of the caregivers (and also of the people in care) are also shaped by traditional forms of knowledge as well as concrete structures and institutions of work. One example is how Christian charitable, functionalist and holistic traditions of care conceptualize the investment and experience of one's own body as "good care".

Another question that is rapidly gaining importance in fieldwork-based research is how the body of the researcher with all its sensory perceptions can contribute, in terms of method, to examining bodies and practices of emotion, a question which in many ways still remains a blind spot in cultural studies. In this area, some fascinating questions are emerging, for example: How do we reflect systematically on both the cognitive and the sensory perceptions of the researcher in the process of research? Is there a conflict between cognition and bodily experiences? Is it possible at all, in a research environment dominated by cognition, to establish a type of research that takes bodily, sensory perceptions seriously?

If culture is expressed directly through the body, if the body can be seen as an interface mediating the translation of expert knowledge into practices and *vice versa*, if scholars in cultural studies want to take an actor- and action-centered approach to research—then we should pay more attention to our own body sensations and their potential as (micro-) ethnographic research instruments. Thanks to their qualitative approaches and their self-reflexive language based on thick descriptions, fieldworkers working in cultural studies possess excellent resources for developing a methodology capturing knowledge that is strongly performative. If researchers reflected on their own body and emotions in the process of research, this would help them to (a) lay out more clearly the *rules of engagement* with the people researched, and (b) theorize the "collective strategies by which we might achieve a better balance of social spheres—market, governmental, civic, personal" (Hochschild 2011). Both might contribute to social change.

Translated from the German by Alexander Gallas

Works Cited

Braun, Sarah (2013), "Hairdressers as Managers of Well-being: A Multi-dimensional Perspective of Emotional Labor in the Service Industry", *in this edition*.

Bröckling, Ulrich (2000), "Totale Mobilmachung, Menschenführung im Qualitäts- und Selbstmanagement", in: Bröckling, Ulrich et al. (eds.), *Gouvernementalität der Gegenwart. Studien zur Ökonomisierung des Sozialen,* Frankfurt am Main: Suhrkamp-Taschenbuch Wissenschaft, 131–167.

Dunkel, Wolfgang, and Weihrich, Margit (2013), "From Emotional Labor to Interactive Service Work", *in this edition*.

Götz, Irene (2012), "Körper-Wissen als Arbeitspraxis in der postfordistischen Dienstleistung. Einführung in ein Panel über normative und gelebte Berufsprofile in Altenpflege, Friseurgewerbe und Mutterschaft", in: Gertraud Koch, and Bernd Jürgen Warneken (eds.), *Wissensarbeit und Arbeitswissen. Zur Ethnografie des kognitiven Kapitalismus,* Frankfurt am Main, New York: Campus Verlag (Arbeit und Alltag), 121–126.

— (2013), "Encountering Arlie Hochschild's Concept of 'Emotional Labor' in Gendered Work Cultures—Ethnographic Approaches in the Sociology of Emotions and in European Ethnology", *in this edition*.

Götz, Irene, Birgit Huber, and Piritta Kleiner (eds.) (2010), *Arbeit in "neuen Zeiten"*. *Ethnografien und Reportagen zu Ein- und Aufbrüchen*, München: Herbert Utz Verlag (Münchner ethnographische Schriften, Band 7).

Gugutzer, Robert (2006), "Der *body turn* in der Soziologie. Eine programmatische Einführung", in: Robert Gututzer (ed.), *Body Turn. Perspektiven der Soziologie des Körpers und des Sports*, Bielefeld: Transcript, 9–53.

Hochschild, Arlie Russell (1983), *The Managed Heart. Commercialization of Human Feeling*, Berkeley, Los Angeles, London: University of California Press.

Koch, Gertraud (2011), *Working Paper to the International Workshop in Honor of Arlie Russell Hochschild, UC Berkerley: Working Cultures at the Crossroads of Emotion, Commodification and Globalisation. Debating Spaces of Resistance and Boundary Work. 12./13. November 2011, Zeppelin University Friedrichshafen.*

Matuschek, Ingo et al. (2008), "Subjektivierte Taylorisierung als Beherrschung der Arbeitsperson", in: *Umkämpfte Arbeit. PROKLA 150. Zeitschrift für kritische Sozialwissenschaft*, 38, 1, 49–64.

Schweiger, Petra (2011), *"Wir haben zwar Geduld, aber keine Zeit." Eine Ethnografie subjektivierter Arbeitsstile in der ökonomisierten Altenpflege*, München: Utz Verlag.

Stemmer, Renate (2006), „Pflegeklassifikationen und der Anspruch umfassender Pflege", in: Gudrun Piechotta, and Norbert van Kampen (eds.), *Ganzheitlichkeit im Pflege- und Gesundheitsbereich. Anspruch-Mythos-Umsetzung*, Berlin et al.: Schibri-Verlag, 78–98.

Voß, G. Günter, and Rieder, Kerstin (2005), *Der arbeitende Kunde. Wenn Konsumenten zu unbezahlten Mitarbeitern werden*. Frankfurt am Main: Campus Verlag.

Being Creative with Time Binds: Solo-entrepreneurs Negotiating Work and Private Life

Birgit Huber

What market society is doing to us

Already in the 1980s, Arlie Russell Hochschild analyzed processes of commodification as they take place when emotions are managed at the workplace (1983). The years after she followed this interest in her examinations of processes of de-limitation, analyzing employees in a large multinational company, where boundaries blurred between work time and family time (2001). Later Hochschild's research targeted points of entry for market culture in the family sphere (2005). Hochschild's crucial question remains today: "What forces drive us to take part in processes of commodification, and how do we control and resist them?" The role that individuals play in selling their own labor power or in allocating their labor potential is a central theme in the study of labor, corporate and work culture by European ethnologists. Their studies are marked—not only in the sphere of labor studies—by the common position that familiar, routinized and day-to-day life should not be described in terms of "'fate' [...], of passive impotence or as swimming in an ocean of constraints, obligations, routines" (Kaschuba 1986: 479; this and all further translations of German sources by the author[1]). In the course of everyday life, "active and creative competence find their expression in material production and social reproduction [...], a mode of appropriation of social spheres and modes of experience and their coordination in cultural patterns" (ibid.). The research tradition of worker studies emerged in European Ethnology/German Folklore Studies in the 1970s.[2] Acts of creative

---

1 My thanks to Andreas Hemming for his careful reading and correction of the English language manuscript.

2 This sub-discipline found its institutional expression in the creation of a commission on "worker culture" in the German Society for European Ethnology/Deutsche Gesellschaft für Volkskunde in 1980. The 1990s witnessed a paradigm shift, which was reflected in the renaming the commission "work culture studies" in 1998. The "corporate culture studies" of the 1990s also focus on the perspective of employees and laborers (e. g. Götz 1997).

adaption, of resistance and protest were central.[3] Worker studies was for European Ethnology/German Folklore Studies "the examination of the culture and lifestyle of the wage-dependent, that part of the population that lived on the basis of selling their labor power, for the purpose of identifying a specific worker culture and explaining it from the perspective of the working and living conditions of the working class [...] [as well as] the analysis of creative opposition to objectively existent constraints" (Assion 2001: 255).

The analysis of wage labor in the past, contemporary factory wage labor structures and their appropriation by the workers was an attempt to understand the genesis of capitalism. The "transformation of the examination of worker culture on the basis of class to a cultural analysis of the specific formation of lifestyles" (Kramer 1991: 319) made it possible to pose the crucial question—that is "what market society is doing to all of us" (ibid.)—not only in terms of history but also for the present. From this point of departure my paper will discuss, on the basis of an ethnographic case study in the creative industries, how individuals "do not adapt themselves to the market economy, but adapt the market economy to themselves" (Matuschek et al. 2004: 129). In this extension of the concept of "entreployee" (Voß and Pongratz 1998) the subjective motivation and goals of individual actors are investigated. In doing so the focus is extended to include not only the "in-order-to motives", but also the "because motives" (Matuschek et al. 2004: 135), not only the demands of the employers towards their employees, but also the demands of the employees on their own work. Decisive for success in this process of adapting the market economy to one's own needs and visions of life are not alone, as the ethnographic approach reveals, subjective goals and individual skills. Shared patterns of action and interpretation can be identified that emerge as resources, as their intersubjective negotiation and links to traditional forms and existing symbolic orders.

The field of the creative industries seems to be especially interesting when studying processes of marketization and self-commodification because actors in this field are considered the spearhead of these processes. In general, sociologists have predicted a *"new stage in the commercialization of individual labor power"* [sic] (Pongratz and Voß 2003b: 15; emphasis in the original). The "extended commercialization of labor power and work capacity by the individual" means that the individual must "actively [...] develop and sell not only his manpower and work skills, but his individual work capacity

---

3 The emphasis in European Ethnology/German Folklore Studies is on creativity (Warneken 2006).

including the entire spectrum of personal potential, skills gained beyond the sphere of work, social networks and contacts, private housing space and concrete contributions of further persons such as friends, family members and relatives to the working process" (Voß and Pongratz 1998: 145). Such work and lifestyles are to be found especially among the self-employed (see Pongratz and Voß 2003a: 28–29), particularly in the project-oriented communication and information technology sectors, in the media and cultural professions, in the continuing education sector and in the consulting and IT industries. Following Voß, not only are these highly qualified jobs affected by various forms of de-limitation, such as in terms of time (flexible working hours, which is, from an emic perspective, often little more than an euphemism for temporal de-limitation), space, contents (what is done; project or group work is an example for de-limitation in the direction of self-organization), function (what skills are required), technology, and in aspects of a social and emotional nature. De-limitation appears not only in the context of a business enterprise. The structural association of work with a clearly defined, exclusive sphere of life is increasingly losing all contour. Arlie Russell Hochschild's study of a large multinational company, *Amerco*, (2001) explains why employees acquiesce to blurring boundaries, even if this means severe stress for them. At *Amerco*, employees of both sexes work extended hours, and work time encroaches on and prevails over family time. Family life is subjected to the imperative of a Taylorist time regime. The workers are not forced to act in this way. Rather, as is shown, employers' and workers' interests here go hand in hand. Employees of both sexes earn recognition and appreciation at work, which causes them to feel comfortable and at home and in turn spend even more time at work. Only a few employees resist this Taylorist time regime: "Instead of adapting themselves to a grueling schedule, some workers altered the schedule itself, or tried to" (Hochschild 2005: 349). These "resisters" were the happiest, perhaps because they felt the most in control of their work lives, as Hochschild suggests (ibid.: 350). The price they paid was that they never rose very high in the *Amerco* hierarchy. These actors "were less likely ports of entry for market culture" (ibid.: 351), compared to employees with other "temporal strategies" (ibid.: 339).

Embedded time

In my ethnographic case study in which I accompanied staff members in a small[4] full-service agency and freelancers from the cultural and creative industries in both urban and rurally structured contexts[5], various "spaces of resistance" could be identified; i. e. geographical and social spaces in which actors manage to adapt the market economy to their own needs and desires. This form of observation was made possible by means of a "multi-local ethnography"[6] over a period of four years. That is, six actors were followed intermittently to all sites where they did things that they understood as work. These included not only the site where the respective contract was to be fulfilled, but offices outside of the corporate context, a commonly maintained office-shop combination and offices in residential spaces. The idea was to capture as a whole the role of paid work in the individuals' lives, as it was done by Hochschild in her study on *Amerco*. The women and men whom I accompanied have for several years worked in projects for the studied agency with a focus on corporate communication and the implementation of corporate communication solutions at trade fairs, in print and the internet. They thus operate as part of a "dyad" (Reindl 2000: 425–426).[7] All employees are educated in a variety of disciplines associated with the "new hybrid organisational field of the 'internet industry'" (Mayer-Ahuja and Wolf 2005: 65–66.). These include information and communication technology,

---

4 At the time of fieldwork, the agency had eight salaried and six freelance staff members. In general, the German Internet and multimedia industry is dominated by such small-scale enterprises, which should be kept in mind since it obviously influences the way in which work is organized (Mayer-Ahuja and Wolf 2007: 79).

5 Project-based cooperation on the basis of new communication and information technologies in the culture and creative industries is a well-studied issue in the social and cultural sciences in several European countries and the United States. The focus on urban-metropolitan environments, however, has left unanswered the question to what extent actors outside of these centers are affected by these fundamental changes in lifestyle and self-interpretation. Statistical data reveals that many small and micro-enterprises in Germany are settled outside of the urban centers. It was for this reason that I did research in an agency based in a rurally structured region in southern Germany and whose freelance employees lived distributed across the whole country.

6 On the practice of "multi-local ethnography" see Huber (2012).

7 The term "dyad" describes the phenomenon that enterprises "develop a stable circle of satellites" and the binding dynamic that emerges between them and their client enterprise. In my case, these "stable satellites" are freelance workers who work repeatedly for the same client, but on the whole have more clients and are thus legally, not pseudo-self-employed (Reindl 2000).

advertising, the related spheres of the publishing and graphics industry and tangents on the audiovisual media sector.

A young freelance couple in their thirties was responsible for web design and internet services in the agency studied. The couple lives in an urban centre known for its culture and creative industries in Germany and combines several forms of paid work in a flexible and well organized manner. They thus provide a unique and dynamic portfolio of services in earning their livelihood in a sector marked by project work. Despite this fact, the couple does not practice an extended self-commodification. The work schedule and daily life of both partners, Anne and Neo, consist to a large extent of activities that are financially unsatisfactory but agree with individual life goals as well as with experiments in terms of time and leisure management and living together. Several years ago, Anne and Neo began what Neo describes as an "extreme psychological experiment". Together with four friends they opened a combination of shop and office that they financed jointly. They share an apartment with two of these friends, a third partner lives in the building next door. The fourth friend left the common project after a few months to find regular employment because he was dissatisfied with the insecurity inherent to freelance work, especially in the media and artistic sector. The different social and spatial spheres – economic, family, friendship, public and private – are closely intertwined in this context. Neo and Anne practice a mix of livelihood strategies (Kramer 2001: 338) that include web design and Internet-service providing, the production of handmade lifestyle products and individualized clothing with a local flair, short term contracts with the local arts college, and media art production. The activities associated with internet concepts and web design, like those for the studied agency, are valued inasmuch as they are financially productive. The activities that Anne and Neo appreciate most in terms of content are the production and presentation of Neo's and his friends' media artwork and Anne's work designing clothing and interiors. These activities nevertheless do not contribute significantly to securing their livelihood. As for the separation of work and private spheres, of work and leisure, an "organic separation of lifeworlds"[8] (Kleemann 2005: 336) is practiced. Concerning temporal strategies, the individual actors each have their own rhythm. It is often the case that several partners are in the

---

8 Here an individualized differentiation of co-present work and private spheres must be created by the subjects themselves. The "'mechanical' separation of spheres in the industrial-modern mode of living is replaced by a post-industrial-modern mode, the logic of which is based on an 'organic' separation of these spheres" (Kleemann 2005: 336).

same place, but each follows his or her own particular time and activity phases. Franko, a partner in the shared office-shop combination, regularly watches TV or eats while Anne and Neo are working at their laptops. From time to time Franko goes for a jog spontaneously, taking those present at this moment with him. Anne enjoys the blurred boundaries in terms of time, space and social relations. This includes, on the other hand, unintended interruptions, which she at times sees as a problem. For her, the office is

workplace, meeting point, a big part of my life. We often sit together in the yard and talk about work. Or our friends are here. Or some watch television while others work. […] We want to work here. But the fact that we sit in a shop window means that many people simply come in—and that is the point. But if we happen to have a lot to do, it can be annoying of course.

Neo, on the other hand, has already started organizing his time and space more stringently:

In the past I hung out here [in the shared offices] for hours. But doing so constantly is not really a lot of fun. […] Now I am paying attention to practicing something like quitting time („Feierabend", translated by Huber).

When I asked him what "quitting time" means to him, Neo answered: "To stop working when I don't feel comfortable anymore and lose interest." At the same time, Neo is making an effort to organize his time flow not only according to the pleasure principle. One of his strategies is to complete the tasks he does not like every morning when he first comes to the office. To delimit work time, Neo abstains from using the Internet in their apartment, "happily", as he comments. For Franko, by contrast, the perfect way of work is the blurring of every temporal boundary, "to feel the flow". This is what he likes best about his work as a media artist, more than getting awards and staging exhibitions. He practices it in the shared rooms: "That the day goes by and I do not notice it. […] Being completely absorbed, enjoying, not noticing time passing." In doing so, Franko has developed a sense of time which is clearly different to that of his surroundings, concerning, for example, daytime activities.

Production between commodification and a self-determined way of life

How is it possible that such diverse, self-determined temporal strategies are practiced and that labor potential is used for personal purposes, especially considering the fact that the actors, working as freelancers, are directly confronted with the market economy? A comparison to Hochschild's study in a large company may help to explain these findings. The employees at Hochschild's Amerco, particularly the managerial staff, are convinced that they must dedicate almost their whole lives to the company. Their time, even at home, is aligned with the needs of the company as an extended work place. This temporal strategy is embedded in a stabilizing cultural context. Firstly, the company does not support other temporal strategies, such as fathers taking paternity leave (Hochschild 2001: chapter 9) or employees reducing their overtime or working part time (ibid.: chapter 7). People practicing such uncommon and undesired temporal strategies are not at or near the top of the *Amerco* employee hierarchy. Secondly, only a small minority of employees do so, and colleagues do not acknowledge such kind of "resistance" positively (e.g. ibid.: 111).

There are three core factors that allow for Neo, Anne and their partners in the office to practice individual temporal strategies and to balance personal needs and economic demands: acknowledgement from various quarters, the renouncing of a Fordist career model and way of life, and a constant market position.

The young couple and their partners practice a socially non-hegemonic, post-industrial-modern lifestyle and are very conscious of this fact.[9] Moreover, collective forms of activity and patterns of interpretation have emerged—accompanied by numerous conflictual negotiations—over a period of two years that allowed for a joint professionalization of livelihood activities in the office and the maintenance of utility value orientation at the same time. Products and services that serve securing the common livelihood are systematically marketed. At the same time, the common idea of the higher value of certain activities is not lost out of sight. As in the past, the utility value of the manufactured products is paramount. If a potential customer's wishes do not meet Neo and Anne's standards in terms of design and aesthetics, these jobs may even be turned down. Financial losses are accepted

---

9 For details see Huber (2012).

and free labor contributed for the purpose of maintaining the infrastructure of the common office. This resistance can be interpreted as a way of gaining and keeping control of one's life and as a protection against being fully commodified as a person.

Other factors stabilize these forms of self-determined control and self-determined commodification as well. Like many other IT-service professionals in the 1990s (see Manske 2007: 94) Neo and Anne started their professional careers in the IT sector by helping friends and their families with their computers and websites. At the same time they earned a professional qualification, i. e. a university degree in media design (Neo) and media technology (Anne). In the meantime they understand their work as a profession in the traditional sense, including the corresponding social expectations in terms of roles and standards. In addition, the couple established the common office together, that is, the respective partner was involved from the very start in the construction of their life concept. Both work to the same extent in the common office. Their work and lifestyle model is supported by their local environment. Here, in a peripheral urban quarter looking to gain in prestige, the common office has become an object of identification for neighborhood residents. Neo, Anne and their friends are in a position to generate symbolic capital to a degree that would be impossible in other parts of the same city or in other cities. In addition to the recognition from their neighbors, the lively contact with the local arts and media college milieu is supportive. Individuals in this social environment organize activities such as lectures and exhibits in the common office, and professors from the arts and media college faculty support them economically in the form of work contracts and assistance in grant applications.

In Hochschild's case, problems of time management derive to a significant degree from the fact that the employees have family and children. Anne, Neo and their partners did not have any children when I was doing field research with them. At the end of my fieldwork, Anne was pregnant. This is a typical professional biographical watershed at which point actors who like Anne and Neo have emerged out of "student-subcultural networks of like-minded individuals" adopt conventional lifestyles and forms of work (Kleemann 2005: 266). The couple moved into the neighboring house. Their behavior towards me changed at that time as well. While they were very open for visits, the couple did not find time for a last meeting. But the "extreme psychological experiment" remained, despite the change in family status. It did not become a mere biographical interval. Today the common office is operated in the same manner as it was during my fieldwork. The partners can look back on a large number of financially successful projects, and just as many that correspond to their own ideals of quality design. Media art and handmade designs remain a priority for all actors. They have together managed to establish and maintain "work patterns of playful experimentation" and an "unconventional attitude" that can be considered a hallmark of a post-Fordist labor patterns (Seifert 2004: 90).

Market entry by use of space and selling strategies

It can be seen in my case of freelancers in the cultural industries that it is not the temporal strategies that form the port of entry for market culture (i. e. "beliefs and practices that are based on the premise that the acts of buying and selling constitute an important source of identity"; Hochschild 2005: 339–340). Instead it is the use of space and selling strategies of self-made products that open the private for the market here. As Orvar Löfgren discovered for the new economy of the 1990s in general, not only has a new kind of economy and market logic evolved but a "cultural logic" (Löfgren 2003: 75). "It was in many senses a very 'cultural economy' that was emphasized, in which the technologies of imagineering, performance, styling and design played important roles" (ibid.: 76). "In order to establish yourself as an interesting actor or an investment object in a rapidly changing world, impression management was an important tool" (ibid.: 80). To understand the ways in which the new economy has been materialized and localized, ethnographies of both centers and peripheries have to be conducted (ibid.: 86). Having done so, in my study phenomena that have been identified in the urban context (e. g. Lange 2007) could also be found in a rurally structured region. Private living space is used for the presentation of hand-made products and a concommitant life-style. A public self-fashioning takes place, among other things by means of the prominent display of material objects inherent to the individuals' lifestyle. These objects acquire thus an aura of authenticity and of a creative lifestyle that in turn becomes a unique selling point and is bought with the product. The actors, in turn, gain a distinct position by means of this self-fashioning. Anne and Neo, for example, have installed a bar counter in their office which they use flexibly, as a bar when the office is used for public events, for self-presentation and for the display of products. At other times they use it as a table for their shared daily breakfast.

The case of another freelancer, Christopher, shows that similar forms of self-representation and presentation of the products emerge in a rurally structured area. Christopher is responsible for the digital design of trade fairs and the material production of the designed exhibition stands at the media agency at the core of the research. At the same time he produces hand-made furniture and one of a kind interiors. He sees the living room with integrated kitchen of his three-generation-household and even the bathroom as a showroom for potential customers. The fact that even the bathroom in which he designed the interior – and is used as any other bathroom is used – is included in his self-presentation might be interpreted as evidence of marketization, especially considering the fact that a bathroom is a typical backstage area (Goffman 1959). But upon closer examination, this form of self-presentation and use of space practiced by the freelancers Anne, Neo and Christopher, is not a mere port of entry for market culture. In fact, in Christopher's case it is not a result of marketization at all. He does not need to sell his hand-made products in order to earn a living; he does so on the basis of other jobs, for example for the studied agency. This self-presentation in the case of the urban freelance couple is used as marketing strategy, but also used for non-marketed purposes. All three try to enhance the status of their local environment, be it a peripheral urban quarter or a peripheral rural region. The office serves as a point of identification in an area that was said to have drug problems until recently. Christopher produces old-style artifacts typical for the region (e. g. a special type of ski) and tries to promote their in his words "authentic" use. The peripheral areas in which the actors live and work thus gain in social value.

To conclude, the freelancers accompanied in this study do not merely adapt themselves to the market economy, but adapt the market economy to themselves. In doing so they rely on shared patterns of action and interpretation as stabilizing resources. These patterns can be either negotiated jointly, as in the urban case of Anne, Neo and their partners. Or they can be based on social roles and spatial patterns that have evolved over generations and have their origin in traditions of small scale family businesses in various craft trades, as in the case of Christopher in a rural structured area.

Works Cited

Assion, Peter (2001), "Arbeiterforschung", in: Rolf Wilhelm Brednich (ed.), *Grundriß der Volkskunde. Einführung in die Forschungsfelder der Europäischen Ethnologie*, Berlin: Dietrich Reimer Verlag, 255–279.

Götz, Irene (1997), *Unternehmenskultur. Die Arbeitswelt einer Großbäckerei aus kulturwissenschaftlicher Sicht*, Münster: Waxmann.

Goffman, Erving (1959), *The Presentation of Self in Everyday Life*, Garden City, New York: Doubleday.

Hochschild, Arlie Russell (1983), *The managed heart: The commercialization of human feeling*, Berkeley: The University of California Press.

— (2001), *The time bind: When work becomes home and home becomes work*, New York: Henry Holt and Company.

— (2005), "On the edge of the time bind: Time and market culture", in: *Social Research*, 72, 2, 339–354.

Huber, Birgit (2012), *Arbeiten in der Kreativindustrie. Eine multilokale Ethnografie der Entgrenzung von Arbeits- und Lebenswelt*, Frankfurt am Main, New York: Campus.

Kaschuba, Wolfgang (1986), "Mythos oder Eigen-Sinn. 'Volkskultur' zwischen Volkskunde und Sozialgeschichte", in: Utz Jeggle, Gottfried Korff, Martin Scharfe, and Bernd Jürgen Warneken (eds.), *Volkskultur in der Moderne. Probleme und Perspektiven empirischer Kulturforschung*, Reinbek bei Hamburg: Rowohlt, 469–507.

Kleemann, Frank (2005), *Die Wirklichkeit der Teleheimarbeit. Eine arbeitssoziologische Untersuchung*, Berlin: edition sigma.

Kramer, Dieter (1991), "Unter welchen Bedingungen ist Arbeiterkultur-Forschung heute noch interessant?", in: Wolfgang Kaschuba, Gottfried Korff, and Bernd Jürgen Warneken (eds.), *Arbeiterkultur seit 1945 – Ende oder Veränderung?* Tübingen: Tübinger Vereinigung für Volkskunde, 314–319.

— (2001), "Kulturmuster für Lebensplätze. Eine mentale Infrastruktur für die Zeit nach der Vollbeschäftigung", in: Siegfried Becker (ed.), *Volkskundliche Tableaus. Eine Festschrift für Martin Scharfe zum 65. Geburtstag von Weggefährten, Freunden und Schülern*, Münster: Waxmann, 327–343.

Lange, Bastian (2007), *Die Räume der Kreativszenen. Culturepreneurs und ihre Orte in Berlin*. Bielefeld: transcript.

Löfgren, Orvar (2003), "Working for the new economy—The new gilded age", in: Sabine Hess, and Johannes Moser (eds.), *Kultur der Arbeit – Kultur der neuen Ökonomie. Kulturwissenschaftliche Beiträge zu neoliberalen Arbeits- und Lebenswelten*, Graz: Institut für Volkskunde und Kulturanthropologie, 73–88.

Manske, Alexandra (2007), *Prekarisierung auf hohem Niveau. Eine Feldstudie über Alleinunternehmer in der IT-Branche*, München, Mering: Rainer Hampp Verlag.

Matuschek, Ingo, Frank Kleemann, and Cornelia Brinkhoff (2004), "'Bringing Subjectivity back in'. Notwendige Ergänzungen zum Konzept des Arbeitskraftunternehmers", in: Hans J. Pongratz, and G. Günter Voß (eds.), *Typisch Arbeitskraft-unternehmer? Befunde der empirischen Arbeitsforschung,* Berlin: edition sigma, 115–138.

Mayer-Ahuja, Nicole, and Harald Wolf (2005), "Arbeit am Netz. Formen der Selbst-und Fremdbindung bei Internetdienstleistern", in: Nicole Mayer-Ahuja, and Harald Wolf (eds.), *Entfesselte Arbeit – neue Bindungen. Grenzen der Entgrenzung in der Medien- und Kulturindustrie,* Berlin: edition sigma, 61–108.

— (2007), "Beyond the hype. Working in the German Internet Industry", in: *Critical Sociology,* 33, 43–71.

Pongratz, Hans J., and G. Günter Voß (2003a), *Arbeitskraftunternehmer. Erwerbsori-entierungen in entgrenzten Arbeitsformen,* Berlin: edition sigma.

— (2003b), "From employee to 'entreployee': Towards a 'self-entrepreneurial' work force?", in: *Concepts and Transformation,* 8, 3, 239–254.

Reindl, Josef (2000), "Scheinselbständigkeit. Ein deutsches Phänomen und ein ver-korkster Diskurs", in: *Leviathan,* 4, 413–433.

Seifert, Manfred (2004), "Arbeitswelten im Wandel. Zur Ethnographie der Arbeits-bedingungen und Arbeitsauffassungen", in: *Rheinisch-westfälische Zeitschrift für Volkskunde,* 49, 57–94.

Voß, G. Günter, and Hans J. Pongratz (1998), "Der Arbeitskraftunternehmer. Eine neue Grundform der Ware Arbeitskraft?", in: *Kölner Zeitschrift für Soziologie und Sozialpsychologie,* 50, 131–158.

Warneken, Bernd Jürgen (2006), *Ethnographie popularer Kulturen,* Wien: Böhlau Verlag.

Encountering Arlie Hochschild's Concept of "Emotional Labor" in Gendered Work Cultures: Ethnographic Approaches in the Sociology of Emotions and in European Ethnology

Irene Götz

I first encountered Arlie Russell Hochschild through reading her modern classic *The Managed Heart*[1] during my ethnographic study on gendered work cultures in a large bakery (Götz 1997). Ever since this first encounter, I have been observing that Hochschild's approach often coincides with the research interests of an expanding community of work ethnographers in the discipline of European Ethnology.[2] In this essay, I will point out some of these striking similarities by focusing on the influence of her books on my own ethnographic work. Yet before discussing my research, I will sketch some of the characteristics of Arlie Hochschild's work and terminology, looking through the lens of a cultural anthropologist. I will conclude this essay with a preliminary summary, which will provide a short account of some of the key characteristics of the ethnographic approach to work life in the service sector.

Arlie Hochschild—a Cultural Anthropologist?
A Holistic Perspective on Emotional Labor

Because of her particular way of approaching research, Arlie Hochschild would probably not object if she were adopted as a cultural anthropologist for her approach to research. In fact, this has already happened: In 2006,

---

1 Hochschild (1983). In this essay, I will cite the 20th edition of 2003 (Hochschild 2003a).
2 For an overview of the current development of work ethnography in European Ethnology, see Götz (2010). The work ethnographers in Germany, Austria and Switzerland are organized in the *Kommission Arbeitskulturen* der *Deutschen Gesellschaft für Volkskunde* (see its publications, for example, the latest collection of essays, edited by Koch and Warneken (2012), on http://www.dgv-arbeitskulturen.de/).

she received the Conrad Arensberg Award of the American Anthropological Association[3]. In the introduction to the latest German edition of *The Managed Heart*, sociologist Sighard Neckel (2006) points out that she uses an approach similar to that of cultural anthropology: an *inductive and creative, situational approach based on a variety of data and perspectives*. Working like a cultural anthropologist/ethnologist, Arlie Hochschild has collected a wide range of oral and written material for all her books—without following strict "evidence-based" and standardized research plans.

In *The Time Bind*, Hochschild (1997) focused on the specific organizational culture of a "Fortune 500 company" called Amerco, and she analyzed the unwritten laws governing the workplace. She looked at this culture from different perspectives and revealed its interconnectedness with family life. Hence, her approach to research is definitively similar to what European Ethnologists do, who also focus on *micro-analysis*, on *case studies* centered on the attitudes and practices of subjects. In this monograph, Hochschild traced the company's new family policy and its failure to make women (and men) take advantage of the parental leave and part-time work arrangements available. She developed creative strategies in order to explore individual work-life-arrangements and the "time binds" of men and women with different places in the hierarchy at the workplace: She spent time in the company's parking lots in order to check who goes to work on Sundays, and she visited kindergartens with the aim of analyzing the time binds of the children of dual-career couples, who receive an hour of condensed "quality time" with their parents after dinner.

In other words, Arlie Hochschild *followed the actors* in their daily work routines like an ethnographer, and sometimes she also accompanied them to their homes to learn more about the personal cost of doing both a challenging job and the "second shift" at home: A surprising number of dual-earner couples still have to cope with powerful traditional value systems. Interviews with couples from different social classes, both used in an earlier book from 1989 called *The Second Shift* and in *The Time Bind*, revealed that traditional gender and class ideologies were affecting the couples and were at odds with their intended—and pretended—egalitarian arrangements of sharing paid work and house work.

As Arlie Hochschild showed in *The Second Shift* (1989), the male workers, especially in the expanding service sectors, are torn between traditional

---

3 This award was established by the Society for the Anthropology of Work in 1991 to recognize contributions to the field.

feeling rules[4] and more modern demands, for example, accepting or even supporting the careers of their wives. Hochschild explained the logic and individual coping strategies of the traditional *"economy of gratitude"* informing housework: According to this value system, the husband should be thanked for his "help" around the house, as doing such a "female" job cannot be expected of the traditional breadwinner. These inner and outer conflicts have several consequences for the individual's "management" of his or her feelings. As Arlie Hochschild showed in her case studies, the management of feelings and the acts of balancing inner tensions are essential parts of the daily, fragile emotion work necessary for sustaining private relationships as well as keeping an (often precarious) job.

According to Arlie Hochschild, it is necessary for scholars working in this area to widen their perspectives and to include in their research both work cultures and the private life worlds of the actors. Otherwise, they will not be able to detect the complex, multi-faceted inner and outer strategies of identity work and of accommodation to existing social structures pursued by the actors. Arlie Hochschild never limited her research field to either the work life or the reproduction sphere, but regarded *both of them as interconnected realms located in a single social field.* As a result, she succeeded in providing deep insights into everyday struggles and the daily transfers from home to work life (and vice versa), which involve values, beliefs, attitudes, gendered hierarchies, practices, emotions, services and commodities.

In the light of the interconnection of the two domains and the expansion of the service sector, which tends to colonize "the whole personality" and leads to the "Commercialization of Intimate Life" (Hochschild 2003b), Arlie Hochschild developed a *broad and open concept of work.* This coincides with "our" own, open approach in work ethnography (see Herlyn et al. 2009): Work can neither be restricted to paid work nor to visible work practices altering the outside world. As a result, Hochschild's concept takes into account both the *inner,* invisible processes of "emotion work" and the effects of this inner management of feelings, which, taken together, constitute "emotional labor". As Hochschild (2003: 7) puts it:

I use the term emotional labor to mean the management of feeling to create a publicly observable facial and bodily display; emotional labor is sold for a wage and therefore as *exchange value.* I use the synonymous terms emotion work or emotion management to refer to these same acts done in a private context where they have *use value.*

---

4 See Hochschild (1979) and Hochschild (1983), especially in chapter 4.

Thus, emotional labor "requires one to induce or suppress feeling in order to sustain the outward countenance that produces the proper state of mind in others" (Hochschild 2003: 7). Emotional labor is observable in the body language and interactions between the service worker and the client; it is objectified and guided by commercial directives and bought and sold on the market.[5]

Moreover, work is always *gendered work*. This is due to the different socialization of men and women, which is reflected in traditional gender roles. There are still many jobs that rely on employees making use of their experiences as housewives. This aspect of the work usually does not have to be remunerated, for the skills and feelings involved are still considered the "natural" gifts and instincts of a mother. Many low-wage service jobs are a domain of female work.[6] In her bestseller *The Managed Heart*, Arlie Hochschild depicted how Delta Airlines' training centers and manuals relied on the "emotional memory" of female private work contexts: Young flight attendants were trained to recall these in order to manipulate their emotional behavior towards problematic passengers (see Hochschild 2003: chapter 6). Focusing on normative instructions and trained feeling rules as well as on interviews with the flight attendants, trainees and supervisors, Arlie Hochschild analyzed the numerous normative demands of this type of "home-like" emotional labor, as well as particular incidents and various practices connected to it. Like perfect "hosts" at a dinner party, they were expected to serve their "friends" with never-ending patience and sincere friendliness. They had to learn that the "passenger has no obligation to return empathy or even courtesy" (Hochschild 2003: 110). If the "guests" got angry or afraid, it was the job of the flight attendants to suppress their own anger and fear, and soothe them like a mother who calms down her angry or anxious children. The supervisors trained the recruits, according to this "cabin-to-home analogy", to use the "company language", which contained standardized "expressions of empathy" (Hochschild 2003: 109–113).

In Arlie Hochschild's research the subjects have always been conceptualized as *active persons*, even if they have to cope with manipulating feeling rules in a challenging, alienating workspace. This shifting focus on the subjects' practices and their dependence on given structures again reveals the similarities between a cultural anthropological approach and Hochschild's work (see Götz 2010). Although Hochschild—somewhat pessimistically—

---

5 See Hochschild (2003), chapter 1, 4–6.
6 Concerning the "gendered labor market" in Germany, see Beck-Gernsheim (1976).

highlights how the structure of this commercialized world is increasingly alienating people through stealing and commodifying their authentic feelings, she emphasizes the agency of the subjects. This is demonstrated by her use of concepts such as "surface acting" and "deep acting" (which is deliberately not called reacting!).[7]

"Deep acting" refers to Constantin Stanislawski's "method acting" technique: He taught professional actors and actresses to recall emotions from their personal "emotional memory"—a situational performing practice of recalling (Stanislawski 1961). Accordingly, the service workers of Delta Airlines have to educate themselves either to feel "serious" friendliness or aggression vis-à-vis their clients. "Surface acting" accords to superficial behavioral rules from manuals; in contrast, the transformations of the self in question go deeper and, therefore, may cause more severe psychological damage if they are applied in commercial contexts. Arlie Hochschild has warned us of this state of affairs on many occasions. If a service worker has to sell her feelings in the service industry day by day, her emotions are rearranged and her entire personality becomes a commodity.

In the process, she (or he) might lose her (or his) inner voice and sense for genuine feelings, which are important "signals" helping people to grasp and interpret situations and the attitudes of other people they interact with.[8] Even though Hochschild developed—in a critical elaboration on Erving Goffman[9]—a more differentiated *concept of emotional acting*, some action theorists criticized her concept of alienation for treating subjects merely as victims who can do nothing but adapt to challenging structures (see Neckel 2006: 22).

This objection does not seem to be justified, for Hochschild always considered the actors' own creativity in subverting the rigid rules and demands of their companies. For example, she showed how the flight attendants managed to develop strategies of coping with unfriendly customers who had offended and humiliated them; in fact, they even found covert ways of paying them back for their nasty behavior—a sublime form of revenge (see Hochschild 2003: 114). It is this sensibility for subversion and resistance that brings Arlie Hochschild's attitude towards research close to that of European

---

7 See chapter 3 in Hochschild (2003).

8 As Hochschild puts it with reference to Freud: "Emotional states—such as joy, sadness and jealousy—can be seen as the senders of signals about our way of apprehending the inner and outer environment." (Hochschild 2003: 119 and 230 ff.)

9 Hochschild (2003: 224–228) blamed Goffman for neglecting the fact that the subject is a person with agency, who has to manage an inner life when displaying a special emotion.

Ethnologists: "We" also consider it a primary task to learn more about subversive strategies and, to an extent, encourage workers to use them as instruments of political empowerment and change (see Götz 2010; Herlyn et al. 2009; Koch and Warneken 2012).

Arlie Hochschild has always chosen and reflected on her case studies thoroughly. Her intention is to develop her conceptual framework and hypotheses building on the solid basis of *well-selected and well-arranged examples*. Just like in the work studies of ethnologists, there is always an emancipatory attitude and tone in her writings. The flight attendants had the task of managing their feelings in order to create a homelike atmosphere of wellbeing, trust and safety; in contrast, the bill collectors of Delta Airlines (Hochschild 2003: 138–147) operating on the backstage were obliged to train themselves according to antagonistic, more "male" feeling rules: They had to create an anonymous and frightening climate of distrust and humiliation which helped to "convince" defaulting customers in an aggressive and intimidating way to pay their bills. Although they were obliged to behave aggressively, some of them also attempted to find hidden ways of bailing-out clients.

These research conceptions and practices of field research are reminiscent of the *phenomenological approach* in ethnology, which is based on "thick descriptions" (Geertz 1973) and interpreting culture as a "web" of interwoven symbols, practices and meanings. In accordance with this ethnographic and casuistic way of representing and textualizing field material, Arlie Hochschild tells stories about her characters.

Her narrative includes case studies; she focuses emphatically on the perspectives of the actors and their practices of managing divergent impulses and feeling rules. However, this is always conceptualized with reference to the corresponding socio-cultural and economic context. Arlie Hochschild's research has always covered both the *macro- and the micro-levels of the field*— as well as different layers and perspectives, such as the different hierarchies, departments and gendered subcultures of a company.

Although Sighard Neckel emphasizes the closeness of Arlie Hochschild's approach to cultural anthropology in his introduction to *The Managed Heart*, he sticks to the old prejudice against 'under-theorized' ethnographic work in one respect: He sees a crucial difference between ethnological and sociological case studies. According to him, only the latter are able to extract, from exemplary cases, more general statements on the social structures of life worlds (Neckel 2006: 15). Hochschild's books are brilliant examples of such an inductive and explorative way of developing and 'sensing' theoretical concepts, but the ethnographic work of European Ethnologists also theorizes the data produced in an inductive fashion and with the aim of developing more general explanations of everyday life and concepts describing it.

Participant Observation in a Bread Factory—Theorizing Gendered Work Cultures through the Lens of the Female Ethnographer's Emotions

Why do (mostly female) shop assistants in a bread factory still earn less money than their (male) co-workers, who work either as mostly unqualified bakers or as suppliers delivering bread to the shops? This question and my observation of deeply rooted gender segregations in the work environment of this company motivated me to conduct an ethnographic field study on corporate culture. For the next three years (in the mid-1990s), a highly industrialized bakery with about 100 shops spread all over southern Germany became my research field (Götz 1997).

I investigated the interactions between the female shop assistants on the one side, and the male suppliers and the customers on the other. Their interactions formed part of the everyday work routines in this highly rationalized and standardized work setting. I learned about the daily routines in the different departments of this company by means of conducting interviews and nosing around in the shops and store halls, the bureaus and the bakery, by attending training courses and participating in Christmas parties and meetings and, last but not least, by digging in the company's archive. Step-by-step, I identified the special ingredients of the professional honor of every job, of its particular reputation and problems.

I was nosing around in the role of a trainee on an internship, and seemed to be mostly useless for the hard work of the bakers. I had to cope with distrust on the work floor—and with official restrictions whenever I seemed to be too interested in "serious" problems concerning, for example, unsatisfied workers. Especially the shop assistants, who in the end accepted me as a "colleague," tried to instrumentalize me for their particular needs, hoping to become more "visible"—for example, in terms of work overload and a lack of recognition from their supervisors.

There were various instrumentalizations of, and projections on, my person, and they helped me to become socialized into the gender-dominated life worlds characterizing the different work places. I was treated as somebody who did not fit into this work environment—at least in the male-dominated areas. I got into this position due to my lack of physical strength and toughness—and because women daring to stay after having experienced that they do not fit in must have "other interests." I fled this work place because I was afraid of sexual assaults, through which the men seemed to compensate for the "mistake" of allowing a younger woman into a work environment that obviously was supposed to be reserved for males. Through this "mistake," I learned about their values, and how they would have supposedly treated any woman who would have demanded to get one of these "male" jobs that were "better" regarding payment and status. These more or less subtle conflicts of power between males and females were still handled in those days by staying in one's "own" restricted work environment, and the personnel office of the company openly supported this policy.

In other words, I managed to gain deeper insights into the unwritten rules and values of the workers on the shop floor by thoroughly reflecting on my role in the field. I grasped these rules and role patterns by studying how cultural roles were projected on my person—and I often found these projections inadequate and disturbing. This is what Arlie Hochschild hints at, when she states that feelings have to be taken seriously: They are important "signals", which reveal the nature of certain situations.[10]

When I started my internship in the shops, I was confronted with an environment completely different from that of the male dominated workplaces. I immediately found myself appropriated for all the routine work which had to be done. As a young woman, I had to be trained for the job of a shop assistant by experienced "mothers". So they taught me the "right" emotions to be used for different types of customers, and to decorate the shop artistically, and—most importantly—to keep everything clean and nice. Again, I experienced what this "female" work culture is like through having to play cultural roles—and through my sensory experiences and feelings. Thanks to the shop assistants' strict lessons, I felt detached, sometimes amused, bored, or even humiliated. Through this introspective stance, by reflecting on why I felt this way, I could get a glimpse of their feelings and a sense of their more or less conscious attitudes to their jobs and role models.

---

10 See footnote 8.

Why did the shop assistants emphasize the virtue of being a housewife? They presented the superiority of housewives as a necessary precondition for doing their jobs. This enabled me to understand that there are few other skills to be proud of in an unskilled and badly paid job. Through intensive contacts and my daily observations in the shops, I learned that the women attempted to present themselves as honorable and qualified shop assistants who draw their self-esteem from the very values and skills they have acquired at home. They gained their self-confidence from being working housewives who managed to do challenging part-time jobs in the bakery in addition to their home duties; in other words, they were able, at last, to transfer their confidence into a professional setting, where they received a salary and gained a certain reputation for their labor. Moreover, by teaching me how to become a good, responsible shop assistant, I sensed that they felt a certain satisfaction: For the moment, they were superior and could turn the existing social hierarchies and power relations upside down.

"This job is not for a man!"—The Devaluation and Revaluation of the Informal Knowledge of Housewives

When I observed how the shop assistants supervised other trainees in their shops, I realized that my feelings had shown me the right way to interpret this "female" work culture. Some shop assistants as well as the workers from the personnel office explained in my interviews that the company preferred to employ experienced housewives "as they were able to learn the job within 14 days". Like the supervisors of the flight attendants in *The Managed Heart*, they referred to the housewife's "emotional memory" when they explicitly stated that a mother has all the necessary "practical" qualifications, such as serving (their children), cleaning (the house), multi-tasking and handling food skillfully.

For example, I observed during a workshop for shop assistants that the company explicitly expected them to make use of their expertise gained from cooking for their families. The supervisor encouraged a group of middle-aged shop assistants to test some of the recipes at home that were on the flyers handed to the customers in the shops. These flyers contained recommendations on how to use the products on sale, for example, organic "dark" rye flour. The women replied that their conservative husbands would neither like this "dark" flour nor the organic pasta made of it. The supervisor joked: "Then you better turn off the light before dishing up the pasta for your husband!" This joke reflected the supervisor's persistence. She tried to make use of the women's informal knowledge as housewives. Moreover, the company attempted to change the women's cooking habits and thus to colonize the private time of their employees as well as the taste of their families.

"Please, use dark (organic) flour for baking a cake, it tastes wonderful", said the supervisor in alluring manner. A shop assistant responded: "If the company pays for it, then, yes." The supervisor was astonished: "But you bake at home anyway!" All shop assistants replied with laughter: "No, we don't bake cakes anymore, we have no time!" The supervisor did not give in. She stated with urgency: "So, your homework for our next training session next week is to find out what you can bake with the organic flour!" A week later, she checked the results of this exercise.

This example highlights how the company expects their employees to identify with its products at almost any cost. This process of "socialization" partly has to take place at home. The company relied on, and strengthened the interconnection of the domains of work and home, as well as colonizing the women's time and abilities as domestic workers without paying for this extra service and the extra skills required. These strategies of "educating" the workers' tastes resulted from the idea of shaping their consciousness according to the corporate identity and language of the company, which praised the tasteful, sustainable and organic products. Furthermore, this example highlights normative demands of subjectification advancing into the realm of a formerly Fordist workplaces characterized by clear-cut boundaries between work and non-work.

The closeness to housework and reproduction work seemed to be one reason for the relatively low wages of the shop assistants. As my case study on the workshop showed, the form of housework in question is traditionally considered to be based on the "natural" tasks of caring and cooking, which mothers and wives have to do anyway. According to these "gender stereotypes", the "labor of love" is not "real" work at all—and this stereotype devaluates the status of all jobs that show a certain closeness to housework. In line with these traditional ways of devaluing female work, the job advertisements of the company explicitly looked for women and offered part-time positions only.

"You can't offer this part-time job to a man!" This was the response of a manager from the personnel office when I asked her why the job of a shop assistant seemed to be restricted to women. According to her, a man would not be able to support his family with a part-time job. She also explained that most of the women, who started to work in one of the shops "for a few hours a week" after their children had left home, were only planning to earn "a little money" while their husbands remained the main breadwinner. As I learned in the field, this assumption and the corresponding official corporate language of "part-time jobs for mothers" were a euphemism for the fact that many shop assistants worked almost full-time in addition to their "second shift" at home. Many of them did not have well-earning husbands and had to look after themselves.

Yet, what seemed unacceptable for men was presented as a good deal for women, especially for those with low qualifications. The company's ideology of empowering middle-aged women by offering them "part-time work" and a "second income" was a distorted account of the situation of these women, who were often forced to do precarious jobs such as these, which did not pay a living wage. Thus, the logic behind these policies of the company contributed to fixing gender roles and gender inequality in the workplace. This in turn served to justify the wage level, which was lower than in "male" unskilled jobs, for example in the bakery. The inter-linkage between unequal payment and status and the gendered evaluations of work seemed to be taken for granted in the personnel office and on the shop floor.

The most striking issue in this context was the perception of the few young men who worked in the shops, and who were eye-catching exceptions in those days. The jobs were only considered adequate for either young students on university vacation or for "really odd guys" who were "satisfied with low pay". The treatment of these men, who were seen as funny exceptions, revealed that being a shop assistant in a bakery was considered a female domain.

Female jobs are assigned a lower status; concerning the different "status shield" at work for men and women, the parallels between the bakery and Arlie Hochschild's observations in the plane cabins are obvious. There were jokes mirroring this difference in social status and the diverging expectations concerning male and female careers. Similar to the male flight attendants, the young helpers in the shop were asked by the customers, in a humorous manner, if they now had become the "boss" in the shop. The male flight attendants were asked whether they had plans to become managers, and as authorities, they were also treated with more respect (Hochschild 2003: 174–186). Nevertheless, male workers in the shop and in the cabin were often mothered. Arlie Hochschild and I observed quite similar processes where mother-son-relationships were transferred to the workplace. In my case, the experienced mothers kept her "sons" from doing dirty and "humiliating" jobs like cleaning the shop floor. What they saw as natural tasks for the female trainees, the "daughters", was called a "vicitimization" when it concerned the young men: "I won't let him clean the floor when there are enough women in the shop!" If a young man was able to explain the recipe of a special kind of bread or was cleaning the floor thoroughly, he was almost admired for this "exceptional" behavior. As Arlie Hochschild showed, some male flight attendants tended to "bow out" of the "hard jobs" of handling babies or "old folks", preferring to deal with young attractive female passengers (Hochschild 2003: 176).

Flirting was a popular practice among the male bread sellers and their female customers. Male customers tended to look down on men dressed in the white apron of the shop assistants. Some of the more conservative customers and suppliers of the company treated the men who "served" customers as weak "mother's boys" who had sold out their male virtues of strength and dominance. In doing so, the gendered stereotypes characterizing work cultures were, once again, fixed and enforced. "Female work" is downgraded by the still wide-spread attitude of regarding it unacceptable for "real" men.

"My most awful customer"—Stories on Emotional Labor in a Highly Standardized Work Environment

Another amazing issue, from my academic perspective, was the notion that most of the shop assistants regarded their job as "independent" work, which offered them a lot of responsibility and opportunities for being creative.

Thus, I wrote about another "contradiction" that I observed: the contradiction between a highly standardized work environment, which regulates every hand and body movement in the narrow shop. This standardization follows the idea of a Fordist, highly functional work place design. It is a form of job engineering and rationalization policy that allows the company to exchange the employees from one day to another or recruit unskilled (and therefore badly paid) workers. These workers will at once come to terms with the strictly organized order in the shop. Selling bread had more to do with working on an assembly line than with being "challenged" by the independent responsible work of a seller who must convince people.

This was the very moment when I discovered Arlie Hochschild's book *The Managed Heart*. Suddenly I began to understand: What these job assistants actually did was the hard job of everyday emotional labor: being friendly and being patient even with the most unfriendly, impatient customer. Such emotions had to be performed within a high-speed and physically straining work culture.

As I learned from Arlie Hochschild's book, emotional work requires training; the corresponding practices are governed by feeling rules. Considering this novel hypothesis, I became aware of several training materials, for example, a video which was used for training new shop assistants. The video and some manuals about being a good seller explicitly fixed and standardized these feeling rules and role models.

In this video, the main mottos of the training—"Friendliness trumps everything!" and "The customer is king!"—are illustrated with the help of a number of practical scenarios. The film sequences present two women aged around 50. They are behind the sales counter of the shop, dressed conservatively in white, clean aprons. Their outward appearance—"neither too fashionable nor too extreme in their bodily constitution"[11]—matches the conservative corporate image of the company and the anticipated taste of the middle-class customers, who can afford to buy expensive organic products. The slight Bavarian dialect of the two shop assistants emphasizes the regional, "traditional Bavarian" image of the brand and helps—as an integral part of the folkloristic shop aesthetics—to advertise the products. The company is looking for a special type of woman who is prepared to treat the customers according to the following ideal:

With never-ending patience and discreet helpfulness, the shop assistant finds out about the customers' wishes. With alertness and courtesy, she asks regular customers how they are. With her perfect memory, she easily remembers their names and favorite bread. With great concentration, she keeps eye-contact while hurrying to find the ordered product. With the correct order in mind, she wraps the bread, and with natural helpfulness, she puts it in the bag provided by the customer. With professional competence, she gives advice to new or insecure customers, identifying the right kind of bread for them by finding out about their individual tastes. With persuasive power, she addresses unusual requests. With compassion and regret, she comforts an old

---

11 As the personnel officer once stated, see Götz (1997: 105 ff.).

woman whose favorite bread is sold out. With the experience of a housewife, she identifies the bread suitable for a certain meal. With the strictness of a mother, she calms down "naughty" children—the customers of tomorrow (see Götz 1997: 108 f.).

Another means through which I grasped the relevance and *real* practices of the emotional labor at work was *storytelling*. I asked the shop assistants to tell me about critical incidents concerning their "most awful customer", and what I held in my hands in the end were about 40 narratives about "ugly", "unclean", "impatient", "aggressive" customers who did not behave at all like good customers. For example, they did not regard organic bread production highly, or did not believe in it, calling the organic production process a "lie", which insulted one of the shop assistants deeply. She told me about her "most ugly client" in a very annoyed tone. This incident revealed that she really believed in the officially propagated values of this organic bakery or at least was loyal to this key concept of the company.

From these violations of the interaction rules, I was able to extract the norms and feeling rules and understand them better, as well as how important emotion work was for the shop assistants' self-esteem and self-image. This was part of the "mysterious" pride and peculiar notion of doing "independent" work in a responsible position in the company that I could not understand at the beginning of my research.

In the end, I wrote a book that tried to bring together informal and formal rules and values and the practices of different work cultures. It turned out to be a book that approached Arlie Hochschild's theses on emotional labor.

A Remark on the Significance of Ethnographies

Ethnographic case studies in general adopt a holistic approach based on analyzing micro- and macro-contexts and revealing a range of perspectives by insiders. The examples presented by Arlie Hochschild and those from my dissertation project demonstrate that qualitative research produces deep insights into the construction of emotional labor, as well as into the different ways in which workers and customers deal with their feelings by adopting individual and collective social practices.

Moreover, fieldwork allowed the researchers to be close to the workers and customers. With their sensory apparatus and through the involvement of their own bodies, they experienced whether the workers are "deep acting"—or whether they are just "surface acting", that is, performing a feeling in the sense of Hochschild (2003: 35–48). In addition, the micro-analytical approach allows the researchers to reflect on, and judge, how emotional labor and feeling rules are embedded in (a) existing pragmatic settings at work and (b) broader social, moral and political frames that are often at odds with these settings.

Ethnographic research enables us to understand the "sentient self" (Hochschild 2003b: 78) in complex processes of interaction. In other words, ethnographic studies explore the "emotion vocabulary" with which the interactive partners themselves interpret their interactive procedures of service. They describe whether people are attached to or detached from one another and committed or uncommitted to their work—and whom they blame for their situation, or who they think is in charge. Through participant observation and individual narratives, we learn "what social situations or rules call feelings forth or tuck them under", as Arlie Hochschild had it (Hochschild 2003b: 78). Ethnographic fieldwork is able to delineate that feelings are produced, to a certain degree, by the pressures of an economized work environment.

Coming Back to the Class Issue and the Two Sides of the Service Sector

In my bakery project I covered one example of the expanding number of precarious jobs in the service sector of postindustrial societies. The example of the shop assistants was not part of the "bright" side of the service industry, that is, skilled jobs where certain forms of emotional labor are in demand and estimated highly. This "bright" side concerns the friendly yet commercialized aspects of a wealthy, aspirational society dominated by the middle class. Here, emotional labor—an essential aspect of the services provided by, for example, hairdressers, fitness trainers, personal and financial consultants, and family therapists—is regarded highly and rewarded accordingly. Here, emotional "gifts" and services constitute a resource for regeneration or an investment in the future: The clients see them as a way of improving their "human" or financial capital and boosting their employability and career opportunities. Here, in the rhetoric class, at the family consultant's, at the bank, emotional labor is, for both counselors and clients, a valuable tool as well as a result and a benefit of the work carried out.

However, the transformation of the "whole personality" according to feeling rules and the corresponding danger of alienation seem to be a more severe challenge for highly skilled service workers. On the whole, the precarious, often female service workers, for example in shops or fast food restaurants, have more superficial contacts with customers. Most of the time, they have to cope with feelings of anger, frustration and being oppressed. Yet they cannot easily be forced to transform their convictions or even their personality.

Post-Fordist labor markets are characterized by a climate of precariousness and insecurity; working class service workers, for example shop assistants or nurses in nursing homes for the elderly as well as flight attendants, currently have to cope with the *devaluation* of the immaterial, emotional aspects of their work and with *de-skilling*. This is one of the problems of the unskilled shop assistants working in the standardized chain stores of big, international companies selling fast food, cheap clothes and—in the IT sector—novel immaterial communication services. The flipside of these branches of the service industry are often less stylish and polished and less friendly work places. These functional, sober, and often antiseptic work environments do not have much in common with the "glamorous" offices of highly skilled consultants. Nevertheless, the staff tries to set or fulfill standards of good service or care.

The general question is: Under which conditions are emotions valued and remunerated adequately, and, conversely, what contributes to the downgrading of immaterial work? I contend that a whole range of interlinked factors play a role, such as the expected benefit of a particular service for the client's contentment at work, career, fitness and employability; the question whether the care or the service offered can expected to be an investment in more efficient work patterns; the social and vocational status of both the service worker and the client; the supply and demand for a certain service in this diversified sector of the economy; and the traditional down- and upgrading of work in a gendered labor market. In addition to this, body work and service work—traditional domains of women, which are often reminiscent of hard and dirty physical labor—are valued less than those forms of "clean" knowledge work that allow the worker to keep a more distant relationship to the client or patient.

Obviously, this is a class issue, and class also determines the "value" of service and care work as a capital. All these work environments, be they public or private, are, in one way or another, deeply influenced by the processes of the subjectification, deregulation and rationalization caused by the predominance of unrestricted market forces and strategies of neoliberal restructuring. The values of post-Fordism and the hegemonic practices of 'reengineering' reflect a new 'spirit of capitalism' centered on 'employability' and commodification (Boltanski and Chiapello 2006). The new economic strategies and practices have not only transformed Fordist institutions, but they have also advanced into the organization of family life[12], which becomes more and more dependent on 'outsourced' care work.

This essay intended to bring together Arlie Russell Hochschild's approach to research and work studies in European Ethnology; it aimed at pointing out the similarities, influences, and coincidences in conceptual, methodological and empirical matters. I hope to have contributed to intensifying the fruitful intellectual exchange between "us"—the next generations of cultural anthropologists exploring subjectification and commodification of emotions, knowledge and "personality"—and Arlie Hochschild, the pioneer of the sociology of emotions.[13]

Works Cited

Beck-Gernsheim, Elisabeth (1976), *Der geschlechtsspezifische Arbeitsmarkt*, Frankfurt am Main: Campus Verlag.

Boltanski, Luc, and Eve Chiapello (2006), *The new spirit of capitalism*, New York, London: Verso Books.

Geertz, Clifford (1973), "Thick description: Toward an interpretive theory of culture", in: Clifford Geertz, *The interpretation of cultures: Selected essays*, New York: Basic Books, 3–30.

Götz, Irene (1997), *Unternehmenskultur. Die Arbeitswelt einer Großbäckerei aus kulturwissenschaftlicher Sicht*, Münster, München: Waxmann.

---

12 Another recent project at the Munich Institute for European Ethnology was a case study on urban, middle-class mothers who felt obliged to conform to the ideals of "professionalized" motherhood, following "best practice" principles of raising children. See Schmidt, Götz (2010).

13 Finally, I want to thank Alexander Gallas for polishing my English and doing a wonderful job in editing this article.

— (2010), "Ethnografien der Nähe – Anmerkungen zum methodologischen Potenzial neuerer arbeitsethnografischer Forschungen der Europäischen Ethnologie", in: *Arbeits- und Industriesoziologische Studien*, 3, 1, 101–117. http://www.ais-stud ien.de/uploads/tx_nfextarbsoznetzeitung/Goetz.pdf.

Herlyn, Gerrit, Johannes Müske, Klaus Schönberger, and Ove Sutter (eds.) (2009), *Arbeit und Nicht-Arbeit. Entgrenzungen und Begrenzungen von Lebensbereichen und Praxen*, München, Mering: Rainer Hampp Verlag.

Hochschild, Arlie Russell (1979), "Emotion, feeling rules, and social structure", in: *American Journal of Sociology*, 85, 3, 551–575.

— (1983; 2003a), *The managed heart. Commercialization of human feeling*, Berkeley, Los Angeles, London: University of California Press.

— (1989), *The second shift: Working parents and the revolution at home* (with Anne Machung). New York: Viking Penguin.

— (1997), *The time bind: When work becomes home and home becomes work*, New York: Metropolitan/Holt.

— (2003b), *The Commercialization of intimate life: Notes from home and work*, San Francisco, Los Angeles: University of California Press.

Koch, Gertraud, and Bernd Jürgen Warneken (eds.) (2012), *Wissensarbeit und Arbeitswissen. Zur Ethnografie des kognitiven Kapitalismus*, Frankfurt am Main, New York: Campus Verlag.

Neckel, Sighard (2006), "Die Kultur des emotionalen Kapitalismus – eine Einleitung", in: Arlie Russell Hochschild, *Das gekaufte Herz. Die Kommerzialisierung der Gefühle*, Frankfurt am Main, New York: Campus Verlag, 13–24.

Schmidt, Petra, and Irene Götz (2010), "Supermami – Rabenmutter. Antagonistische Leitbilder und Subjektivierungsansprüche im Bereich Familienarbeit", in: Irene Götz, Birgit Huber, and Piritta Kleiner (eds.), *Arbeit in "neuen Zeiten". Ethnografien und Reportagen zu Ein- und Aufbrüchen*, München: Herbert Utz Verlag, 165–180.

Stanislawski, Constantin (1961), *Die Arbeit des Schauspielers an sich selbst. Teil 1: Die Arbeit an sich selbst im schöpferischen Prozeß des Erlebens*, Berlin: Henschel.

Biographical Notes

Sarah Braun, MA is a PhD student and research assistant at the Institute of European Ethnology in Munich. From 2005 to 2010 she studied Folklore/European Ethnology (major) as well as Legal Science and Psychology (minor) at the LMU Munich, with her Magister awarded in 2010. The topic of her Magister thesis was "Feelings in 'the Normal Working Day'. Emotional Capital—Emotional Labor as a Hairdresser's Service". From December 2010 to December 2012, she was a mentee in the LMU Excellence Initiative's mentoring program for emerging female academics in the Department of Cultural Studies.

Paul Brook is a senior lecturer in Sociology of Work and Employment at the University of Leicester's School of Management having previously worked at Manchester Metropolitan University and the Open University. Before becoming an academic he was a researcher and speech-writer for the Union of Shop, Distributive and Allied Workers (UK). He has published widely in the areas of emotional labor, service work, labor power and labor process theory, including articles in *Work, Employment and Society, Capital & Class* and *Culture & Organization*. He is a member of the Work, Employment and Society Editorial Board, an Associate Editor for the *International Journal of Management Concepts and Philosophy* and was secretary of the British Universities Industrial Relations Association (BUIRA) from 2007–10.

Dr. Wolfgang Dunkel studied Sociology at the Ludwig-Maximilians-University Munich and received his diploma in 1986 (thesis on emotional labour in elder care). He received his Dr. phil., also at LMU Munich, in 1993 (thesis on the conduct of everyday life of nurses) and has been working in several sociological research projects. Since 2001 he has been a researcher at the Institute for Social Science Research, ISF München. His research interests include interactive service work, service science, sociology of emotions, work and health, and qualitative methods. Recent publications include: Dunkel, Wolfgang and Margit Weihrich, (eds.) (2012), *Interaktive Arbeit. Theorie, Praxis und Gestaltung von Dienstleistungsbeziehungen*, Wiesbaden: Springer VS; Dunkel, Wolfgang and Frank Kleemann (eds.) (2013), *Customers at Work. New Perspectives on Interactive Service Work*, Houndmills: Palgrave Macmillan (in press).

Dr. Stefanie Everke Buchanan studied American Studies and European Ethnology at Eberhard Karls University Tübingen and Humboldt University in Berlin. She received her PhD in German Studies from Monash University, Australia, in 2007 for her dissertation on *The Construction of Cultural Identity: Germans in Melbourne*. In the following years, she worked as a lecturer and research fellow at Monash University and the University of Konstanz. Since 2011, she has been a research fellow and lecturer in the Department of Communication and Cultural Management at Zeppelin University. Her areas of research interest include migration, cultural identity, bilingualism and education.

Prof. Dr. Irene Götz studied European Ethnology and History in Freiburg/ Breisgau and Munich (LMU). In 1994, she completed her doctoral degree based on an ethnographic case study of gendered work cultures (published by Waxmann-Verlag in 1997). In the 1990s she held several research positions at LMU Munich and Humboldt University Berlin. Having mainly published on work ethnography so far, her habilitation project led her into a new research field: Funded by a Habilitation Grant of the German Research Foundation (DFG) in 2001/02, Irene Götz finished her habilitation on "German Identities. The Rediscovery of the National after 1989" at HU (published in German by Böhlau-Verlag in 2011). After guest professorships at HU and the University of Innsbruck/Austria she has been working as a full professor in the department of European Ethnology at LMU Munich since 2007. Her main research fields are work ethnography and new nationalism in Europe after 1989.

Prof. Em. Arlie Hochschild, PhD: A University of California Berkeley sociologist, Arlie Hochschild's books include *The Outsourced Self, The Managed Heart* (German translation by Campus Press), *The Second Shift* (German translation by Zolnay), *The Time Bind* (German translation by Verlag Leske Budrich), *The Commercialization of Intimate Life*, and the co-edited *Global*

Woman: Nannies, Maids and Sex Workers in the New Economy (Suhrkamp). The essay in this book is drawn from her forthcoming collection of essays entitled *So how's the family? and other essays* (University of California Press, August 2013). She is the winner of Guggenheim, Fulbright and Mellon Research awards as well as the American Sociological Association's Jessie Bernard Award, and its 2000 Public Understanding of Sociology Award. Three of her books were selected as "notable books of the year" by the *New York Times Book Review* and plays have been based on two. Her work has been translated into 16 languages. She has begun work on the interface of emotion, fantasy and politics.

Dr. Birgit Huber studied European Ethnology, German Literature and Sociology at the University of Passau and the University of Freiburg. She worked as a university assistant at the University of Bonn and the University of Tübingen. She received her PhD in European Ethnology from the Ludwig-Uhland-Institut für Empirische Kulturwissenschaft at the University of Tübingen for her dissertation on "Working in the creative industries. A multilocal ethnography on blurring boundaries of paid work and private life". From 2006 to 2009, she was a Research Fellow at the Max Planck Institute for Social Anthropology in Halle/Saale, researching on Catholics in East Germany. After that, she worked as a researcher and university lecturer. Since 2011, she has been a university assistant at the Institute of Historical Science and European Ethnology at the University of Innsbruck, Austria. Her areas of interest include work cultures, post-Fordism, multi-local ethnography, transnational Catholic movements, interreligious dialogue, and the internet.

Prof. Dr. Gertraud Koch is a cultural anthropologist and holds the chair for Communication Studies and Anthropology of Knowledge in the Department of Communication and Cultural Studies of Zeppelin University in Friedrichshafen. Her research interests are in the fields of working cultures, spatial research and digital anthropology. Current research projects focus on cultures of diversity in vocational education and diversity in processes of urban gentrification. She is the speaker of the research cluster *Urban & Regional Diversities* at Zeppelin University and of the *Commission for Digital Cultures* in the German Society of European Ethnology.

Dr. Nancy Konvalinka, PhD, is a cultural anthropologist in the Department of Social and Cultural Anthropology at the National Distance Education University (UNED) in Madrid. Her areas of interest are kinship, gender, family, and life course, as well as anthropology of work and care. Her ethnographic research in rural and urban contexts in Spain has been published in various articles and her book *Gender, Work and Property. An Ethnographic Study of Value in a Spanish Village,* published by Campus Verlag, deals with gender-differentiated emigration and changes in the organization of family farms. At present, she has a grant from the Wenner-Gren Foundation in the United States of America to study late-forming families in Madrid and their organization of care-giving activities. She is also a member of a Spanish I+D project on late-forming families.

Dr. Caroline Ruiner studied Sociology and Economics at Goethe University Frankfurt am Main. She received her doctoral degree in Sociology from the University of Augsburg in 2009 for her dissertation on the development of intimate relationships. In the following year, she worked as a research associate at University of Augsburg on the inclination and the success of women founding a business and their familial backgrounds. Since 2010, she has been a research associate and lecturer in the Institute of Work Science, Chair for Human Resources and Work Process Management at Ruhr-Universität Bochum. Her areas of interest include new forms of employment and the flexibilization of work, psychological contracts and fairness in employment relationships.

Dr. Jeremy Schulz: In 2010 Jeremy Schulz earned his PhD thesis in the Department of Sociology at the University of California, Berkeley for his dissertation entitled *Work and Life in the Balance.* His dissertation research examined the influence of societal environments and cultural contexts on the ways in which French, Norwegian, and American professionals experience and organize work, family, and private life. His article *Zoning the Evening: Constructing the Evening Work-life Boundary among French, Norwegian, and American Business Professionals* received the Shils-Coleman Award from the theory section of the American Sociological Association. Most recently Jeremy Schulz held an NSF funded postdoctoral fellowship at Cornell University's Center for Economy and Society where he launched a project exploring stances towards debt tied up with "productive" goods and services such as education and medical care and how these stances intersect with gender and class identities. His recent publications include *Talk of Work* published in *Theory and Society*. He has also done research and published in several other areas, including theory, qualitative research methods, sociology of ideology, and sociology of consumerism.

Petra Schweiger, MA: Since 1995, Petra Schweiger has been working as a physiotherapist in different therapeutic settings. Additionally, she has been trained as a practitioner in the Feldenkrais Method since 2011. In 2009 she received her master in European Ethnology, Social and Cultural Anthropology and Social Psychology at the Ludwig-Maximilian-University in Munich. Petra Schweiger is currently working on her doctoral thesis after a year working as a research assistant at the Department of European Ethnology at the Ludwig-Maximilian-University Munich. Her areas of interest are anthropology of work, elder care and medical anthropology. Her master thesis was based on field work in a nursing home conducted in a research project on precarious work under the supervision of Prof. Dr. Irene Götz. It was published in 2011 in a book series (Münchner ethnographische Schriften) and bears the title *"Wir haben zwar Geduld, aber keine Zeit". Eine Ethnografie subjektivierter Arbeitsstile in der ökonomisierten Altenpflege.*

Dr. Margit Weihrich studied Sociology at Ludwig-Maximilians-University in Munich and received her diploma in 1986. After this she worked at the University of the Armed Forces Munich where she received her Dr. phil. in 1998 (thesis on the conduct of everyday life in east Germany during the "Wende"). Currently she is a researcher at Augsburg University. Her research interests include social theory, institutional analysis, sociology of work (especially interactive service work) and qualitative methods. Recent publications include: Dunkel, Wolfgang and Margit Weihrich (eds.) (2012), *Interaktive Arbeit. Theorie, Praxis und Gestaltung von Dienstleistungsbeziehungen*, Wiesbaden: Springer VS; Böhle, Fritz and Margit Weihrich (eds.) (2010), *Die Körperlichkeit sozialen Handelns. Soziale Ordnung jenseits von Normen und Institutionen*, Bielefeld: transcript; Böhle, Fritz and Margit Weihrich (eds.) (2009), *Handeln unter Unsicherheit*, Wiesbaden: VS.

Index

International Labour Studies –
Internationale Arbeitsstudien

Klaus Dörre, Dieter Sauer,
Volker Wittke (Hg.)
Kapitalismustheorie und Arbeit
Neue Ansätze soziologischer Kritik
2012. 513 Seiten. Band 1
ISBN 978-3-593-39657-6

Karin Scherschel, Peter Streckeisen,
Manfred Krenn (Hg.)
Neue Prekarität
Die Folgen aktivierender Arbeitsmarktpolitik –
europäische Länder im Vergleich
2012. 316 Seiten. Band 2
ISBN 978-3-593-39656-9

Klaus Dörre, Karin Scherschel, Melanie Booth (Hg.)
Bewährungsproben für die Unterschicht?
Soziale Folgen aktivierender Arbeitsmarktpolitik
2012. Ca. 350 Seiten. Band 3
ISBN 978-3-593-39797-9

www.campus.de/wissenschaft   Frankfurt. New York

Cultural Studies

Nancy Konvalinka
Gender, Work and Property
An Ethnographic Study of Value
in a Spanish Village
2013. 294 pages. ISBN 978-3-593-39661-3

Tina Weber
Drop Dead Gorgeous
Representations of Corpses
in American TV Shows
2011. 267 pages. ISBN 978-3-593-39507-4

Christian Huck,
Stefan Bauernschmidt (eds.)
Travelling Goods, Travelling Moods
Varieties of Cultural Appropriation
(1850–1950)
2012. 261 pages. ISBN 978-3-593-39762-7

Hans Peter Hahn, Karlheinz Cless,
Jens Soentgen (eds.)
People at the Well
Kinds, Usages and Meanings of
Water in a Global Perspective
2012. 316 pages. ISBN 978-3-593-39610-1

Michael Nentwich, René König
Cyberscience 2.0
Research in the Age of Digital
Social Networks
2012. 237 pages. ISBN 978-3-593-39518-0

Monika Grubbauer, Joanna Kusiak (eds.)
Chasing Warsaw
Socio-Material Dynamics of
Urban Change since 1990
2012. 336 pages. ISBN 978-3-593-39778-8

Michi Knecht, Maren Klotz,Stefan Beck (eds.)
**Reproductive Technologies
as Global Form**
Ethnographies of Knowledge, Practices,
and Transnational Encounters
2011. 386 pages. ISBN 978-3-593-39100-7

Tsypylma Darieva, Wolfgang Kaschuba,
Melanie Krebs (eds.)
Urban Spaces after Socialism
Ethnographies of Public Places
in Eurasian Cities
2011. 325 pages. ISBN 978-3-593-39384-1

Elahe Haschemi Yekani
The Privilege of Crisis
Narratives of Masculinities in Colonial and
Postcolonial Literature, Photography and Film
2011. 320 pages. ISBN 978-3-593-39399-5

Julia Bernstein
Food for Thought
Transnational Contested Identities and
Food Practices of Russian-Speaking
Jewish Migrants in Israel and Germany
2010. 451 pages. ISBN 978-3-593-39252-3

www.campus.de/wissenschaft

campus
Frankfurt. New York